A Global Agenda

Issues Before the United Nations
2011-2012

Edited by Irwin Arieff
Foreword by Timothy E. Wirth

Published by the United Nations Association of the United States of America, New York, New York
Production of "A Global Agenda" was made possible by a generous grant from Korea University
facilitated by the World Federation of United Nations Associations

UNITED NATIONS ASSOCIATION, USA Inc.

Published in the United States of America
by the United Nations Association of the United States of America.
801 Second Avenue, New York, N.Y. 10017

Copyright © 2011 by the United Nations Association of the United States of America Inc.
UNA-USA is a program of the United Nations Foundation.

All rights reserved. No part of this publication may be reproduced, stored in a retrieval system or transmitted in any form or by any means, including electronic, mechanical, photocopy, recording or otherwise, without prior permission in writing from the publisher.

ISBN 978-0-9845691-3-7

Printed in the United States of America

Advisory Board: Steven A. Dimoff, A. Edward Elmendorf, Park Soo Gil, Bonian Golmohammadi, Patrick Madden, Minh-Thu Pham, Courtney B. Smith

Consulting Editor: Barbara Crossette

Executive Editor: Dulcie Leimbach

Editor: Irwin Arieff

Articles Editor: Betsy Wade

Assistant Editors: Mirva Lempiainen, Simon Minching

Photo Editor: Joe Penney

Designer: Laurie Baker, Cohoe Baker Design cohoebaker@nyc.rr.com

Indexer: Simon Minching

Assistant Researcher: Alma I. Hidalgo

Editorial Assistant: Vicky Liu

Front cover: Protesters in Cairo's Tahrir Square in February 2011.
Reuters Photo/Suhaib Salem; photo illustration by John Penney

Back cover: Refugees from the uprising in Libya line up for food at a transit camp in neighboring Tunisia in March 2011.
UN OCHA Photo/David Ohana

Contents

Introduction *Patrick Madden*	vi
South Korea and the United Nations *Park Soo Gil*	viii
About Korea University *Kim Byoung-Chul*	x
About WFUNA *Bonian Golmohammadi*	xii
Editor's Note *Irwin Arieff*	xiv
Contributors	xv
Foreword *Timothy E. Wirth*	xxvi

Chapter 1 New Day in the Arab World — 1

The People Want; the UN Must Help Them Achieve *Rima Khalaf*	2
A Next Chapter in Human Rights *Louise Arbour*	6
Libya in Revolt: Testing the Responsibility to Protect *Allan Rock*	11
Talking Points	17

Chapter 2 Fault Lines — 19

Lord's Resistance Army: Terror Roams Central Africa *Ida Sawyer*	20
Balance and Perseverance: The Case for Continued Engagement With Iran *Joseph Cirincione and Benjamin Loehrke*	26
In Somalia, Banking as Usual Is Rather Unusual *Liat Shetret*	31
The Nuclear Outliers *Jayantha Dhanapala*	35
North Korea and the UN: An Uneasy Relationship *Daniel A. Pinkston*	41
International Puzzle: Ending a Decade of Afghan War *Jeffrey Laurenti*	46
Talking Points	51

Contents

Chapter 3 A Change of Pace on Human Rights — 53
A New Human Rights Council? *Jacques Fomerand* — 54
Why Are Special Human Rights Procedures So Special? *Ted Piccone* — 59
Iraqi Refugees: Still There *Elizabeth Ferris* — 62
In Support of the Complaint Procedure *Helmut Volger* — 66
Talking Points — 69

Chapter 4 Building Peace and Keeping It — 71
The False Promise of 'Free and Fair Elections' *Mike McGovern* — 72
South Sudan: The Path Forward *Amir Osman* — 76
UN Intervention Rescues Ivory Coast by a Hair's Breadth *Richard Gowan* — 80
Margot Wallström: UN Watchdog on Sexual Abuse in War *Barbara Crossette* — 84
Somalia's Life as a Piracy Center *Evelyn Leopold* — 87
Talking Points — 91

Chapter 5 UN Perspectives — 93
Washington and Turtle Bay: Hop on the Roller Coaster *James Traub* — 94
People and Ideas for the Next Secretary-General *Thomas G. Weiss* — 98
Picking the UN Leader Should Be More of a Contest *Simon Minching* — 102

Touching the Lives of Half the World *Barbara Crossette*	105
Help Wanted for Work That Makes a Difference *Gus Feissel*	110
Why UN Reform Remains an Elusive Goal *Minh-Thu Pham*	114
What the United Nations Loses to Academic Indifference *Helmut Volger*	117
Talking Points	121

Chapter 6 Global Aid: Questions of Supply and Demand 123

Planet Earth: Serving Billions Each Day *Abigail Somma*	124
Which Path to Food Security? *Nathanial Gronewold*	129
After the Millennium Development Goals: What Next? *Hélène Gandois*	134
The Changing World of International Aid *Alexander Shakow*	137
Talking Points	141

Chapter 7 Pulling Together and Crossing Borders to Improve Heath 143

Polio Comeback: A Sad Lesson From Nigeria *Betsy Pisik*	144
Health: From an International Concern to a Global One *A. Edward Elmendorf*	150
Saving Women's Lives in Pregnancy and Childbirth *Adrienne Germain*	154
Talking Points	157

Contents

Chapter 8 Chasing War Crimes While Changing the Lineup	159
Electing International Criminal Court Judges: Merit Over Politics *Bill Pace and Matthew Heaphy*	160
A New Criminal Court Prosecutor *Richard Dicker and Param-Preet Singh*	163
70 Years of Evolution in Prosecuting War Crimes *Dan Plesch and Shanti Sattler*	166
Talking Points	171
Chapter 9 Curtailing the Damage to Our Ailing Earth	173
At Climate Talks, Small Steps Add Up to Strides *Karen Freeman*	174
Standing Up to a Tide of Garbage *Karen Freeman*	183
Talking Points	185
Appendices	187
Appendix A: Important Dates in United Nations History	188
Appendix B: The UN System	192
Appendix C: Composition of the Secretariat *Compiled by Simon Minching*	193
Appendix D: Operations and Budgets *Compiled by Simon Minching*	194
Appendix E: Acronyms and Abbreviations	206
Appendix F: Glossary	215

Appendix G: Nobel Prizes	230
Appendix H: Top Contributors of Peacekeeping Funding *Compiled by Simon Minching*	232
Appendix I: Top Contributors of Uniformed Personnel *Compiled by Simon Minching*	233
Appendix J: Global Summary of the HIV/AIDS Pandemic *Compiled by Simon Minching*	234
Appendix K: Millennium Development Goals and Targets	236
Index	238
UNA-USA Membership Application	243

Introduction

Patrick Madden
Executive director, UNA-USA

The United Nations Association of the United States of America is a vibrant nationwide network of local chapters and individuals dedicated to building understanding of and support for the ideals and work of the UN among the American people.

As a grass-roots volunteer organization, its heart rests with the members—UNA-USA members develop and carry out public programs that highlight the efforts of the UN; host educational events for young people to instill a global competency; and advocate with elected officials to focus their attention on why the UN is relevant to the entire country.

"A Global Agenda" is a vital UNA-USA publication that adds to the dialogue on the UN in auditoriums, classrooms, meetings and homes across the U.S. and beyond.

Nothing has captured the world's attention so far in 2011 more than the Arab Spring. In Rima Khalaf's opening essay, "The People Want," she discusses how the UN faces new challenges in that regional landscape. Through an economic, political and cultural lens, Khalaf rightly notes that the most impressive element of the uprisings is how regular citizens—those at the grass roots—were finally heard. They demonstrated (literally) that they were ready to reclaim their voice in how their country governs. Khalaf considers the UN's current and future role in this region and how it can bring progress despite lingering uneasiness.

As academics, nongovernmental organizations and governments ponder the impact of the Arab Spring country by country, the UN was front and center when it took unprecedented actions under the Responsibility to Protect (R2P) doctrine. Allan Rock's "Libya in Revolt" essay, for example, details the progression of the UN's adoption of R2P as member countries debated national sovereignty against humanitarian atrocities. The R2P principle made historic headlines when the Security Council acted against the Libyan government and NATO's forces were directed to step in. Rock looks at what has unfolded since and what it may mean for the future of R2P.

Daniel A. Pinkston's "North Korea and the UN" digs deeper than the common nuclear defense issues of the day. Walking readers through the history and shifting relationships of the 1940s and 50s of the West and North Korea, one quickly realizes how the country's current diplomatic and defense postures complicate regional geopolitics and keep the country in regular conversations at the UN.

In "Which Path to Food Security?" Nathanial Gronewold reports on the concerning pattern of farmers in the developing world in relation to the recent thinking of the World Bank, the UN and other international development agencies. The food crisis and the struggles of farmers is not a new issue, but the focus of international institutions on "market solutions" in lieu of large infrastructure projects and other traditional solutions is explored carefully in Gronewold's essay.

With the ever-shifting confluence of global issues facing the UN, authors Thomas G. Weiss and Simon Minching look at the secretary-general position in their independent essays. Minching studies the process of selecting candidates for the UN's top post and why reform may be needed in the near future. Weiss emphasizes that UN executive leadership in Ban Ki-moon's second term should harness the power of the institution by raising its profile and empowering UN staff across the organization.

These are but a few of the issues covered in "A Global Agenda" and in front of the UN. The weight of any single topic could fairly stand alone and easily fill the covers of a book. The UN's work certainly deserves such study and consideration. With the range of writing and opinions expressed in the book, we aim to demonstrate the strengths, challenges and breadth of the UN in the global conversation.

South Korea and the United Nations

Park Soo Gil
President, World Federation of United Nations Associations

This edition of "A Global Agenda" is published at a time of heightened expectations for the United Nations in the organization and across the international community. Perhaps nowhere is this more apparent than in South Korea, the home country of Secretary-General Ban Ki-moon.

Ban's election to lead the UN five years ago spurred national pride and a sense of responsibility, and his unanimous re-election in June renewed this spirit of engagement and prompted Korea to play an even more active role on the international scene.

His country's leaders can rightly value the credit that Ban brings to Korea, but more important, I believe they will increase their commitment to the UN's goals. Both the Korean government and the general public view his re-election as an affirmation of his performance as well as a stimulus for the country's efforts to tackle the pressing issues of our time by creating, in the words of Ban, a "stronger UN for a better world."

Korea will continue to support the world body's efforts to address climate change. Since the government's announcement of the "Low Carbon Green Growth" policy in 2008, Korea has given priority to dealing with carbon dioxide emissions and promoting sustainable development. By strengthening its partnerships on green technology, Korea intends to help solidify the shift from an energy-intensive to a green-growth paradigm.

On the development front, Korea will continue to press for countries to reach the Millennium Development Goals by participating in the global partnership that can help lift countries and populations out of poverty. During the Group of 20 summit in Seoul, leaders endorsed the Korean initiative, "Seoul Development Consensus for Shared Growth." Based on its own experience of speedy and successful development, Korea will continue to bridge the concerns of donor and recipient countries to contribute to the shared goals of peace, prosperity and respect for human rights.

Other Assistance Goals in View

Toward these noble aims, Korea will, I hope, increase its official development assistance and continue to fulfill other international commitments. This is critical to meeting the world's growing expectations of Korea, which has proven that political maturation and socioeconomic development can be achieved in one generation.

As a committed contributor to UN peacekeeping (in the Top 10), Korea will continue supporting work to prevent and respond to conflicts around the world. Currently, 600 Korean soldiers serve in nine peacekeeping missions, including Lebanon and Haiti. Based on the country's strong commitment, Korea will seek ways to intensify its support for peacekeeping. And in a reflection of the country's commitment to global peace and security, it will also be host for the 2012 Nuclear Security Summit meeting next year.

In addition to these activities, Korea will continue to participate in efforts to reform the UN, especially the Security Council. There has been no breakthrough in efforts to reconcile the positions of the countries seeking a larger number of permanent and nonpermanent members and those, like Korea, hoping to expand only the number of nonpermanent seats. Separately, Korea is likely to seek a second term as a nonpermanent member of the Security Council in 2013-14.

In all its efforts to support the UN, Korea will benefit from the publication of "A Global Agenda," as will everyone who has an interest in international affairs and the world body's work.

Having worked at the permanent mission of South Korea to the UN on three occasions, I can confidently say that this book is required reading not only for diplomats stationed in New York and in Geneva but also for officials at foreign ministries around the world. It has become a valuable aide-mémoire for all people engaged on the global scene, from veteran diplomats to students aspiring to international careers.

As we move into Ban's second five-year term, I hope that all readers of this book will use the lessons in its pages to take action to achieve a better world.

About Korea University

Kim Byoung-Chul, President, Korea University

Korea University's commitment to excellence extends beyond the classroom and the campus to the world. In South Korea and abroad, it strives to prepare students and faculty to help solve social and humanitarian problems.

That is why Korea University has worked with the United Nations Association of the United States of America to support publication of the 2011 issue of "A Global Agenda." The book is an indispensable guide to the UN and the crucial international challenges it faces.

Korea University was established in 1905 with the guiding principle of "national salvation through education" and is dedicated to independent learning and modern education. Since its founding, the university has stood at the forefront of every major turning point in Korean history. Graduates have served as leaders in every sector of society, giving the university the status of a beacon for the nation.

The university's main campus in Anam-dong, a neighborhood in north-central Seoul, was built in 1932 under the guidance of its president at the time, Kim Sung Su. The Anam campus now covers 8.5 million square feet; a second campus in Sejong, in the province of Choongchung Nam Do, is 4.3 million square feet. As it matures, Korea University is also growing academically; it currently comprises 22 colleges and divisions and 23 graduate and professional schools. It enrolls 27,000 undergraduates and more than 10,000 graduate students, with 3,201 faculty members renowned in their fields and devoted to research.

Korea University can compete with the world's best. In 2010, it was ranked 191st in the Quacquarelli Symonds Ltd. World University Ranking and 29th in the Quacquarelli Symonds Asia league table.

Korea University is also a leader in the globalization of higher education in South Korea. It has international agreements with 769 institutions in 79 countries, and in the past year, 1,062 of its students studied abroad in exchange or visiting programs. This semester, 2,277 foreign students from 89 countries are studying at our university.

Yearly, the university's International Summer Campus—a program conducted entirely in English—serves as an educational hub where students worldwide gather to experience Korea and engage in intercultural dialogue.

In recognition of its work, the institution has become the first Korean university to be a member of Universitas 21, a network of 23 leading research-intensive universities in 13 countries, and the Association of Pacific Rim Universities, with 42 members. In addition, Korea University successfully hosted "Universitas 21 Annual General Meeting and Symposium" in 2009 and is expecting to host the 2012 Association of Pacific Rim Universities' senior staff meeting in March.

The university is rigorously expanding its horizons at home. Its Division of International Studies and Graduate School of International Studies conduct all their courses in English. A distinguished faculty directs courses in international commerce, international relations, trade and security.

The Division of International Studies has also hosted a model United Nations with the UN Development Program and the UN High Commissioner for Refugees and a model meeting of the Group of 20, among other international activities. Housing the UN Development Program policy office in the International Studies Building will significantly contribute to the enrichment of international studies research and education.

To provide its students with the best possible education, the university offers an innovative general curriculum. Its new Office of General Education is aiming for a broader range of subject matter. The Korea University Social Service Organization was set up to advance knowledge and nurture future leaders of society.

With broad ambitions, Korea University is well on its way to becoming a leading world-class institution. ■

About WFUNA

Bonian Golmohammadi, Secretary-General
World Federation of United Nations Associations

The United Nations global community has faced many challenges in 2011, including the earthquake and tsunami in Japan and human rights crises in Kordofan, Sudan. It was through these tragic instances, however, that moments of hope and progress have emerged, including South Sudan's acceptance as the 193rd member country of the UN and the promising opportunities of the UN International Year of Youth. Balancing all these challenges and opportunities underscores the importance of applying a cooperative multilateral approach to problems and illustrates the significant role of the UN in managing them as well.

The World Federation of United Nations Associations is a global nonprofit organization representing and coordinating the efforts of more than 100 national United Nations Associations. WFUNA and our member UNAs aim to build a better world through education and awareness raising, policy development and advocacy and multilateral cooperation and development projects. We help provide programs and information on the work of the UN to engage citizens the world over on both the local and international level. WFUNA contributes to a stronger, better UN community through the efforts of like-minded individuals who value cooperation among all people.

WFUNA is proud to once again be a partner in the publication of "A Global Agenda." This year's issue addresses many topics relevant to WFUNA's mission and the work of our member UNAs: international security, climate change, peacekeeping and human rights, among others. The publication is a valuable tool for information and research on the many sectors touched by our work, including diplomats, academics, students, government officials and nongovernment constituents.

WFUNA has programs in the three areas of importance at the UN: peace and security, sustainable development and human rights. We coordinate these programs through our "Global Citizen Campaign," which began in 2009. All programs under this campaign highlight the interconnected nature of global issues, promote the effectiveness and engagement of civil society organizations in such issues and advocate for democratic solutions to international problems. Our programs in the area of peace and security revolve around the concepts of the Responsibility to Protect norm and nuclear disarmament. Programs in the area of sustainable development are centered on climate change and enhancing progress on the Millennium Development Goals. Our program in human rights is focused on increasing the capacity of civil society organizations to engage in human rights mechanisms at the UN and in their respective countries.

We at WFUNA believe strongly in the power and future of youth at the UN. We provide programs that engage young people around the world in the work and processes of the UN. Our "Handbook for Establishing a National Youth Delegate Programme to the United Nations" guides readers through the steps of becoming a youth delegate. To support the UN International Year of Youth, we have held youth seminars in Europe and South America and continuously focus on facilitating youth participation in all our projects and programs. We appreciate the innovation and passion that youth bring to many aspects of our work.

With recent successful training programs and events in many parts of the world—Argentina, Armenia, the Democratic Republic of Congo, Kenya, Norway and Switzerland—WFUNA remains committed to bringing the ideals and activities of the UN to citizens in all member countries. "A Global Agenda" aids in these efforts as well. We hope that this publication inspires you to get involved in creating a world of peaceful cooperation, sustainable development and human rights for all, too. ■

Editor's Note

What an extraordinary year. To name just a few history-changing events, think back to the Arab Spring, the double whammy of the Security Council and its human rights counterpart taking on the Libyan leader Muammar el-Qaddafi and the precedent-setting UN peacekeeping effort to help oust the loser in a contested presidential election in Ivory Coast.

The goal of "A Global Agenda: Issues Before the United Nations 2011-2012" is to help people think about what is going on in the world and explore what the UN role should be in all of these politically charged events. As its many authors make abundantly clear, the book is centered on the fundamental belief that nations working together offer the best promise of solving the world's biggest challenges, and that the UN is in a unique position to help because it alone offers every country a seat at its table.

I am grateful to—and humbled by—our writers, who worked tirelessly to make this such a compelling book. We hope you will read it, talk about it and share it.

I also owe thanks to Dulcie Leimbach, the executive editor, for her creativity, hard work and unstinting support. And I salute my crackerjack editorial team: Consulting Editor Barbara Crossette, Copy Editor Betsy Wade, Assistant Editors Mirva Lempiainen and Simon Minching, Designer Laurie Baker, Photo Editor Joe Penney, Assistant Researcher Alma Hidalgo and Editorial Assistant Vicky Liu. ■

–*Irwin Arieff, New York, August 2011*

Contributors

[The views expressed in this book belong to their authors alone]

Louise Arbour, a Canadian, has served as president and chief executive officer of the International Crisis Group since July 2009. She was the United Nations High Commissioner for Human Rights from 2004 to 2008. In 1999, she was appointed to the Supreme Court of Canada, and before that she served as chief prosecutor for the International Criminal Tribunals for the former Yugoslavia and for Rwanda. Arbour has received numerous awards and honors, including some 30 honorary doctorates. She has been named commander of the French Legion of Honor and most recently was a recipient of the 2010 North-South Prize, together with the former president of Brazil, Luiz Inácio Lula da Silva.

Irwin Arieff has edited "A Global Agenda: Issues Before the United Nations" for a second year; he contributes regularly to other UNA-USA publications. He worked for Reuters for 23 years in Washington, Paris and New York and at the United Nations before leaving daily journalism in 2007. Arieff earned a master's degree in journalism from Northwestern University, and before that served three years in the Peace Corps, specializing in rural development in Senegal and Mauritania.

Laurie Baker is a partner in Cohoe Baker, an award-winning graphic design firm for leading publications and other companies, including The New York Times, The Wall Street Journal, Andersen Consulting and Mercedes-Benz of North America. Baker has worked as a freelance art director and designer for UNA-USA, Storey Books, Travel Holiday magazine, the Leukemia Society, the Metropolitan Museum of Art and CBS. She holds a master of fine arts from the University of Michigan.

Joseph Cirincione is president of the Ploughshares Fund, a global security foundation, and author of "Bomb Scare: The History and Future of Nuclear Weapons." He has been vice president for national security at the Center for American Progress, director for nonproliferation at the Carnegie Endowment for International Peace and has served on the professional staff of the Armed Services

Committee of the U.S. House of Representatives. He is a member of the Council on Foreign Relations and has been appointed to the International Security Advisory Board to the U.S. Secretary of State.

Barbara Crossette is a regular contributor to The InterDependent, UNA-USA's online magazine, and is also the UN correspondent for The Nation. She was UN bureau chief for The New York Times from 1994 to 2001 and earlier its chief correspondent in Southeast Asia and South Asia. She is the author of "So Close to Heaven: The Vanishing Buddhist Kingdoms of the Himalayas," "The Great Hill Stations of Asia" and a Foreign Policy Association study, "India: Old Civilizations in a New World." Crossette won the George Polk award for her coverage in India of the assassination of Rajiv Gandhi in 1991 and the 2010 Shorenstein Prize for her writing on Asia. She is a member of the Council on Foreign Relations and a trustee of the Carnegie Council on Ethics in Foreign Affairs.

Jayantha Dhanapala is president of the Nobel Peace Prize-winning Pugwash Conferences on Science and World Affairs, vice chairman of the governing board of the Stockholm International Peace Research Institute and a member of other international advisory boards. He was UN under secretary-general for disarmament affairs from 1998 to 2003. As a Sri Lankan diplomat, Dhanapala served as ambassador to the U.S. from 1995 to 1997 and as his country's representative to the UN in Geneva from 1984 to 1987. He also held diplomatic posts in London, Beijing and New Delhi and represented Sri Lanka at many international conferences. Among others, he chaired the historic Nonproliferation Treaty Review and Extension Conference of 1995. He was director of the UN Institute for Disarmament Research from 1987 to 1992. Dhanapala holds many international awards and honorary doctorates and has published five books and several articles in international journals.

Richard Dicker has been director of Human Rights Watch's International Justice Program since its founding in 2001. Dicker also led Human Rights Watch's multiyear campaign to establish the International Criminal Court. He monitored the Slobodan Milosevic trial in The Hague and traveled often to Iraq before and at the start of the trial of the deposed president, Saddam Hussein, for war crimes. A former civil rights lawyer in New York, Dicker graduated from New York University Law School and received his master of laws from Columbia University.

A. Edward Elmendorf is a former president and chief executive of UNA-USA, a post he assumed after 40 years as an international and national civil servant. He started his international career in the U.S. Foreign Service at the U.S. Mission to the UN under Ambassador Adlai Stevenson. He later became a UN staff member, and in 1970 began a 30-year career at the World Bank, where he focused on health in Africa. After retiring, he taught at Johns Hopkins University and consulted for the World Bank, the World Health Organization, the UN Development Program and the U.S. Institute of Medicine. He has served for 15 years as an officer or board member of USA-UNA's largest chapter, in the national capital area. He graduated magna cum laude in German literature from Yale, has a master's degree in economics from George Washington University and a master's in public health from Johns Hopkins.

Gus Feissel worked for 35 years at the United Nations, involved in diplomacy and negotiations on political and economic issues. In those capacities, he was special assistant to the under secretary-general for Economic and Social Affairs and associate director in the UN Center on Transnational Corporations. In addition, he worked in conflict resolution and peacekeeping on the political side, serving as assistant secretary-general and chief of mission of the UN Operation in Cyprus. He did his undergraduate work at Hunter College and his graduate studies at New York University and the Institute of Political Studies in Paris.

Elizabeth Ferris is a senior fellow in the Foreign Policy Studies Program at the Brookings Institution in Washington, and a co-director of the Brookings-London School of Economics project on internal displacement. Before joining Brookings in 2006, Ferris worked for 20 years in international humanitarian response, most recently in Geneva, at the World Council of Churches. She has been a professor at several U.S. universities and served as a Fulbright professor to the Universidad Autónoma de México in Mexico City. Her most recent book, "The Politics of Protection: The Limits of Humanitarian Action," was published by Brookings in 2011.

Jacques Fomerand joined the UN Secretariat in 1977, where he followed economic, social and coordination questions in the Office of the Under Secretary-General for International Economic and Social Affairs. From 1992 to 2003, he was director of the UN University office in North America. He has since taught at Columbia University, John Jay College of Criminal Justice, Seton Hall University, Occidental College and New York University, among others. He has published extensively on matters related to the UN and is completing a study on human rights.

Karen Freeman is a freelance journalist and journalism educator who left The New York Times in 2007 after 15 years as an editor on the national, science, editorial, business and technology desks. She was science editor at The St. Louis Post-Dispatch and was an associate professor of journalism at Pennsylvania State University. Freeman was a Knight International Journalism Fellow in Moldova in 2006 and continues to teach in Eastern Europe. She lives in Dublin.

Hélène Gandois is a training associate with the UN Institute for Training and Research in New York and a visiting research scholar at the College of Staten Island, City University of New York. She has served in various positions at the UN, the United Nations University and the Carnegie Council for Ethics and International Affairs. She holds a Ph.D. in international relations from Oxford University.

Adrienne Germain worked for women's equality in the 1970s and 80s with the Ford Foundation, including four years in Bangladesh as the foundation's country representative. For 26 years, she led the International Women's Health Coalition, creating policy innovations through the UN system, heading advocacy efforts for sexual and reproductive rights and health and helping build local organizations in Africa, Asia and Latin America. Germain is now president emerita of the coalition. She is also a member of the Council on Foreign Relations, the editorial board of Reproductive Health Matters, the Human Rights Watch Women's Division Advisory Committee and the International Health Partnership Evaluation Advisory Group. She also served on the Millennium Development Goal project task force on child mortality and maternal health.

Bonian Golmohammadi was elected secretary-general of the World Federation of United Nations Associations in August 2009. Previously, Golmohammadi served as secretary-general of UNA-Sweden for eight years. Under his leadership, UNA-Sweden increased its budget from $1 million to $5 million and expanded its staff from 10 to 30 full-time employees. Golmohammadi also introduced several programs, including a bilateral international project in more than 10 countries; among them, China, Georgia, the Democratic Republic of Congo and Uganda. Since 2005, Golmohammadi has also served as president of the UNA Europe Network. In addition, he has served on the advisory boards of the Swedish Ministers for Development, international development corporations and UN entities. Before joining UNA-Sweden, Golmohammadi worked with consultancy and private businesses in Sweden and the Czech Republic. He has a degree in political science and studied international law, human rights and philosophy at Stockholm and Uppsala Universities.

Richard Gowan is an associate director of New York University's Center on International Cooperation. He is also a senior policy fellow at the European Council on Foreign Relations. In 2005 and 2006, he coordinated the first edition of the Annual Review of Global Peace Operations, the most extensive source of data and analysis on peacekeeping in the public domain.

Nathanial Gronewold is the New York and UN bureau chief for Environment and Energy Publishing, which produces the newswire services Greenwire and ClimateWire and Environment and Energy Daily. Gronewold has reported on the UN for seven years, including covering its response to rising food costs, beginning with the sharp increase in commodity prices from 2007. He previously wrote articles from the UN for the Canadian Press, The Economist and Nikkei, a Japanese financial newspaper.

Matthew Heaphy is a legal consultant to the Coalition for the International Criminal Court, working on its ICC elections campaign, and in that capacity is a legal adviser to the secretariat of the Independent Panel on ICC Judicial Elections. Heaphy also serves as deputy convener of the American Nongovernmental Organizations Coalition for the International Criminal Court, formerly a program of UNA-USA. Heaphy previously worked as an associate legal officer in Trial Chamber I at the UN International Criminal Tribunal for the former Yugoslavia in The Hague and interned as a law clerk to Judge Anita Usacka at the International Criminal Court. He also worked as an antitrust litigation lawyer in San Francisco.

Alma I. Hidalgo is an intern with UNA-USA, a program of the United Nations Foundation. She is a master's candidate at the New School, with a focus in international affairs. While studying abroad in Egypt, she worked at the Better World Foundation, collecting information on human trafficking. Hidalgo has a bachelor's degree in journalism from the State University of New York at Oswego.

Rima Khalaf is a UN under secretary-general and executive secretary of the UN Economic and Social Commission for Western Asia, in Beirut. She served as director of the Regional Bureau for Arab States with the UN Development Program from 2000 to 2006, initiating projects to promote good governance, human rights and human development in Arab countries. She was the principal architect of the pioneering Arab Human Development Report series and has received numerous international prizes, including the Prince Claus Award and the King Hussein Leadership Prize. Before joining the UN, Khalaf served in senior government posts in Jordan, including deputy prime minister, industry and trade minister, planning minister and head of the ministerial economic team. She has also participated in international commissions, including the High Level Commission for the Modernization of the World Bank Group Governance. Khalaf holds a bachelor's degree in economics from the American University of Beirut and a master's in economics and a Ph.D. in system science from Portland State University.

Kim Byoung-Chul is the president of Korea University, the 18th person to hold this post, which he assumed in December 2010. He first joined the university as a professor in 1985 and has since served as the head of facility management, dean of the School of Life Sciences and Biotechnology, provost and executive vice president. He graduated from Seoul National University with a major in animal husbandry, earned a master's degree from the Graduate School of Korea University and holds a Ph.D. from the University of Göttingen.

Jeffrey Laurenti is senior fellow and director of foreign policy programs at The Century Foundation and a member of the Council on Foreign Relations. He was UNA-USA's executive director of policy studies until 2003 and also served on its board. He was deputy director of the United Nations Foundation's initiative in support of Kofi Annan's high-level panel on global threats, challenges and change in 2003 and 2004, a candidate for the U.S. House of Representatives in 1986, senior issues adviser to Walter Mondale's 1984 presidential campaign and from 1978 to 1984 was executive director of the New Jersey Senate. He is the author of numerous monographs and articles on international peace and security, terrorism, UN reform and other topics. Laurenti graduated Phi Beta Kappa and magna cum laude in government from Harvard University and earned his master's degree in public affairs from Princeton University's Woodrow Wilson School of Public and International Affairs.

Dulcie Leimbach is the editor of The InterDependent, the online magazine published by UNA-USA and the United Nations Foundation, covering news and features on the UN (www.theinterdependent.com). She was a writer and editor at The New York Times for more than two decades, working on most news desks, including Business Day, Editorial, Metro, Special Sections, Style, Sunday Magazine and Week in Review. Her writing has also appeared in The Washington Post, Ms., Salon and literary journals, and she has taught news writing and reporting at Hofstra University. Leimbach has a B.S. in journalism from the University of Colorado and an M.F.A. in creative writing from Warren Wilson College.

Mirva Lempiainen is a freelance journalist and graduate of the international reporting program at the City University of New York Graduate School of Journalism. Her articles have been published in the U.S., Finland and Australia. She spent the summer of 2010 training young journalists in the Maldives through a grant from Davis Projects for Peace.

Evelyn Leopold is a freelance writer and regular contributor to the Huffington Post, based at the United Nations, where she served as UN bureau chief for Reuters for 18 years. She was awarded a gold medal in 2000 by the UN Correspondents Association. She is the chairwoman of the Dag Hammarskjöld Fund for Journalists and is a member of the Council on Foreign Relations, the Overseas Press Club and the Newswomen's Club of New York. At Reuters, she also served as a news editor for North America, the African region editor and associate editor worldwide. In addition, she writes for The InterDependent, UNA-USA's online magazine.

Vicky Liu has a master of science in global operations management from Stony Brook University. She interned at the Business Council for the UN for one year in addition to writing articles for The InterDependent.

Benjamin Loehrke is a research associate at the Ploughshares Fund, a global security foundation. He earned his master's in public policy from the University of Maryland with a certificate in intelligence analysis. He is also a graduate of Indiana University.

Patrick Madden is executive director of UNA-USA. Before assuming the post in February 2011, he served four years as president and chief executive officer of Sister Cities International, building a network of U.S. cities partnering with more than 2,000 international communities on economic development, humanitarian, cultural and education programs and exchanges. Before that, he held senior positions at the Association of Performing Arts Presenters and the Smithsonian

Institution's National Portrait Gallery. Madden also teaches graduate seminars in fund-raising at George Mason University.

Mike McGovern is assistant professor of anthropology and director of Graduate Studies in African Studies at Yale. He is the author of "Making War in Côte d'Ivoire" and the forthcoming "Unmasking the State: Making Guinea Modern." From 2004 to 2006, he was the West Africa Project Director of the International Crisis Group.

Simon Minching was a UNA-USA policy intern in 2008 and has been a contributor to the organization's publications, "A Global Agenda," and the online magazine, The InterDependent. Minching is a recent graduate of the University of Chicago, where he received a master of public policy degree. He holds a bachelor's degree in government and politics from St. John's University.

Amir Osman is a senior policy analyst for Africa at the Open Society Foundations. There, he campaigns for Africa at the UN Secretariat, the UN Security Council and UN country missions. Previously, Osman was the senior director of policy and government relations for the Save Darfur Coalition. With the coalition president, Osman worked on domestic and international policy, advocacy and outreach to the U.S. government, foreign governments, regional and international institutes, media and nongovernmental organizations. Before that, Osman was the Sudan program officer for the Cairo Institute for Human Rights Studies. He also worked on research projects with the Forced Migration and Refugee Studies Program at the American University in Cairo.

Bill Pace has served as the convenor of the Coalition for the International Criminal Court since its founding in 1995. He is the executive director of the World Federalist Movement-Institute for Global Policy and is a co-founder and steering committee member of the International Coalition for the Responsibility to Protect. He has been involved in international justice, rule of law, environmental law and human rights for the last 30 years. He previously served as the secretary-general of The Hague Appeal for Peace, director of the Center for the Development of International Law and director of Section Relations of the Concerts for Human Rights Foundation at Amnesty International, among other positions.

Park Soo Gil is president of the World Federation of United Nations Associations and the current chairman of the Policy Advisory Committee of South Korea's National Human Rights Commission. He is also a professor at Korea University's Graduate School of International Studies, teaching on international organizations and the UN. From 1984 to 1998, he served as South Korea's ambassador to Morocco, Canada, the UN in Geneva and the UN in New York. From 1963 to 1998, he held a variety of positions at South Korea's Ministry of Foreign Affairs and Trade, including director-general of treaty affairs, deputy minister for political affairs and chancellor of the Institute of Foreign Affairs and National Security. Park also was a member of the UN Subcommission on the Promotion and Protection of Human Rights. He graduated from the Korea University College of Law and has a master's degree from the School of International Affairs and Public Administration at Columbia University.

Joe Penney is a freelance photojournalist who covered the 2011 elections in Nigeria for Reuters and the 2010 presidential election in Guinea for Reuters and for CNN. His photos, which can be viewed at www.joepenney.com, have appeared in Le Monde, The New York Times (foreign news and Lens blog), Reuters, Time, Newsweek (cover of Africa edition), The InterDependent and The Montreal Mirror. His work was part of an exhibition at the Musée National du Sport in Paris and was awarded a merit prize in the Yonhap International Press Photo Awards 2011. He is a graduate of McGill University in Montreal and was the photo editor for UNA-USA's "A Global Agenda" in 2010.

Minh-Thu Pham is director of public policy at the United Nations Foundation. She was previously chief of staff for the UN secretary-general's special envoy for malaria and served as policy adviser in the executive office of the secretary-general under both Kofi Annan and Ban Ki-moon, where she developed and carried out policy on UN reform, worked on the U.S.-UN relationship and helped to integrate peace-building throughout the UN system. She also served in Bosnia-Herzegovina to carry out the Dayton Peace Accord and worked with refugees in East Africa through the UN and humanitarian and advocacy organizations. She has a master's in public administration from the Woodrow Wilson School of International and Public Affairs at Princeton and a bachelor's degree in history from Duke. She is a term member of the Council on Foreign Relations, a fellow of the Truman National Security Institute and a board member of the Coalition for Asian-American Children and Families.

Ted Piccone is a senior fellow and deputy director for foreign policy at the Brookings Institution. His most recent publications include the report, "Catalysts for Rights: The Unique Contribution of the UN's Independent Experts on Human Rights," and the book, "Shifting the Balance: Obama and the Americas." Piccone has held various leadership and policymaking positions in the government, nonprofit and legal arenas, including eight years as a foreign policy adviser in the Clinton administration. An honors graduate of Columbia Law School and the University of Pennsylvania, he also served as counsel for the UN Truth Commission for El Salvador.

Daniel A. Pinkston is a senior researcher and deputy project director with the International Crisis Group. Before joining the Crisis Group, he was the director of the Asia Nonproliferation Program at the James Martin Center for Nonproliferation Studies. He has a doctorate from the University of California, San Diego, and served as a Korean linguist in the U.S. Air Force.

Betsy Pisik has reported on development issues, human rights violations and armed conflict from the UN and the field for the last decade. She has covered conflict and abuse in Iraq, Afghanistan, Pakistan, the Democratic Republic of Congo, Ethiopia, Israel, Palestine, Lebanon and Syria, among others. She reported from Nigeria recently on a grant from the Washington-based International Reporting Project. Pisik is a graduate of the University of Maryland.

Dan Plesch is the director of the Center for International Studies and Diplomacy at the University of London's School of Oriental and African Studies. He is the author of "America, Hitler and the UN," and "The Beauty Queen's Guide to World Peace," which led to the world disarmament initiative, the Strategic Concept for Removal of Arms and Proliferation. In 1986, he founded the British American Security Information Council and directed it from Washington until 2001, when he became the senior research fellow at the Royal United Services Institute for Defense and Security Studies in London.

Allan Rock is president of the University of Ottawa. He previously served as Canada's ambassador to the United Nations, where he led the successful Canadian effort to secure adoption of the Responsibility to Protect doctrine at the UN's 2005 Global Summit. Before serving at the UN, he held senior posts in the Canadian Government, including Minister of Justice and Attorney-General of Canada, Minister of Health and Minister of Industry. He had earlier spent 20 years in the practice of law in Toronto, and is a Fellow of the American College of Trial Lawyers.

Shanti Sattler is a post-conflict reconciliation and development consultant who has worked for nongovernmental organizations in conflict and post-conflict zones in Africa and Asia. She was based in Phnom Penh, Cambodia, for several years at the start of the Khmer Rouge Tribunal proceedings. She is a graduate of the International Relations and Peace and Justice Studies Programs at Tufts University and is a research assistant at the Center for International Studies and Diplomacy at the University of London's School of Oriental and African Studies.

Ida Sawyer is a researcher for Human Rights Watch, based since January 2008 in Goma in eastern Democratic Republic of Congo. She regularly documents attacks on civilians and other human rights abuses in conflict zones of eastern and northern Congo and presses government authorities and UN officials to help end abuses, provide more effective civilian protection and justice for victims. She has written extensively on the human rights situation in Congo. Before joining Human Rights Watch, Sawyer was a freelance journalist in Cairo; researched the origins of the Lord's Resistance Army in northern Uganda; and worked with a Ugandan organization to set up a youth education program for former child soldiers. A native of Washington, D.C., she holds bachelor's and master's degrees specializing in human rights from Columbia University.

Alexander Shakow held various high-level positions at the World Bank from 1981 to 2002, including director of external affairs and strategic planning as well as executive secretary of the IMF/World Bank Development Committee. Since 2002, he has been an independent consultant for numerous international entities, including Unicef, the Food and Agriculture Organization and the Global Fund to Fight AIDS, Tuberculosis and Malaria. From 1968 to 1981, Shakow held many senior posts at the U.S. Agency for International Development and was a staff member of the U.S. Peace Corps from 1963-1968, including director for Indonesia. He received his Ph.D. from the University of London-London School of Economics in 1962.

Liat Shetret is a programs officer at the Center on Global Counterterrorism Cooperation in New York. She is focusing on Somali remittance companies as part of the center's projects on strengthening security, justice and anti-money laundering institutions in East Africa and the Horn of Africa. She previously contributed to the center's work as a consultant, overseeing programming in Ethiopia, Uganda and Djibouti and has conducted research on multilateral responses to terrorism, weapons of mass destruction, terrorist financing and the role of society and human rights in countering terrorism. She is an expert in international security policy, countering violent extremism and Middle Eastern affairs and has served as the Harold Rosenthal Fellow in international affairs to the U.S. House Committee on Homeland Security.

Param-Preet Singh is a senior counsel in Human Rights Watch's International Justice Program, researching, advocating and writing on international justice issues relating to the International Criminal Court and the International Criminal Tribunal for the former Yugoslavia. She also works on strategies to encourage national prosecution of serious international crimes, including in Bosnia and the Democratic Republic of Congo. Previously, Singh worked as a lawyer with the UN Mission in Kosovo and in the federal Department of Justice in Toronto. She is a graduate of the University of Alberta and the McGill Law School.

Courtney B. Smith is associate dean of the John C. Whitehead School of Diplomacy and International Relations at Seton Hall, where he is also an associate professor and director of the UN Intensive Summer Study Program. His teaching and scholarship focus on international organizations, particularly the UN. Smith has published on global consensus-building, Security Council reform, the secretary-general, peacekeeping, the U.S.-UN relationship, the UN Year of Dialogue Among Civilizations, peace-building, human rights and teaching about the UN.

Abigail Somma has worked as a writer and editor for the United Nations, the World Bank, think tanks and media outlets. She has a master's degree from Johns Hopkins University's School of Advanced International Studies and a bachelor's degree from Villanova University. Her first play, "Beneath the Hush, a Whisper," is slated for production at the Workshop Theater Company in New York.

James Traub is a contributing writer for The New York Times Magazine, where he has worked since 1998. He has written extensively about international affairs and especially the United Nations. His weekly column on foreign policy, Terms of Engagement, appears on foreignpolicy.com, the Web site of Foreign Policy magazine. In 2006, he published "The Best Intentions: Kofi Annan and the UN in the Era of American World Power."

Helmut Volger has written and edited several books about the UN, including "A Concise Encyclopedia of the United Nations," of which the second revised edition was published by Brill Academic Publishers in 2010. He is a co-founder of the German UN Research Network (www.forschungskreis-vereinte-nationen.de) and a contributor to The InterDependent, UNA-USA's online magazine.

Betsy Wade, the first woman hired as a copy editor by The New York Times, is a former head of the paper's foreign copy desk. She was news editor in the Times's UN bureau in 1967 and afterward was on the team of editors whose work won a Pulitzer Prize for the Pentagon Papers project. Before retiring from The Times, she wrote the Practical Traveler column.

Thomas G. Weiss is presidential professor of political science at the City University of New York Graduate Center and director of the Ralph Bunche Institute for International Studies, where he directed the UN Intellectual History Project from 1999 to 2010 and was president of the International Studies Association in 2009-10. He was also chairman of the Academic Council on the UN System from 2006 to 2009, editor of Global Governance, research director of the International Commission on Intervention and State Sovereignty, and research professor at Brown University's Watson Institute for International Studies. In addition, he served as executive director of the Academic Council on the UN System and of the International Peace Academy, was a member of the UN Secretariat and a consultant to several public and private agencies. He has written or edited some 40 books and 175 articles and book chapters about multilateral approaches to international peace and security, humanitarian action and sustainable development.

Timothy E. Wirth is president of the United Nations Foundation and the Better World Fund. He has led the foundation since it began in 1998. Wirth spent more than 20 years in the U.S. Congress, representing Colorado in the House of Representatives and in the Senate. Wirth started his political career as a White House Fellow under President Lyndon Johnson and served as deputy assistant secretary for education in the Nixon administration. In 1970, Wirth returned to Colorado and successfully ran for the U.S. House of Representatives in 1974. He was elected to the U.S. Senate in 1986 where he focused on environmental issues, particularly global climate change and population stabilization. From 1993 to 1997, he served in the U.S. Department of State as the first under secretary for global affairs.

Foreword

Timothy E. Wirth
President, United Nations Foundation

The spirit of the United Nations is embodied in its work addressing the problems that no single country can tackle on its own. The UN's scope—its presence is literally everywhere around the world—gives the global body unique capacity in:
- Defending human rights
- Fostering peace and prosperity around the globe
- Expanding women's rights
- Protecting the environment and combating climate change
- Delivering solutions for health

These priorities are more important today than at any point in the UN's history. The world's population will pass the seven billion mark this year and is on course to reach nine billion by 2050. The impacts of climate change are becoming more widespread, including extreme weather, exacerbated natural disasters and a new phenomenon: climate refugees.

As the struggle for democracy and human rights continues in dozens of countries worldwide, the international community convenes at the UN to find the best ways to support such struggles. The civil war in Libya and the uprisings in Bahrain, Egypt, Tunisia and Yemen demonstrate how rapidly the balance of power can shift within a nation and a region, emphasizing the value of cooperation in international responses to complex situations. As I write this, famine grips the Horn of Africa and the UN is on the front lines of the response, highlighting the importance of collective international action to address major humanitarian crises.

The ultimate demonstration of the importance of international burden-sharing is evident in the work of the UN Department of Peacekeeping Operations. UN peacekeeping accepts the most difficult assignments, ones that no country wants to handle alone. After all other interventions fail, the agency stabilizes regional and interstate conflicts, facilitates free and fair elections and protects civilians during humanitarian crises. UN peacekeepers, who today serve more than 200 million people across 15 operations in the most difficult circumstances, should be thanked for putting themselves on the line every day to protect our collective security interests.

In 2012, UN Secretary-General Ban Ki-moon will begin his second five-year term at a critical time. With his vision and leadership, the UN can build on its momentum to tackle our most important collective issues, while at the same time modernizing the organization so it is better prepared to address the global challenges of the future.

The UN's top role on climate change is critical to addressing the one challenge that will affect every person on earth. In his first term, Ban put climate at the top of the global agenda. In his second term, he will continue to move toward a global agreement that can be reached only with international cooperation through the UN system.

Ban will also maintain a focus on the Millennium Development Goals. They draw world attention to our most important challenges: ending hunger and extreme poverty, achieving universal primary education, promoting gender equality, reducing child mortality, improving maternal health, combating HIV/AIDS and other diseases, ensuring environmental sustainability and developing global partnerships. The secretary-general will also continue to champion support for women and girls in the developing world, which not only helps advance the gender equality and health goals, but also has a multiplier effect on the other Millennium Development Goals.

Under Ban's leadership, the UN will continue the process of modernization, creating streamlined internal processes, developing and recruiting a new cadre of international civil servants and enhancing communications—all to ensure maximum return on the global investment in the UN.

Readers of "A Global Agenda" know that even as nations work together through the UN to combat climate change, protect human rights, maintain collective security and expand women's rights, the support of individuals, civil society, corporations and foundations is also essential to meeting these goals. At the United Nations Foundation, we pride ourselves on connecting people, ideas and resources to the UN by mobilizing the energy and expertise of visionaries, businesses and nongovernmental organizations. To learn more about our programs and campaigns, visit www.unfoundation.org.

With unprecedented challenges come unparalleled opportunities. As we look forward to the global agenda of the coming year, we see opportunities to work together for a safer, more secure world, with greater opportunity and prosperity for all. ■

A woman delivers a message in Cairo's Tahrir Square in January.

Floris Van Cauwelaert

New Day in the Arab World

2   **The People Want; the UN Must Help Them Achieve**
Rima Khalaf

6   **A Next Chapter in Human Rights**
Louise Arbour

11   **Libya in Revolt: Testing the Responsibility to Protect**
Allan Rock

17   **Talking Points**

The People Want; the UN Must Help Them Achieve

Rima Khalaf

All revolutions are impossible, until they become inevitable, Leon Trotsky once said. Though the uprisings rocking Arab countries this year have caught the world by surprise, for most Arabs the question was not whether they would happen, but rather when they would be inevitable.

The Arab Human Development Report series, written by Arab intellectuals and published by the United Nations Development Program starting in 2002, maintained that Arab countries were in deep crisis. Arabs enjoyed few of their universal rights. Some were suppressed by occupying powers and others by authoritarian regimes.

The former were best exemplified by an Israeli occupation, condemned by several UN General Assembly Resolutions as a violation of the UN Charter and the principles of international law, that for decades has denied Palestinians their freedoms and their collective right to self-determination. Within most Arab states, suppressed freedoms, minimal respect for human rights, lack of voice and political accountability, corruption and rising inequality and unemployment contributed to the marginalization of the majority and growing frustration and anger. Though fear kept a lid on action, this dual oppression created a combustible mix that awaited a trigger.

A police officer in the little known town of Sidi Bouzid in Tunisia unknowingly provided that trigger on Dec. 17, 2010, when she humiliated a street vendor named Mohamed Bouazizi and seized the fruits he had been selling. He decided he had had enough of the regime's dehumanizing treatment and set himself afire. Less than a month later, the region exploded and an authoritarian ruler was boarding a plane to never return.

Citizens of the region were inspired. "The people want …"—the main slogan of all the revolutions—encapsulated their sentiment in its purest form. Some "wanted" to topple their regime, others to reform it. What they all "wanted" was freedom, respect for their dignity and social justice. People realized, for the first time, that what they "want" can matter and that they have the voice and power to make it happen.

A Wind Blew Through With Mixed Results

Six months later, it is hard to name an Arab country that did not witness popular protest in one form or another. However, the results of these protests have so far been mixed. While Egyptians and Tunisians succeeded in overthrowing "dynastic" presidents, other despots cling to power by brute force.

The outlook for the region is not clear yet. But one thing is certain. It will not regress to its pre-Dec. 17 condition. It is on a new trajectory. The barrier of fear has been shattered. Intimidation seared into peoples' consciousness through decades

Flickr/Jonathan Rashad

Egyptians celebrate in Cairo's Tahrir Square after President Hosni Mubarak announces his resignation on Feb. 11, 2011.

of oppression has been transformed into defiance. Mindsets have been changed irreversibly.

What kind of political projects will emerge is one part of the uncertainty that lies ahead. Though the probability that all Arab countries will shift to democracy in 15 to 20 years is high, their paths toward that goal will vary. This will depend not only on the changing balance between the ruler and the ruled, but also on the interests and actions of major international and regional powers affected by the change.

This new regional landscape poses new challenges to the UN. The difficulty is compounded by a lack of a single prototype to deal with.

Though often referred to as an Arab Spring, the climate in Arab countries today is more of a concurrent four seasons. While Egypt and Tunisia may represent a potential Arab Spring, three other situations are emerging: countries where the ruling elite is promising meaningful political reforms; countries where the political struggles have degenerated into government-led violence, increasing the potential for civil conflict; and countries where the political establishment was able momentarily to deflect demands by citizens for greater democratization, through a range of social and economic transfers.

First Group May Move More Rapidly

For the first category of countries, Tunisia and Egypt, the probability of shifting to democratic governance in five years is high despite serious challenges. Drafting new constitutions and holding fair and transparent elections in the coming months would pave the way for democratic institutions and solidifying a democratic culture.

Current economic difficulties will prove to be short lived. Returns from fairer and more transparent markets will probably outweigh short-term losses. More challenging in the short term will be stabilizing the security situation, reforming and rehabilitating the security sector and clarifying the role of the military.

The prospects for countries like Libya and Yemen are more complicated. Months of violence will leave tens of thousands of refugees and serious damage to the countries' infrastructure. The fighting may also leave societal fissures that need to be repaired. Unlike Tunisia and Egypt, Libya and Yemen had institutions for judicial, economic and military affairs that were originally weak. They will require rebuilding, not just modernizing. Though in Libya financial resources will not be in short supply, their absence in a country like Yemen could be a binding constraint.

In all countries, the UN can make significant contributions through its humanitarian, political and development arms. It can provide electoral assistance, support transitional justice, and mobilize donor support for countries like Tunisia and Egypt. It should continue to offer mediation and humanitarian assistance where conflicts necessitate it; and it should not shy away from exposing human rights abuses and advocating reform where needed.

Respect for a Strong History

In rendering assistance, the UN and other international donors should be careful not to assume a "know-it-all" attitude. Human resources in Arab states were suppressed but not nonexistent. The region is home to some of the most notable intellectuals and experts in fields ranging from writing constitutions to building institutions.

A most inspiring dialogue is currently taking place in Arab countries. The people—the bastion of these revolts—have reclaimed the public sphere as a space for critical debate, dissent and discussion. They are probing the boundaries between the individual and the collective, and looking into new social contracts on which to base the relationship between governments and citizens and the reciprocal boundaries of rights and obligations.

An unprecedented battle of ideas is raging in the streets, coffee shops, meeting rooms and on the screens of national and pan-Arab media. Issues shunned for too long are now being looked at head on. What kind of country do we want? Religious, secular or civil? What economic models should be pursued and how can social justice be ensured? And given the vivid ethnic and religious diversity that characterizes the region, the question of citizenship and identity once again takes center stage.

Positions in the discussion are not static. They unfold and develop and spread into new domains. The intensity and the diversity of issues increase as the uprisings evolve. Groups formed in the furnace of street protests are starting to chart different paths as they move from toppling a regime to building a new one.

UN organizations can contribute by providing space to those who are still deprived of it, and voice to those traditionally marginalized. They can provide training to youth on how to organize politically, since young people were among the main protagonists of the revolutions. But their strength, their non-hierarchical nature, has become their Achilles heel as they compete for votes against well-entrenched forces. Support to societal organizations, including labor unions, can focus on negotiation skills to ensure the protection of basic human and labor rights.

The UN can also enhance the debate by factoring global experiences. Transitions to democracy in Latin America, Africa, Asia and Eastern Europe are rich with experiences and lessons that the Arab world can benefit from.

The UN Also Must Learn

UN agencies can also make an important contribution in the development sphere. Yet this requires that they revisit the development framework they have advocated in the past to learn from obvious failures. For too long, the UN and international financial institutions operated on the assumption that sound social and economic policies can, in and of themselves, bring about growth, prosperity and human development.

Recent events exposed this as a fallacy. The absence of public participation in decision-making and abuse of human rights cannot be excluded from consideration when it comes to eradicating poverty or achieving equitable development. Addressing these knotty challenges requires a holistic approach that grasps the interrelationships between the economic, social and political.

The UN can be a valued partner in fulfilling the promise that the Arab Spring holds. But the UN has to change the way it does business. It has to regain the trust of the people.

In a recent Gallup Poll on public support for the UN, 9 of the top 10 disapproving countries were in the Middle East. The political UN was seen as a supporter of the old regimes against the wills and rights of their peoples. The Security Council is accused of double standards particularly when it comes to Palestinian rights. The development arm may be seen in a better light, but still needs to reinvigorate itself.

As people learn how to hold their rulers to account, they will not spare the UN. Dealing with autocratic rulers is often easier than dealing with democracies, particularly teething ones. However, supporting a democratic dream is by far more rewarding. ■

A Next Chapter in Human Rights
Louise Arbour

At no time in recent history have the people of the Arab world been so close to realizing the promise of human rights as now. Tired of corruption, repression and despotism, populations have mobilized in unprecedented numbers to demand their rights.

Starting in December 2010, this wave of public protest swept away the Tunisian and Egyptian regimes and inspired hope for change across the region. Yet, while these events seemed to herald a new era for the region, violence in Libya, Bahrain, Syria and elsewhere has tempered that hope.

The uprisings in Egypt and Tunisia, though far from straightforward, appear in retrospect as somewhat easier cases. In contrast, civil war and international intervention in Libya; sectarian undertones—possibly even overtones—of government repression in Bahrain; a multiplicity of actors in Yemen, and the wider implications of the unrest in Syria make these situations more complex and less predictable.

But all the events still share common features, principally a clear demonstration of the idea that rights withheld will be seized, not just claimed.

Indeed, while all the implications may not be understood for many years, two aspects are striking. The first is the central role played by human rights: however the uprisings have been framed, at their heart lie demands for political freedoms, social equality and economic justice. In Tunisia and Egypt at least, these demands have led to previously unimaginable changes. The second is the relatively robust action taken by the United Nations Human Rights and Security Councils, particularly in comparison with the past.

A New Type of Revolution

The uprisings shattered myths. They have shown that significant change does not depend on a few leaders or figureheads, but on people coming together to demand their rights. The uprisings have overturned many beliefs about what constitutes stability. They have made clear that change is not always dictated by the great powers. They have brought into question any assumption that Islam is the core issue in the region's politics. And they have demonstrated that a deep-rooted desire for more freedom can inspire great passion, even after decades of repression.

In these ways, the events in Tunisia, Egypt, Libya, Yemen, Syria, Bahrain and elsewhere have demonstrated the true value of the international human rights agenda. What the protesters and insurgents share is not just a revolt against political repression but a broader rejection of unconscionable economic and social inequities. It is tempting to downplay the significance of one or the other factor, but it is truly their combination that is lethal to oppressive regimes.

While occupying seats on the UN Human Rights Council, representatives of these very regimes gave lip service to human rights. But pleading cultural sensitivity, they cynically reshaped concepts until they were scarcely recognizable, rejecting as exclusively Western basic political rights and freedoms. What we are seeing in the Arab world is a rejection of this impoverished vision of human rights and a reaffirmation of what authoritarian rulers always seek to deny: that human rights are universal and indivisible.

Much has been made in recent months of the role of social networks. World War II was described as the war of the radio; the Vietnam War as the war of television; the first Gulf War was seen as the war of CNN and rolling news networks; the wars in Iraq and Afghanistan were the campaigns of the Internet era. Now, some say, we are witnessing social networking revolutions. But while Twitter and Facebook facilitated the unfolding of these mostly leaderless movements and while they have become a powerful means of transmitting the voice of civil society, these instruments do not make revolutions: injustice does.

The lesson is fundamentally positive. Despite the frustration, obstruction and politicization of human rights at the international level, recent events—in Tunisia

UNHCR Photo/Helene Caux

Children play in a Tripoli street on a tank used by the Libyan leader, Muammar el-Qaddafi, against antigovernment forces in the port city of Misurata. The fighting in Misurata drove tens of thousands of Libyans from their homes in spring 2011.

New Day in the Arab World 7

and Egypt at least—show the broader power of the concept of rights. The people of the Arab world have made it clear that however paralyzed the international community, even the most repressive regimes can be shaken. Simply put, we are encountering a new form of revolution, where people rise to overturn authoritarian regimes on the basis of no ideology beyond hostility to economic and political injustice.

Now Old Failures Are Manifest

In demonstrating the desire of people of the Arab world for full economic, social, political and civil rights, the Arab Spring has also thrown into bold relief the failure of the international community to protect these rights in the past, and the weakness of the UN's framework for human-rights protection. While international law places both positive and negative obligations on countries for the benefit of individual people, there is no adequate mechanism for the enforcement of those rights.

It seems self-evident that countries should not themselves judge whether they adequately discharge such obligations. But this is what happens at the international level. There is no international human rights court. The 47-nation Human Rights Council is certainly not a court: it is a forum of nations, an explicitly political body—that purports to be guided by legal principles.

The 15-nation Security Council is similarly constrained by politics, perhaps even more so, given the veto power of the five permanent members, Britain, China, France, Russia and the United States. As a result, neither the Human Rights Council nor the Security Council has a shining record on taking action or even speaking out against abuses.

A troubling recent demonstration of tendencies toward inaction followed the civil war in Sri Lanka in May 2009, when the government finally defeated the separatist Tamil Tigers. Then, the Human Rights Council welcomed the government's efforts for peace and condemned all attacks by the Tamil Tigers on civilians. While the UN has estimated that the closing months of the war saw as many as 40,000 civilians killed in indiscriminate government attacks in supposed "no-fire zones," the council did not refer to the government's gross rights violations; instead, it applauded the government's commitment to the promotion of human rights.

The Security Council response was even more woeful. For reasons of great-power politics, the matter never appeared on the council's agenda.

Libya Brings a Robust Response

In stark contrast, both the Human Rights Council and the Security Council took robust measures after recent violence in Libya.

The Human Rights Council strongly condemned violations there, called on the government to protect its population and urged the authorities to respect the popular will of their people. It decided to dispatch an independent commission of inquiry to investigate alleged violations and make recommendations on accountability measures.

The Security Council took an even firmer stance, imposing sanctions, referring the situation to the International Criminal Court and eventually, authorizing UN members to use "all necessary measures" to protect civilians, a move that led to military attacks on the part of NATO and other powers.

The councils' actions are seen in some quarters as raising hope for future protection through the UN. The actions of the Security Council have brought into focus two tools of potentially significant benefit to the cause of civilian protection: the Responsibility to Protect doctrine adopted by a UN world summit in 2005, and individual criminal responsibility.

These tools point toward a further yielding of national sovereignty in favor of a larger concept of human security. They show concern for civilians at risk, and pay some heed to humanitarian and legal considerations alongside political ones. That said, the highly political context of the two councils cannot be forgotten, and one should be cautious about ascribing too much to the Libyan resolutions as precedents.

New Era for Civilian Protection?

So, are these developments a true vindication of principle over self-interest and a retreat of the political agenda in the face of legal and humanitarian claims?

The answer is unclear. The ideas of shields for international human rights and the safety of civilians are inextricably linked to political bodies. I have long advocated a separation of the justice and political agendas, and would prefer to see an International Criminal Court with no connection to the Security Council. But

Rais67

Tunisians demonstrate against the government in January 2011. Their Jasmine Revolution led to the ouster of President Zine el-Abidine Ben Ali and helped spark uprisings across the Arab world.

this is neither the case nor the trend. As for the Responsibility to Protect, it is clear that military intervention for the protection of civilians must come with a council mandate. This is the price to pay to prevent abuse of the doctrine.

Political input will therefore always be inevitable. That politics accommodated —in part—humanitarian concerns in Libya is encouraging, but does not necessarily signal a new era in civilian protection. Nonetheless, there is much that the UN can still do.

For all the emphasis on military intervention, economic sanctions and judicial accountability, the best form of civilian protection is to prevent deadly conflict in the first place. A vital part must be securing the human rights of oppressed peoples so that they do not feel the need to take matters into their own hands. This idea lies at the heart of the Universal Declaration of Human Rights, which holds that "…it is essential, if man is not to be compelled to have recourse, as a last resort, to rebellion against tyranny and oppression, that human rights should be protected by the rule of law… ."

Wonderful though it is to see the people of the Arab world seizing the rights that they have long been denied, the turbulent spring has carried a heavy human cost that could perhaps have been avoided had the UN and the Human Rights Council acted more effectively in the past. Properly conceived, the Human Rights Council should act as the prime forum for the prevention of deadly conflict. Human rights violations are, to varying degrees, precursors to most internal conflicts.

Many of the reference points used by human rights organizations are also used in assessing the risk that conflict might break out or in developing recommendations to end conflicts. Firm, timely action by the Human Rights Council at the earliest stage of abuses, and an end to pandering to dictators and despots, would have a significant impact and avoid the appalling consequences of inaction.

A Lesson Is Upon the Wall

Of course, this sort of preventive action requires significant political will. But recent events might provide impetus. Dictators have been shown that, even without international support, their people will not tolerate abuse and corruption. They have seen that failure to uphold standards can have tangible consequences.

Similarly, the international community has been shown the lengths to which people will go to secure their freedoms. Ultimately, these events have shown that oppression, corruption and abuse, left unchecked, will eventually provoke rebellion and instability. Both authoritarian rulers and international leaders must now realize that crafting a peaceful solution earlier in the day provides a better outcome for all involved.

The people of the Arab world have shown extraordinary courage. Frankly, though, they shouldn't have to; the situation should never have been allowed to deteriorate so far. I hope the international community, and the Human Rights Council, will realize that reactive and interventionist responses are not sufficient. Only by concentrating on preventing conflict in the first place will it maximize civilian protection. This is the challenge for the UN, and as current events are so starkly demonstrating, this is one it can't afford to ignore. ■

Libya in Revolt:
Testing the Responsibility to Protect
Allan Rock

When United Nations members in 2005 unanimously adopted the bundle of principles known as "the Responsibility to Protect" (or R2P), it was uncertain whether the concept would ever move from a mere political declaration to a recognized international norm, let alone a basis for Security Council action.

The adoption of R2P was expressed in just two paragraphs of a 40-page declaration formally approved at the 2005 global summit by a unanimous vote of the General Assembly.

The summit, and the balance of the declaration, dealt with subjects as widespread as international development assistance, counterterrorism and security, disarmament and nonproliferation, peace-building and UN management reform. In those circumstances, it was easy to assert—and many did—that R2P was either an afterthought or an oversight: a radical notion that many believed would never have been approved as a stand-alone proposal, but that had survived only because the membership was too distracted by larger and more controversial issues.

R2P has not only endured, but by serving as a foundation for a Security Council resolution adopted in response to the crisis in Libya, it has provided a framework for a new approach to national sovereignty and an instrument of unique value for the protection of populations when the failures of their own governments expose them to mortal risk.

The Case for Intervention

R2P elicited strong reactions from the moment it was first proposed in 2001 by the International Commission on Intervention and State Sovereignty, appointed (through the leadership of the government of Canada) after several mass atrocities within the borders of UN members. The Bosnian massacre in Srebrenica and Rwanda are only the most prominent that come to mind.

Those appalling events of genocide, ethnic cleansing and crimes against humanity shocked the world. Calls for "humanitarian intervention" as the events unfolded were met with the objection that each country's government is master of its own affairs, even, it seems, when that involves slaughtering its own people, or standing by while others do so. Those who resisted action referred to the UN Charter, which expressly prohibits intervention "in matters which are essentially within the domestic jurisdiction of any state."

The commission debated whether the principle of national sovereignty confines the international community to being a bystander when civilian populations face mass murder carried out or enabled by their own governments. Is sovereignty a shield to prevent all outside interference? The moral case for intervention in such cases is easily made, but can there be a legal justification for doing so?

Reasoning that sovereignty entails not only rights but responsibilities, the commission concluded that each government's most fundamental responsibility is to protect its citizenry from mass murder. If the government is unwilling or unable to do so, with the result that there is a risk of significant loss of life, the responsibility shifts to the international community to take steps—including military intervention if needed—to prevent or stop the atrocity.

A Major Change After 360 Years

In this sense, the adoption of R2P was truly revolutionary, changing the notion of national sovereignty by introducing an exception to the hitherto absolute nature of a country's prerogatives.

In 2007, the historian and Churchill biographer Sir Martin Gilbert asserted: "Since the Peace of Westphalia in 1648, noninterference in the internal policies even of the most repressive governments was the golden rule of international diplomacy. The Canadian-sponsored concept of 'responsibility to protect' proposed the most significant adjustment to national sovereignty in 360 years."

Despite its significance, R2P had seemed an unlikely candidate for approval in the run-up to the 2005 global summit. For one thing, the focus of the world's attention had, on Sept. 11, 2001, shifted away from humanitarian intervention to issues of security. Furthermore, R2P was being debated in the toxic environment created by the 2003 invasion of Iraq. Depicted by many as an illegal and

UNHCR Photo/Helene Caux

Tripoli Street in Misurata on Libya's Mediterranean coast. Government forces besieged the rebel-held city in March 2011.

illegitimate means of regime change by an imperialistic Pentagon, the Iraq invasion deepened long-standing suspicions among developing countries about the motivations of the U.S. and Britain.

The resulting distrust created an atmosphere that was hardly conducive to the adoption of a principle calling for outside intervention in countries' domestic affairs, no matter how noble the purpose cited.

An Alteration of View

Despite these long odds, the summit's declaration recorded unanimous agreement in these terms:
- "Each individual State has the responsibility to protect its populations from genocide, war crimes, ethnic cleansing and crimes against humanity [including] the prevention of such crimes."
- "The international community, through the United Nations, also has the responsibility . . . to help protect populations from genocide, war crimes, ethnic cleansing and crimes against humanity. In this context, we are prepared to take collective action, in a timely and decisive manner, through the Security Council, in accordance with the Charter, including Chapter VII . . . should peaceful means be inadequate and national authorities manifestly fail to protect their populations from genocide, war crimes, ethnic cleansing and crimes against humanity."

The reference to the Charter's Chapter VII opens the way for the Security Council to make its demands binding under international law, if it chooses to, adding military intervention to the list of possible collective actions.

Notwithstanding the apparent clarity of these commitments, the post-summit commentary about R2P's prospects was highly cynical. Many observers wondered how long such a decision could stand, given the hostile reaction among developing countries to Western-led interventions following Iraq and Afghanistan.

Others questioned whether the political will to invoke R2P could ever be generated, no matter the circumstances. Even in such a case, it would of course be necessary to overcome the potential vetoes of China and Russia, notoriously reluctant to countenance UN "interference" in the affairs of sovereign nations.

Predictions of a short lifespan for R2P acquired greater currency from widespread reports of "buyers' remorse" among developing nations who had gone along (in some cases very reluctantly) with R2P rather than stand apart from the crowd.

And so an expectation grew that opponents would find ways to have the General Assembly reconsider if not reverse the adoption of R2P.

Survival Despite Countercurrents

But the two paragraphs and their powerful idea proved remarkably durable.

Within seven and a half months of adoption by the General Assembly, the doctrine had been reaffirmed by the Security Council and then invoked by the council in creating a protection force for civilians caught in a civil war in Darfur in western Sudan.

When the General Assembly scheduled a special debate on R2P in the summer of 2009, the doctrine's opponents seemed to have found their moment: an opportunity to roll it back and to narrow or revoke the broad and unanimous commitment. But of the 94 nations in the debate, the clear majority were generally very supportive. The resulting resolution was benign.

After that there finally arose a cautious sentiment that perhaps R2P had indeed taken root: that it was here to stay, as an emerging standard of international conduct.

The question remained, however, whether it would ever be applied and brought to life.

If R2P proved hardy enough to survive a difficult infancy, even its strongest supporters were left to wonder whether it would fulfill its potential. In case after case, those who saw it as a new and effective instrument to prevent or stop mass killings were disappointed.

Whether in Darfur or the Democratic Republic of Congo, Zimbabwe or Sri Lanka, the targeting of civilian populations continued unabated.

Had anything really changed?

Making History With Libya

That question was answered with the transformation of R2P from emerging concept to operational principle through the adoption by the Security Council in the spring of 2011 of the second of two resolutions dealing with the crisis in Libya after the brutal response of its leader, Col. Muammar el-Qaddafi, to peaceful protests that developed in his country in January.

The first resolution, adopted Feb. 26, referred the situation to the International Criminal Court and imposed an arms embargo. Apart from the unanimity of the vote in favor of referral to the court (unusual because of longstanding U.S. opposition to the court), the resolution was hardly ground-breaking.

It was the second Libya resolution that made history.

That resolution, adopted March 17, imposed a no-fly zone over Libya and authorized "all necessary measures" to protect civilians and enforce the arms embargo. Taken in its entirety, the measure clearly gave a green light to military intervention. The vote was 10-0 with five abstentions: Brazil, China, Germany, India and Russia. Since permanent members have veto power, a "no" vote by China or Russia would have killed the measure.

The resolution expressly reiterated the responsibility of the Libyan authorities to protect the population and asserted that the "widespread and systematic attacks" being carried out by the government against its own citizens might amount to crimes against humanity.

The resolution did, however, expressly rule out an occupying force, thus reassuring the Arab world and others that this operation would be unlike either Iraq or Afghanistan.

What was it about Libya that impelled the Security Council to move so fast and so far in applying R2P? A number of factors set the stage for these dramatic developments.

A Situation Impelling Action

The first was the nature of the Qaddafi regime's response as unrest and then civil war engulfed Libya early in 2011.

Authorities in Libya responded with increasing violence and aggressiveness as rebels seized control of one town after another in the early weeks of the uprising. In contrast with Tunisia and then Egypt, where the despots fled in the face of popular demonstrations and the armed forces refused to attack the population, the Libyan military (and paid mercenaries) turned their arms on the dissidents.

When rebel forces took control of the eastern city of Benghazi, Qaddafi threatened to attack and kill them and vowed that "there would be no mercy or compassion." His words and deeds—especially given his history of criminality and irrationality—demonstrated a real risk of mass atrocity as the ruthless Qaddafi forces bore down on the over-matched rebels and the vulnerable civilian population of Benghazi. To a world still feeling the shame of inaction, in Rwanda, in Srebrenica and elsewhere, the time had come to act.

A second crucial factor was the encouragement and support of regional organizations.

The Security Council expressly took note of the condemnation by the League of Arab States, the African Union and the Secretary General of the Organization of the Islamic Conference of the serious violations of human rights and international humanitarian law in Libya.

The council was especially influenced by the decision of the Council of the League of Arab States on March 12 to call for the imposition of a no-fly zone on Libyan military aviation, and to establish safe areas in places exposed to shelling, as a precautionary measure for the protection of civilians.

Finally, it must be said that in contrast to other cases in which supporters of R2P had unsuccessfully advocated strong action (Darfur, for example), circumstances in Libya overall permitted a robust response. Geographically as well as geopolitically, the operation was feasible.

Physical factors that might have inhibited such an intervention elsewhere such as remoteness and terrain did not present obstacles in Libya. Furthermore, air power was uniquely capable of achieving the mission's stated objectives, so that the difficult and divisive issue of organizing and deploying ground forces did not arise. The cumulative effect of these circumstances created a propitious environment for action.

In addition, of course, the Security Council itself managed the political dimension of the case so as to avoid the exercise of a veto and achieve sufficient consensus to permit bold action.

The Americans and the British provided strong leadership. France played an active role in the process leading to the March 17 resolution, perhaps stung by criticism that it had failed to provide early encouragement to the successful revolt in Tunisia. Lebanon's continuous and insistent advocacy for vigorous action helped motivate regional approval. South Africa and Nigeria lent crucial support: without their votes in favor, the resolution would have failed to achieve the 9 votes needed for adoption.

Some of the Security Council members' positions on the resolution elicited surprise (as when Germany abstained, while afterward claiming solidarity with the mission's aims). That Russia and China did not veto the resolution is perhaps a measure of widespread impatience with Qaddafi and of a strong international consensus that he should be stopped.

The Shadow of Regime Change

The stated purpose of the March 17 resolution and the NATO operation that followed was to protect civilians. Repeated assertions, however, by President Barack Obama and the British prime minister, David Cameron, that Qaddafi must leave office created the impression that key NATO actors saw the objective as regime change. The selection of bombing targets in Tripoli, far from the endangered Benghazi population, added to the sense that NATO was aiming at the leadership and not just the military.

There is risk here for the future of R2P as an instrument of protection.

If in this first major foray under the R2P principles, its proponents are seen to have gone beyond prevention and protection and to have taken sides in a civil war, and especially if they are seen to have targeted the country's leader, they will give the doctrine's opponents very powerful arguments for resisting action the next time. The concerns expressed for years by many in the developing world linking R2P with Western imperialism will seem to have been well founded.

The venture has also come under criticism for failing because Qaddafi was not quickly ousted. Ironically, this criticism was often leveled by the same voices who complained of "mission creep," insisting there was no authority for Qaddafi's overthrow.

A clear military result, however, is not necessary to R2P's success. If the doctrine is about protection and prevention, the mission succeeded when the mass murder threatened by Qaddafi in Benghazi was avoided. If a stalemate results (which, at this writing, seems likely) and other political initiatives are required to resolve it—whether through negotiating partition, or a power-sharing arrangement, or both—then so be it.

Finally, there is the question of consistency. Some are asking why similar resolutions and operations were not undertaken in Bahrain, Syria or Yemen, where oppressive regimes have launched deadly attacks on their civilian populations.

There is no easy answer. To be sure, each of those cases presents circumstances that explain, even if they do not excuse, the failure to act in defense of their vulnerable populations. But ultimately, it is very difficult to justify differential treatment when the objective is the protection of civilians from crimes against humanity.

What can be said is that the mere fact that there is no action to protect populations elsewhere is not a reason for failing to do so in Libya.

The March 17 resolution is historic because it is unprecedented. Let us hope that it will, in time, establish a new standard for international responses to protect civilian populations and that such protection will, in the future, be consistently provided. ■

Talking Points

1. The UN response to the developments in Libya was a rare example of vigorous action in support of human rights despite the highly politicized environment in which the Security and Human Rights councils operate. Is this a sign of a UN shift in elevating universal human rights over the sovereignty concerns of individual nations? Or was Libya a unique example of overwhelming international antipathy toward a despotic regime, suggesting that the UN is unlikely to act as forcefully in the future without similar political conditions?

2. With vastly different socioeconomic and political situations across countries in the Middle East, the Arab Spring is hardly a homogenous movement with straightforward solutions that can be easily applied. Will the international community avoid a "one-size-fits-all" approach, uniquely tailoring its aid and support to each country? Given the recent Gallup Poll indicating strong disapproval of the UN among Middle Eastern nations, would the UN be better off pursuing a more discreet role until such negative opinion subsides?

3. The Responsibility to Protect (R2P) doctrine asserts that the international community can act to prevent mass atrocities within a member nation's borders by framing sovereignty as a government's responsibility as well as its right. But the doctrine has been inconsistently applied from crisis to crisis. In weighing a government's actions against its own people, should the UN develop specific benchmarks that, if crossed, would automatically trigger the international community's responsibility to protect?

4. As a thought experiment, 20 years from now, will we look back at the UN's response to the Arab Spring as a success or failure of its ever-changing role in the world?

UNHCR Photo/R.Gangale

Children sift through trash outside a refugee camp in central Somalia. Many Somalis have fled to other parts of the world but send money home via a secretive network of remittance companies. Counterterrorist agencies worry the money could be feeding terrorists.

Fault Lines

20 **Lord's Resistance Army: Terror Roams Central Africa**
Ida Sawyer

26 **Balance and Perseverance:
The Case for Continued Engagement With Iran**
Joseph Cirincione and Benjamin Loehrke

31 **In Somalia, Banking as Usual Is Rather Unusual**
Liat Shetret

35 **The Nuclear Outliers**
Jayantha Dhanapala

41 **North Korea and the UN: An Uneasy Relationship**
Daniel A. Pinkston

46 **International Puzzle: Ending a Decade of Afghan War**
Jeffrey Laurenti

51 **Talking Points**

Lord's Resistance Army: Terror Roams Central Africa

Ida Sawyer

The rebels burned the man's house in northern Congo and abducted his four sons, the youngest 4 years old. Two were killed, he was told, and he knows nothing of the fate of the other two. "We have sad hearts knowing that we've been forgotten and live here at the mercy of the rebels," the man, a 45-year-old in the village of Zangabai told me in April, trembling as he spoke.

Those who obliterated the man's family were from the Ugandan rebel group known as the Lord's Resistance Army, which for 25 years has terrorized remote parts of central Africa, massacring thousands, mutilating men and women and abducting tens of thousands of children into their forces.

Despite the crisis the Lord's Resistance Army has created, the United Nations and its member nations have devoted limited attention and resources to tackling it. Two things would be required: a serious commitment of new UN resources to protect civilians and provide humanitarian aid, and a law enforcement operation able to apprehend the top leaders.

On the face of it, that could be simple enough. But the political will is lacking. Richer countries insist they are too busy in Iraq, Afghanistan and elsewhere to dedicate resources to ending attacks on civilians in a poor and remote area of central Africa. The result is that the people who live with the daily reality of Lord's Resistance Army attacks feel abandoned by their governments and by the international community.

'Realize We Are Humans Too'

In Zangabai, in a remote border region between the Democratic Republic of Congo and the Central African Republic, the father of the four abducted boys tried to hold back his tears as he talked about the attack on his family in November 2010. "I wish the international community would look at what's happening and realize we are humans too," he said.

For two and a half years, I have traveled through some of the most remote areas in central Africa to speak to witnesses and victims of the Lord's Resistance Army; it is part of my work as a researcher for the New York-based organization Human Rights Watch. Often there are no roads, cellphone networks or other kinds of infrastructure. Together with local human rights activists, we traveled by motorcycle through rough forest paths to reach areas where we had heard there had been attacks. Sometimes we were the first outsiders to have visited in years.

One such remote area that I visited was Makombo, in Haut Uele district, in March 2010. We had heard of an attack, but it was impossible to verify without going there. When we arrived and began our work, we were taken aback by the scale of the attack. By listening to dozens of victims and witnesses, we learned that in December 2009, at least 345 people were killed and 250 abducted in a four-day killing rampage. The attack was one of the worst in the Lord's Resistance Army's history, yet it had gone unreported and undocumented for months. The area's isolation meant information had not reached the outside world. We worked to correct that and published a detailed report.

While documenting this and other atrocities, we traveled from village to village of abandoned homes, schools and churches. The people had fled in fear after attacks. We spoke to grief-stricken mothers and fathers whose children were abducted by the Lord's Resistance Army to fight as soldiers. And we heard from children who had managed to escape. They described the abuse they had suffered and how they were forced to participate in atrocities and were often made to kill friends, relatives or others whom the group targeted. Some of the girls told us about rapes they endured by the group's commanders.

The Lord's Resistance Army and its leaders originated in northern Uganda, where their initial aim was to overthrow the government of President Yoweri Museveni. But soon its main activities became attacking civilians and abducting children. Repeated Ugandan military operations eventually pushed the group out of northern Uganda and, in 2005, it relocated to Garamba National Park, a largely uninhabited game park in northern Congo.

The organization leader, Joseph Kony, is a former Catholic altar boy from northern Uganda who sought to overthrow President Museveni and impose a rule based on his own interpretation of the Ten Commandments. Kony has claimed to follow the commands of spirits which only he can hear. The group's current motivations, other than survival, are unclear.

A 12-Year-Old Girl Forced to Kill

A 12-year-old girl I interviewed from Bas Uele district, northern Congo, was held for more than six months by the Lord's Resistance Army. She was held by a Lord's Resistance Army commander who raped her almost daily. She was also forced to kill—she does not remember how many in all—one day it might have been four people, the next day three. She was mostly made to kill adults who had been abducted to transport looted goods.

She told me that combatants refused to release captives alive because they did not want them to tell the Congolese army where they camped. The victims were tied up and made to lie face down on the ground. Then she and other children were forced to beat them on the head with pieces of wood until they died. To make it easier to kill, the combatants taught her to view people as animals. The experience left her deeply traumatized.

Whole communities are left in terror. In late August of 2010 I visited the village of Duru, in northern Congo. Just after we had found shelter for the night in a church, the Lord's Resistance Army attacked the village center. They abducted eight civilians, including three children, less than half a mile from a UN peacekeeping base. Later that night, the group killed three of their captives with machetes.

A woman and a 16-year-old girl who had been abducted were released the next morning. When I interviewed them, they told me the message they had been given for the Congolese army and others in Duru: Lord's Resistance Army fighters are nearby and they will be back soon. The woman and girl then led Ugandan and Congolese army soldiers to the place where the three young men had been killed. I watched family members and neighbors bear away butchered bodies for mourning and burial.

These kinds of attacks are not new phenomena. Though it has operated for more than two decades, there has been no effective strategy to end the group's brutality and protect civilians. Current military operations, which rely on the Ugandan army to tackle the threat, have not succeeded. An urgent rethinking of the issue is required, and the UN should play its part in protecting civilians and ending impunity.

In 2006 after the group moved its base to northern Congo, Uganda and international partners started new efforts to negotiate peace, but talks ended two years later when Kony, its leader, did not sign a final peace agreement.

Joint Operation Is Organized

The Ugandan army launched a new operation with the national armies of Congo, Southern Sudan and the Central African Republic, and with financial and logistical support from the United States. It began on Dec. 14, 2008, with a surprise

UNHCR Photo/P. Taggart

Civilians on the move in a part of the Democratic Republic of Congo that has been terrorized by the Lord's Resistance Army. The group has been attacking civilians, abducting children and spreading terror across central Africa for 25 years.

22 *A Global Agenda 2011-2012*

aerial bombardment of the group's main base, but Kony and other senior leaders escaped and the group's fighters scattered across the remote border region of northern Congo, Southern Sudan and the eastern Central African Republic. Kony and two top lieutenants, Okot Odhiambo and Dominic Ongwen, are sought on arrest warrants issued by the International Criminal Court in 2005 for war crimes committed in northern Uganda, but all three remain at large.

Since September 2008, the Lord's Resistance Army has killed nearly 2,400 civilians and abducted 3,400, many of them children, according to Human Rights Watch and UN documentation. Over 400,000 people have fled in the past few years, including more than 38,000 displaced since the beginning of 2011.

The group's extreme brutality is one reason civilians flee at the first rumor of its presence, and why few want to return. As the girl in Bas Uele reported, its combatants commonly kill their victims—men, women and children—by crushing their skulls with heavy wooden sticks or tying them to trees, then slashing their heads and throats with machetes.

We have learned through interviews with hundreds of former combatants, as well as children and adults who later escaped, how those spared death and taken as hostages are often tied together in long human chains with heavy loads of looted goods on their heads and their backs. The captives are forced to walk dozens of miles a day, often with little or nothing to eat or drink, and are beaten or killed if they go too slowly.

Young boys and girls, abducted to serve as fighters, undergo violent rituals to induct them into the group, and are forced to kill family members, friends and neighbors who try to escape, seem too tired or weak, or are deemed unnecessary by their captors. The physical and psychological scars are permanent.

Kony's Forces Adept at Strategy

Yet Kony should not be dismissed as a mere madman. He and the group's other senior leaders have demonstrated skills at military strategy, surviving in unforgiving forests and jungles, remaining in communication with each other despite wide separations between small groups of combatants and implementing well-coordinated attacks. The Lord's Resistance Army has also clearly become adept at using brutality, fear and brainwashing to turn young children into obedient and ruthless combatants.

The group conducts its activities in remote, underdeveloped parts of countries facing a plethora of other challenges, posing no direct threat to the national governments of the three countries where it currently operates. The national armies of Congo, South Sudan and the Central African Republic are weak, and tackling the Lord's Resistance Army is not a priority for any.

The Lord's Resistance Army is not large. It is estimated to have 200 to 300 combatants, plus the hundreds of abducted children and adults. Unlike most other armed groups in the region, it has no popular support, no clear political objectives and no voluntary recruits. But it is responsible for unimaginable suffering and brutality. Few would object if the group's leaders were apprehended, removing the threat they pose.

This is clearly a situation where intervention by capable forces to help carry out the International Criminal Court arrest warrants and protect civilians would face little opposition. In 2006, UN peacekeepers in Congo conducted an operation against the group's then headquarters in Garamba National Park, where one of its leaders sought by the court was assumed to be hiding. But the mission failed and eight Guatemalan peacekeepers were killed. Since then, UN peacekeepers have made no further attempts to apprehend or pursue the group's top leaders.

UN Peacekeepers—Too Few and Ineffective

The UN Security Council has authorized four UN missions in the central African region in recent years, all dealing with a broad range of problems. None of them has made the Lord's Resistance Army a priority. Overstretched and lacking authority to cross national borders, these missions have failed to protect civilians and have struggled to put in place effective coordination, cooperation and intelligence-sharing.

Peacekeepers from the UN Mission in the Central African Republic and Chad, whose mandate expired in December 2010, were never deployed to the parts of the eastern Central African Republic where the group was operating. The UN Integrated Peacebuilding Office in the Central African Republic is still operational, but it has no peacekeeping capacity and has not been focused on the Lord's Resistance Army.

The UN Mission in Sudan has played a minimal role in protecting civilians in the areas of southern Sudan affected by Lord's Resistance Army attacks. Yet this mission's hands have been full with the recent referendum on independence for South Sudan and violence in other parts of the country.

The UN mission in Congo has done more than any of the other UN missions to address the threat posed by the Lord's Resistance Army, but fewer than 1,000 troops (just 5 percent of the mission's 19,000 peacekeepers, police and military observers) are in the areas affected by the group. No peacekeeping troops are in Bas Uele district, one of the areas worst hit by the group's atrocities, and where Kony has recently been operating, despite repeated calls from humanitarian groups and others for the UN to set up a peacekeeping base there.

The peacekeepers deployed to the parts of northern Congo where the Lord's Resistance Army has been active have been ineffective. The Congo mission, while it has a mandate from the Security Council to protect civilians and support international justice efforts, has a serious shortage of trained and equipped peacekeepers, intelligence analysts, interpreters, helicopters and military assets.

Its strategy of "protection by presence" has had limited effect. Many UN commanders have said they are able to do little more than protect the UN's own bases. In many incidents in the past year, the Lord's Resistance Army has carried out attacks very close to a UN base, such as the one I nearly witnessed in Duru in August of last year. Following these attacks, the peacekeepers have been either unable or unwilling to pursue the assailants and try to rescue the abducted children and adults.

The peacekeeping mission's response is further weakened by having only a very small number of senior-level staff in or near areas where the group is active, with an insufficient number of dedicated political advisers and military liaison officers.

Such senior-level staff could enable the UN to use its good offices to help manage tensions and coordinate intelligence.

U.S. Attention—Providing Some Hope

On May 24, 2010, President Barack Obama signed into law the most widely supported Africa-specific legislation in recent history, committing the U.S. to help arrest or remove the Lord's Resistance Army's top leaders and to protect populations at risk.

This law gave hope to tens of thousands of civilians across the region. Local leaders and activists appealed to President Obama to back his words with decisive actions. Yet more than a year later, little has changed on the ground and few improvements have been made in previously unsuccessful efforts to pursue the group's top leaders and protect civilians.

One of the main problems is that the U.S. continues to rely on the Ugandan army to do the job. The U.S. has provided Uganda with logistical and intelligence support since 2008 in this cause. Yet the Ugandan army, lacking adequate intelligence and rapid reaction capacity, has failed to defeat the Lord's Resistance Army for 25 years. The Ugandan army's main base for its operations against the group is in Nzara, in South Sudan. Uganda is now estimated to have 1,500 troops deployed in the region against the Lord's Resistance Army. The national armies of Congo, the Central African Republic and South Sudan, who work alongside the Ugandan army, are ill-equipped, poorly trained and often are themselves responsible for serious human rights abuses.

Plans to deploy U.S. military advisers to support the regional effort and more effectively direct U.S. military support have stalled.

Many diplomats and policy makers have hoped the African Union will take the lead on dealing with the group. The regional body has recently increased its efforts, promising to facilitate coordinated regional actions. In June, it proposed establishing a regional task force and a joint operations center and appointing a special envoy to tackle the threat. These steps could make an important contribution, but it is unlikely that these efforts on their own will be sufficient to address the serious protection gaps and failures in the current strategy.

Changing Direction

Over 25 years, numerous strategies, nearly all relying on the Ugandan army's leadership, have been tried. While the number of the group's combatants has fluctuated over the years, its ability to attack civilians remains undiminished. Current efforts too closely resemble past ineffective attempts.

If the U.S., the UN Security Council and other concerned parties are serious about giving meaning to international justice and protecting civilian populations at grave risk, then a new strategy and urgent new measures are required.

Significantly increased levels of political, financial and military resources are needed to ensure both that capable forces are pursuing the group's top leaders and that civilians are protected from its brutal attacks. ∎

Balance and Perseverance: The Case for Continued Engagement With Iran

Joseph Cirincione and Benjamin Loehrke

Nuclear diplomacy with Iran is stalemated. Sanctions against the regime are biting but not compelling. Negotiations drift, as neither side seems prepared to compromise.

The relative calm of the current standoff is misleading, however. The illusion of a military solution has faded, but could re-emerge if the stalemate continues. More important, as conflict roils the region, risks rise that a miscalculation could trigger a larger military confrontation.

A frank assessment of the strategic picture indicates that a new, determined engagement with the Iranian people and the government offers the only reasonable chance of resolving this.

Drivers of Iran's Program

There does not appear to be a consensus among Iran's leaders to build a nuclear bomb, but there is agreement to develop the technologies that would permit this in the future. Even that capability is a threat to international security. And it is difficult to say if Iran would stop short of developing weapons. The classic drivers for a nation developing a nuclear capacity—security, international prestige and domestic politics—all give Iran incentives. Unless effective counterincentives are found, it is possible that trends would push Iran over whatever line its leaders may now have in mind.

Iran is, after all, a fundamentally insecure country with many adversaries at its borders. The U.S., Iran's "Great Satan," has a large military presence in Iraq, Afghanistan and the Persian Gulf. Other Middle Eastern nations have enhanced military capabilities and alliances to balance against Iran, largely through partnership with the U.S. Faced with these, Iran's leadership wants to deter the kinds of attacks it has seen on Afghanistan, Iraq and Libya. A nuclear weapons capability could offer that deterrent while reinforcing Iran's ability to project power throughout the region.

Iran also sees its nuclear program as a coin of international prestige and a nationalist rallying point domestically. Mastering the nuclear fuel cycle—chiefly uranium enrichment—is a challenging task few countries have achieved.

This symbol of technological prowess has broad public appeal in Iran, and the regime has used it skillfully to rally political support for an otherwise unpopular government. Support for a nuclear program—though not necessarily for weapons—extends across the political spectrum.

The objective for the international community is to tip Iran's balance of incentives. As the U.S. Director of National Intelligence, Lt. Gen. James Clapper, told Congress in 2011, "Iran's nuclear decision-making is guided by a cost-benefit approach, which offers the international community opportunities to influence Tehran."

The Slow Road to Nuclear Breakout

Reza Shah Pahlavi started Iran's nuclear program, including nuclear weapons research, in the 1960s. This covert nuclear program continued off and on, but its greatest advancements have come over the last decade. In 2002, dissidents disclosed that Iran had secretly built a uranium enrichment facility near the city of Natanz that would allow Iran to produce fuel for nuclear reactors or for nuclear bombs.

That enrichment program is the focus of the Iran nuclear controversy. The U.S. and its partners see Iran's enrichment program as a threat, and would like it dismantled. Iran argues it has the right to peaceful nuclear technology and wants an indigenous enrichment capability. Efforts at compromise have fallen short, and Iran has consistently failed to provide meaningful assurances that its nuclear program is peaceful.

While diplomacy faltered, Iran's nuclear program advanced. It has a large uranium enrichment capacity, with about 8,000 centrifuges installed at Natanz, according to a report by the International Atomic Energy Agency in May 2011. Iran nearly has the technical means to enrich uranium to bomb-usable levels, indicated by its production of about 125 pounds of uranium enriched to 20 percent (weapons-grade uranium is 90 percent). Iran also produced a stockpile of 9,000 pounds of low-enriched uranium—sufficient for building perhaps two or three nuclear warheads if further processed.

Those are the known capacities. Iran may also have covert facilities. Questions remain about Iran's weapons activities, including evidence of past research into technologies necessary to develop a nuclear warhead for a missile.

At the current pace, Iran's nuclear abilities could hit a critical point in the latter part of this decade. It could then reach "break-out capability," giving it the option of rapidly producing weapon cores. But Iran is not there yet, allowing time to find a peaceful resolution.

Broken Engagements

Missed opportunities dot the record of diplomacy between the U.S. and Iran. When Iran was willing to talk, the U.S. was not, and vice versa.

After disclosure of the Natanz facility in 2002, Iran agreed to suspend its enrichment program and permit intrusive inspections under an additional protocol to its safeguard agreements under the nuclear nonproliferation treaty. Tehran also sought discussions with Washington on normalizing relations. The Bush administration, preferring regime change, spurned these efforts and argued for punishing Iran's noncompliance. The opportunity for engagement faded in 2005, as the hardliner President Mahmoud Ahmadinejad came to office with little interest in improving relations with the West.

As Iran's position hardened, the U.S. became more receptive to talks. The U.S. joined multilateral negotiations and also prepared for direct talks. Iran spurned these efforts and stymied nuclear inspections. Judging Iran in breach of its treaty obligations, the UN Security Council adopted a resolution in 2006 requiring Iran to suspend its enrichment activities under Chapter VII of the UN Charter, making the measure mandatory under international law.

Iran's failure activated a series of Security Council sanctions to limit Iran's ability to acquire nuclear and ballistic missile technologies. As three subsequent rounds of sanctions advanced, Iran stalled negotiations, became less cooperative, or escalated the crisis by advancing its nuclear activities. This spiral of noncooperation and tightening sanctions continued, despite attempts at diplomacy near the end of the Bush administration.

President Obama changed the dynamic in 2009, offering to negotiate with Iran without preconditions. But the Iranians balked at the offer. Simultaneously, the U.S. prepared to impose targeted sanctions on Iran if it failed to cooperate in talks.

In June 2009, the streets of Tehran erupted with unrest after a fraudulent election. The regime cracked down on its citizens and hardened its position against the West. The international community soon brought down on Iran one of the strongest multilateral group of sanctions ever imposed—with tougher Security Council sanctions combined with targeted sanctions from the U.S. and its partners.

Reliable reports indicate that while President Obama offered engagement he also sped up secret plans to infect Iran's centrifuge-control systems with the Stuxnet virus. This computer virus appears to have destroyed 1,000 centrifuges in 2009, about one-fifth of those operating at the time.

The triple-track strategy of engagement, sanctions and sabotage appears to have further isolated Iran and considerably slowed, but not stopped, its nuclear program. This bought time, not resolution.

Narrowing Options

A premeditated military strike on Iran is highly unlikely. Elite decision-makers in the U.S., Europe and Israel agree that the costs of a strike on Iran in the near future outweigh the benefits. An attack would not end Iran's program, but would solidify Iran's resolve to get a bomb, destabilize the region, cripple the global economy and overwhelm overstretched militaries. The former Israeli intelligence chief Meir Dagan calls an attack on Iran "a stupid idea."

The greater risk now is war through miscalculation. With conflicts and uncertainty rising in the region, clashes involving Iranian naval forces or allies in Iraq, for example, could spark a war no one wants. Meanwhile, conservative elements in U.S. politics will continue calls for military strikes unless the stalemate is broken soon. These calls could rise during and after the U.S. presidential election.

Iran is more politically and economically isolated than ever before—"strategically lonely," in the words of the Middle East scholar Shireen Hunter. But for sanctions to work they must be part of a balanced strategy with incentives for cooperation. The party under sanctions must also trust they will be lifted if it cooperates. Current U.S. strategy is heavy on sanctions and light on incentives. Lacking this balance, stalemate persists.

U.S. officials appear to accept this status quo, relying on punitive measures and the containment strategy that has been used for decades. Not wishing to take the political risks of increased engagement, officials are "muddling through" until after the U.S. presidential elections, hoping that containment will buy time for negotiations or for collapse of the Iranian regime. If all else fails, this strategy could be adapted to deter a nuclear-armed Iran.

However, the Arab Spring shook the pillars of containment. Key partners in the Middle East, like Egypt and Saudi Arabia, turned their attention toward domestic challenges and away from countering Iranian influence. Meanwhile, Iran attempted to use the opportunity to divide the alliance against it and spark proxy fights with the U.S.

The strategy must adapt to these new dynamics.

Three Steps Toward Progress

Engaging Iran—the people and the regime—provides the most promising path for keeping Iran from the bomb. Effective engagement will require a rebalancing of incentives—an achievable objective—and persistent diplomacy from the U.S. and its international partners.

First, the U.S. needs to ease off threats of crippling sanctions and holster counterproductive military threats. These only strengthen the position of Iran's hardliners, who oppose engagement. Instead of adding pressure, negotiators need to communicate a sequence of steps that Iran can take over time in exchange for

UN Photo/Mark Garten

Mahmoud Ahmadinejad, Iran's president, attending a General Assembly session in New York.

Fault Lines **29**

the gradual lifting of sanctions. A recent report from the Henry L. Stimson Center and the U.S. Institute of Peace said: "U.S. and European leaders should communicate a comprehensive picture of what Tehran has to gain from a mutually acceptable agreement on the nuclear issue. Such an effort cannot be piecemeal."

Second, engagement must be targeted toward achievable goals. Halting the enrichment program is politically infeasible for Iran's leaders. A middle ground is needed. Charles Ferguson, president of the Federation of American Scientists, has proposed a sensible goal: Iran could retain an enrichment program if it comes into compliance with its international obligations, accepts an intrusive inspections regime and provides a complete accounting of past activities. Iran could then continually sell the low-enriched uranium it produces to ensure that it does not have enough material on site to make a bomb.

Together, these measures would help provide confidence that Iran is not diverting nuclear material for nuclear weapons. The International Atomic Energy Agency would have a central role in this proposal. Under its UN mandate, the agency would administer an enhanced safeguards regime with Iran to assure the international community that Iran's program remains peaceful.

Third, the international community could add to the isolation and weakness of the Iranian regime by helping develop a more prosperous and democratic Middle East that can ignore Iran's bluster. The plan announced at the May 2011 meeting of the Group of eight nations (Britain, Canada, France, Germany, Italy, Japan, Russia and the U.S.) for $40 billion for Arab nations trying to establish free and democratic societies is a major step in that direction.

There are no guarantees that engagement will work. No matter how finely crafted an engagement strategy, Iran could simply refuse and continue to advance its threatening nuclear program. Sustained sanctions and other punitive actions will be necessary to demonstrate the substantial costs to Iran of noncooperation. But this adapted strategy has the best potential for success.

The international community has shown unity and resolve in addressing the Iranian nuclear challenge. Now it must show flexibility to engage Iran and build resiliency lest efforts falter. Such perseverance is required to resolve this imposing challenge to global security. ■

In Somalia, Banking as Usual Is Rather Unusual
Liat Shetret

The collapse of Somalia as a functioning country in 1991, a continuing civil war, criminal violence, poverty and large-scale famine have led to an exodus of Somalis from Somalia.

Drawn elsewhere by opportunities for resettlement, work and financial growth, these Somalis have been drawn to diaspora communities in the Gulf, North America, Europe and neighboring East African countries. These communities retain strong clan-based and family ties to those left behind; they regularly send money home to brothers, sisters, children, spouses, parents and grandparents living in economic hardship. Somalis who think about eventually returning to the homeland may also send back money to invest in a future home, a construction project or an education.

Sending money home is a common practice across diasporas globally. The World Bank officially recorded $325 billion flowing in this form to developing countries in 2010.

But remittances in the Somali community are different. They are often referred to as the "lifeline" of Somalia by development and aid agencies, yet at the same time they are perceived as a security risk by counterterrorism and security organizations. A World Bank report from 2006 estimated that $825 million a year is sent to Somalia as remittances; other estimates put the total at well over a billion dollars.

Old Economic Ideas Still Active

Somali remittance companies, like most financial institutions, work on supply and demand. On the demand side, Somalia's environment—that is, its lack of a central banking system and other governmental institutions, its ungoverned spaces and overwhelming dependence on the remittance market—has fostered a habit of informal and unregulated economic activity.

The supply side has created a rapidly growing decentralized global network of Somali companies that offer some traditional banking services such as foreign exchange, as well as general money transfer services. Although transfer companies occasionally move physical currency, they rely more on a settlement process through a central clearinghouse and a network of agents who disburse cash from stockpiles and the nearest part of the network.

In this process, it is the value of the money that is moved and settled. Physical cash does not necessarily change hands unless the value to be transferred is higher than an agent can access. Tens of remittance companies with thousands of agents are linked to one another and to Somalia around the world.

Money transfers are flexible, almost immediate and relatively cheap and are often the only option available. Business transactions are based on trust, reputation and family links, essentially bypassing the regulatory framework found in formal financial institutions.

Remittances in Somalia also fulfill a humanitarian purpose and have a direct impact on food security, the job market and economic development. Telecommunication companies, major import and export businesses, relief organizations and various UN bodies all rely on remittance companies to get value and money into Somalia. Remittances have served a big role in promoting investment in schools and hospitals, have assisted in post-war reconstruction and fostered employment opportunities.

It Moves Under the Finance Radar

At the same time, the Sept. 11, 2001, terrorist attacks focused sudden attention on Somalia's ad hoc system from security and counterterrorism agencies because of the possibility it was financing terrorists.

Somalia's money transfer agents are a geographically diverse and intricately networked system with hundreds of agents and companies. This leaves it vulnerable to exploitation by anyone seeking to support illicit activities in largely lawless and ungoverned spaces throughout the country.

The UN Development Program identifies three types of remittances that loosely identify the various amounts commonly sent through the system:
- $100-$500 per month sent by a person to help family members back home;
- One-time transactions over $100,000 sent as investments, and
- Business activities, averaging $500,000 per transaction.

The New York-based Center on Global Counterterrorism Cooperation, where I work, is studying the Somali remittance sector in hopes of coming up with innovative ideas for strengthening its regulation.

Somali remittance companies, we have found, vary in size, reach (for example, within an urban area or also extending to rural areas, or providing only local services or global), capacity and structure. Some companies are organized as corporate franchises while others are owned by one person, family or clan. These companies often offer services to a very specific clientele according to name, clan affiliation or blood line that solidifies a network of trust.

Efforts to Ward Off Its Dangers

These transactions may or may not follow any international standards or regulations. Such a structure, cash volume and operating environment present challenges and opportunities to countries hoping to regulate remittances along the lines recommended by the Financial Action Task Force.

The task force, comprising representatives from 36 UN member countries, was set up at a Group of 7 summit in Paris in 1989. The goal was to develop procedures to combat money laundering and terrorist financing. The European, North American and Middle Eastern countries represented in the task force are host to many Somali communities. The group recommends that financial institutions, for example, be required to conduct their business with care, know their customers, keep records, track and report suspicious transactions and so forth.

A major challenge is the increasing opacity of the network once the money—or

A remittance outlet in Puntland, Somalia. The Dahabshiil franchise has specialized in money transfers since the 1970s.

Wikimedia Commons/ warsame90

value—has moved beyond countries that enforce their regulations.

As an example, a resident of Britain may enter a foreign exchange bureau or neighborhood kiosk in East London and ask to send £50 to Hargeisa, Somaliland. The sender has probably selected a particular remittance company because of clan affiliation, a personal recommendation or after shopping for the best rates.

It is also extremely likely that the sender is a repeat customer. The sender will pay the transmission fee, usually 5 percent to 10 percent of the amount to be sent. Charities, humanitarian or relief organizations and repeat customers typically receive a significant discount on multiple remittances or large amounts.

British remittance companies must adhere to requirements given in the task force's guidelines. Thus the company will ask the sender to provide a government-issued identification card and may check to see if the sender's name appears on a UN sanction list or a list of names flagged by the U.S. State Department's Office of Foreign Assets Control.

At the start, the company may meet obstacles in checking on the sender. For example, there are many ways to spell a given Somali name, which is customarily made up of multiple names and aliases. Then too, names of the dead remain on lists for a long time; Osama bin Laden and Saddam Hussein are still on the State Department list. Outdated and incomplete lists are a waste of time.

The company will then provide instructions, either by e-mail, text message, phone call or fax to a clearinghouse, often based in Dubai in the United Arab Emirates, for the funds to be paid to the recipient on the other end.

Depending on what the disbursing agent requires, the recipient in Hargeisa may be asked to provide identification. Oftentimes a clan elder accompanying the beneficiary will confirm an identity. This is common since Somali passports and identification documents have long been easily forged.

Recordkeeping on these transactions is sparse and not readily available for inspection. There is certainly no oversight on how that money is then spent and who benefits from it. Not surprisingly, there is no financial transparency in Somalia.

While individual countries are aware of the regulatory challenges they face, and take what measures they can to enforce standards, regulators face significant challenges. They work with restricted budgets and staff and their impact is further limited by political and financial priorities. Linguistic, ethnic and cultural barriers are rife.

Above all, the transfer of funds internationally, whether on the up-and-up, illicit or some of each, cannot occur efficiently without cross-border cooperation and standardized regulatory requirements across jurisdictions.

How to formalize this system and make it transparent and traceable remains a work in progress. The UN Development Program has repeatedly warned that shutting down these networks would likely aggravate Somalia's existing humanitarian catastrophe.

But the credibility of the UN Development Program's own Somalia Remittances Program was damaged when a whistleblower in May 2008 accused it of corruption and fraud.

A View From Both Sides Would Help

While the UN Development Program has looked at the system from a development and humanitarian perspective, international counterterrorism bodies adopt a "security first" stance, focusing on concerns over money laundering and terrorism financing.

Given the interaction between the global financial system and the Somali economy, it makes sense to look at the problem from both perspectives, so that remittances can continue to flow, even as they comply with international safeguards.

The international community has an obligation to develop a realistic understanding of Somalia's underground economy, with the goal of harmonizing the administrative burden placed on remittance companies trying to span the borders of numerous countries, each with its own regulatory requirements.

The international community can also do more to encourage innovation, such as Somali communications companies offering mobile banking services to reach more people while lowering costs.

Remittance companies, for their part, must do more to comply with the requirements of their host countries, train their staffs and adopt international reporting requirements.

Given the vital role they play in the otherwise flailing Somali economy, Somali remittance companies are not likely to disappear anytime soon.

With Somalia unable to regulate this sector, a joint, coordinated and cooperative relationship between counterterrorism, security, development and humanitarian agencies is a good place to start. ■

The Nuclear Outliers
Jayantha Dhanapala

In a world where the global norm is membership in the Treaty on the Non-Proliferation of Nuclear Weapons, countries with nuclear weapons that are not members have come to be identified as outliers.

Some would argue that all countries with nuclear weapons are the outliers, as so few have them. The use of the term has an undeniably pejorative implication but in modern realpolitik—a world of great-power exceptionalism, national interest and sovereignty—no value judgments hold sway.

The nuclear nonproliferation treaty was adopted in 1968 and entered into force in 1970. Over its 41 years, it has gathered five nations with nuclear weapons and 184 without as members pledging to abide by the three pillars of the treaty: nonproliferation, disarmament and the verifiable peaceful uses of nuclear energy. In addition to the five in the treaty acknowledging their nuclear arms (Britain, China, France, Russia and the United States), there are four outside including North Korea, the subject of six-nation talks aimed at getting that country back into the treaty while giving up its nuclear arms.

The countries with nuclear weapons that have a distinct outlier status are:
- Israel, which does not acknowledge having such weapons;
- India, which has de facto recognition through the controversial 2008 Indo-U.S. nuclear cooperation agreement and is seeking membership in the exclusive Nuclear Suppliers Group of 46 nations that oversees global trade in nuclear materials and technology, and
- Pakistan, whose growing nuclear arsenal has prompted international concerns over proliferation of nuclear material and knowhow of the program's father, the notorious A.Q. Khan, as well as the safe custody of its nuclear arsenal in unstable political conditions.

In each of these three cases, the acquisition of expertise and materials has invariably been helped, wittingly or unwittingly, by an established nuclear-armed state among others. According to the latest statistics provided by the Stockholm International Peace Research Institute, the three outliers are estimated to have 250 to 290 nuclear warheads among them.

The world seems to have abandoned hope they will voluntarily give up their nuclear weapons unless all nuclear weapons everywhere are eliminated through a verifiable international convention.

The implications of this tacit acceptance of the outliers are portentous. And yet with each of them enjoying good relations with at least one of the five nuclear-arms nations adhering to the nonproliferation treaty, who also happen to be veto-wielding permanent members of the UN Security Council, their nuclear weapon arsenals have, by and large, escaped unequivocal criticism let alone condemnation. That the three outlier countries never joined the treaty while Iran and North Korea did (although North Korea later pulled out) is cited as another reason a disproportionate criticism is heaped on the latter two. A cynic would see that as a reason for not joining any treaty.

Israel: Neither Confirm nor Deny

Israel has long maintained a policy of nuclear ambiguity, neither confirming nor denying possession of nuclear weapons. Some leaks have been hastily plugged and whistle-blowers like Mordechai Vanunu, who disclosed details of Israel's nuclear program in 1986, have effectively been silenced. The origins of the Israeli nuclear program go back to the late 1950s, and by 1970 it is reported to have crossed the nuclear threshold.

France has been identified as the source of Israeli nuclear expertise and matériel in the early stages. By the 1980s, Israel was seen as having a mature nuclear weapon program centered on the southern city of Dimona. The Stockholm International Peace Research Institute estimates that Israel has 80 nuclear warheads but other organizations, such as the Nuclear Threat Initiative, have estimated 100 to 300 deliverable through its Jericho missiles and Falcon aircraft.

It is also estimated that Israel has more than 1,400 pounds of weapons-grade plutonium—the equivalent of about 130 nuclear warheads. Rumors of Israel's developing tactical nuclear weapons and nuclear-capable sea-launched cruise missiles have not been substantiated. No Israeli doctrine on the possible use of nuclear weapons has been announced, but their deterrent value has not prevented Arab-Israeli wars and persistent attacks across Israeli-held territory.

As the sixth nation in the world to acquire nuclear weapons, and the very first in the Middle East, Israel never overtly tested nuclear devices, as did India, Pakistan and North Korea. A Sept. 22, 1979, event known as the Vela Incident or the South Atlantic Flash has been identified as a test in which Israel and South Africa colluded but details have never emerged.

With a policy of nuclear opacity, Israel did not sign the nonproliferation treaty and, unlike other nonsigners, was not pressured to do so by the U.S. Since countries that had exploded nuclear devices before 1967 qualified to join the treaty as nuclear-armed nations, there is no realistic possibility of Israel's joining without giving up its nuclear arms.

Israel has signed, but not ratified, the 1996 Comprehensive Nuclear Test Ban Treaty, which cannot enter into force until it is ratified by all 44 nuclear weapon-capable countries stipulated in the treaty. It is also a member of the Geneva-based Conference on Disarmament with its partly fulfilled mandate as the sole multilateral negotiating forum to produce treaties on disarmament issues such as a proposed fissile material cut-off treaty.

As the only state in the Middle East outside the nonproliferation treaty, Israel has been strongly criticized in forums like the UN General Assembly's First Committee, which deals with disarmament issues, and the International Atomic Energy Agency with resolutions adopted by overwhelming majorities annually calling on Israel to join the treaty.

A resolution calling for a nuclear-free zone in the Middle East has been adopted repeatedly by treaty members without a formal vote. Further pressure has been added with the 1995 resolutions extending indefinitely the Nuclear Nonproliferation Treaty and calling for a zone free of all weapons of mass destruction in the Middle East. A diplomatic drive by Arab nations in 2010 led members to call for a conference to be held in 2012 aimed at ridding the Middle East of all weapons of mass destruction. Slow progress toward this is likely to aggravate Arab hostility despite the distractions of the Arab Spring and the war in Libya.

India: Detour from a Path of Nonviolence

For many, India's acquisition of the most destructive weapon invented is a contradiction of the philosophy of nonviolence, famously advocated by Gandhi, and of India's moral posture in world affairs.

At the time of independence in 1947, Prime Minister Jawaharlal Nehru placed India firmly on the path to modernization through the development of science and technology including the peaceful uses of nuclear energy. However, others in the leadership harbored ambitions of acquiring nuclear weapons for prestige

Wikimedia Commons/Antônio Milena

An Indian Agni-II intermediate range ballistic missile is displayed on a mobile launcher at a parade in New Delhi. The missile is capable of delivering a nuclear warhead.

Fault Lines **37**

and global power status while Nehru preached nuclear disarmament and a ban on nuclear testing. Thus India resisted all pressures to join the nonproliferation treaty, carrying on a strident campaign against its discriminatory aspect.

In 1974, India, under Prime Minister Indira Gandhi, conducted a nuclear test that was falsely described as "peaceful" but later acknowledged to be a nuclear weapon test. The test, conducted with Canadian nuclear supplies earmarked for peaceful purposes, fueled suspicions about India's nuclear ambitions.

Indian nuclear ambitions—which had led to a similarly clandestine program in Pakistan—were further evidenced by its strong and solitary opposition to the test ban treaty. In 1998, India conducted five underground tests and declared itself to have nuclear arms amidst domestic jubilation, citing a threat from China.

The immediate reaction of Pakistan was to follow suit and the world was suddenly faced with two more nuclear-armed countries outside the nonproliferation treaty, making the goal of a nuclear weapon-free world even more distant. The strong condemnation by the UN Security Council at the time is in strange contrast to U.S.-driven global indulgence and active encouragement of India's nuclear weapon possession today.

India is estimated to have 80 to 100 nuclear weapons. A domestic debate goes on among Indian scientists about whether more tests are needed, although an Indian prime minister has pledged that India would not stand in the way of the entry into force of the test ban treaty. Indian nuclear weapons can be delivered through its Mirage and Jaguar aircraft as well as through land- and sea-based missiles.

India maintains a nuclear doctrine of "no first use" and of having a "credible minimum deterrence." That and the firm civilian control of India's nuclear weapons in a functioning democracy with a credible nonproliferation record have alleviated some of the concerns over escalation of a conflict between India and Pakistan especially provoked by incidents of terrorism.

An agreement between the U.S. and India on civil nuclear cooperation was highly controversial because it legitimized India's acquisition of nuclear weapons selectively, in contrast with a 1998 UN Security Council resolution demanding that both India and Pakistan shut down their nuclear weapons programs. It was also widely seen as a violation of the nonproliferation treaty. It was subsequently approved by the Nuclear Suppliers Group under heavy U.S. diplomatic pressure, but the advantages for the U.S. nuclear industry in sales to India have yet to materialize.

Pakistan: Responding to India

It is widely conceded that Pakistan would not have acquired nuclear weapons if India had not. It is the equalizing weapon to counter a perceived conventional weapon imbalance. Thus Pakistan's rationale for nuclear deterrence is India-specific, especially after the 1971 Indo-Pakistan war, which led to the creation of Bangladesh after Indian intervention. The 1974 Indian test accelerated the program. If Pakistan is to eliminate its nuclear arsenal, India must also do so. In the case of India, however, there must be global disarmament. From a period of nonweaponized deterrence, Pakistan, with its tests in 1998, became an overt nuclear power. It is widely suspected that China provided assistance to Pakistan in developing nuclear weapons.

Pakistan is estimated to have 90 to 110 nuclear weapons using highly enriched uranium, but recent reports indicate a growing plutonium-based arsenal, probably larger than India's, and an increased production of plutonium as fissile material.

The delivery systems are both aircraft and missiles. The perception of inferiority in fissile material stockpiles in relation to India has led to an inflexible Pakistani stance in the Conference on Disarmament on the issue of negotiating a treaty on fissile materials. The Indo-U.S. nuclear cooperation deal has also had adverse repercussions. Chinese firms intend to build two new 340-megawatt light-water reactors at Pakistan's Chashma Nuclear Power Plant. Ironically this has elicited protests from the U.S.

The activities of the A.Q. Khan network and doubts over the safe custody of Pakistani nuclear weapons in a country fraught with terrorist threats and weak governmental controls have made Pakistan a key concern. The discovery that Osama bin Laden had been in Pakistan, either unknown to the Pakistani authorities or with their connivance, can only enhance concerns over the safety of the country's nuclear arsenal. With the history of hostile relations between India and Pakistan, many see South Asia as a likely theater for a limited nuclear war. However, both sides have expressed confidence in their command and control structures and systems.

North Korea, Iran and Syria

The focus of recent international attention has been on the nuclear programs of North Korea, Iran and Syria—countries that signed the Nuclear Non-proliferation Treaty.

North Korea, which withdrew from the treaty in 2003, demonstrated its nuclear weapon capability by conducting tests in 2006 and 2009 and is under sanctions ordered by the UN Security Council. In November 2010, the North's revelation of a new uranium enrichment facility with 2,000 centrifuges to Prof. Siegfried S. Hecker, an American nuclear scientist, has also heightened fears that North Korea may move irreversibly toward nuclear weaponization. However, political negotiations may contain this threat through the six-nation talks in which China, Japan and South Korea have been active.

Iran and Syria represent a different threat since the International Atomic Energy Agency remains unsatisfied that these two countries have fulfilled their obligations under the safeguards agreements signed with the agency.

Both countries assert that their programs are for peaceful purposes. However, the international community is unpersuaded after two recent Iranian declarations: that it would triple its production capacity and transfer 20 percent uranium enrichment from the Natanz site to the Fordow site, giving greater protection to its uranium-purifying centrifuges from possible U.S. and Israeli air strikes.

While no concrete evidence has surfaced proving that the two countries are developing nuclear weapons, their uranium enrichment programs have been of sufficient concern to some nations as to lead to the introduction into Iran by an unknown party of the malicious Stuxnet virus, the bombing of a facility in Syria by Israel, and more recently a move by the International Atomic Energy Agency's 35-nation board of governors to report Syria to the UN Security Council as hindering an agency investigation of a suspected nuclear reactor destroyed in 2007. A military strike against the programs in either country could lead to major unrest and instability in the Middle East and the global preference has been to continue with diplomatic negotiations.

To conclude, all nine nuclear-armed states, whether within the nonproliferation treaty or outliers, present a threat to global security.

Napoleon is said to have remarked: "Bayonets are wonderful! One can do anything with them except sit on them!" Today's bayonets are nuclear weapons, and we are actually sitting on them.

The potential for their use by accident or design, by the nuclear powers themselves or by terrorist groups is too great for the people of the world to accept. ■

IAEA Photo/Kirstie Hansen

Broken metal seals salvaged from North Korean nuclear sites in 2003, when Pyongyang withdrew from the nuclear nonproliferation treaty. Two years later, it declared it had nuclear arms. Inspectors from the International Atomic Energy Agency use the seals to tag safeguarded equipment.

North Korea and the UN: An Uneasy Relationship
Daniel A. Pinkston

The Democratic People's Republic of Korea—North Korea—has had a rather adversarial relationship with the United Nations throughout its history.

It resisted joining the UN until 1991 when it appeared that South Korea would be able to join on its own after the Soviet Union and China disclosed they would no longer block its membership. Although both Seoul and Pyongyang joined in 1991, the national division and the Korean War have affected the UN-North Korea relationship for over six decades.

Historical fate and geopolitics put the Korean peninsula on the fault line of the Cold War. Korea was colonized by Japan in 1910, but with the collapse of the Japanese empire in 1945, the United States and the Soviet Union agreed to establish a temporary demarcation at the 38th parallel to accept the Japanese surrender. Unable to resolve their political differences, the two superpowers worked to establish separate governments in the north and the south.

The General Assembly established the UN Temporary Commission on Korea in 1947 and recommended that elections be held throughout the peninsula no later than March 31, 1948, to establish an independent Korea. However the UN was not granted access to the Soviet zone to carry out and observe elections. As a result, South Korea was established in August 1948, and North Korea the next month.

In June 1950, North Korea invaded the south to unify the peninsula by arms. The Truman administration referred the matter to the UN Security Council, which adopted resolutions in support of South Korea at a time the veto-wielding Soviet Union was boycotting the UN because the Security Council would not seat the People's Republic of China in place of the Republic of China on Taiwan.

Reminders of War Remain in Place

Resolutions adopted by the Security Council in late June and early July called for UN members to assist South Korea and authorized a "unified command" leading these forces to use the UN flag in operations against the north. Sixteen nations provided combat troops to assist South Korea during the war, and the UN command is still present in South Korea, led by a U.S. general.

The UN command also continues to fly the UN flag at the Joint Security Area at Panmunjŏm on the line dividing the two Koreas under the armistice of July 1953, which ended the Korean War. South and North Korean forces continue to stand face-to-face in this area. North Korea regards the command as an illegitimate institution controlled by the U.S.

North Korean doctrine, based on *chuch'e* (self-reliance) and *sŏn'gun* (military first), prescribes totalitarianism and inward-looking development. North Korea is insecure because of chronic concerns stemming from a national division. North Korea's policy is based on a need to unify Korea on its own terms and to maintain a strong military that can balance against the perceived threat of the south and America, its ally.

This posture, and the suspicion of the international community, have led Pyongyang to reject arms control and confidence-building measures with Seoul. As the north continues to fall behind the south economically and technologically, the growing conventional military gap has pushed Pyongyang to look to other tactics, notably nuclear weapons, for its security, which has become the greatest source of conflict between the north and the international community.

A Struggle Over Nuclear Arms

North Korea has demonstrated the long-term political will to invest tremendous resources in developing nuclear weapons and ballistic missiles. The existence of those programs became apparent in the 1980s, and it conducted nuclear tests in October 2006 and May 2009.

The Security Council responded by prohibiting North Korean arms exports, which have been a significant source of foreign exchange for the country. While most nations have respected the ban, Pyongyang continues to defy it. The interdiction of aircraft loaded with North Korean conventional arms in Bangkok in December 2009 is a prime example of this defiance. A shipment of tank parts was intercepted in South Africa the previous month, and there are lingering suspicions about missile and nuclear cooperation with Iran and possibly Myanmar, formerly Burma.

Further ratcheting up its defiance of international arms control regimes, North Korea withdrew from the Treaty on the Non-Proliferation of Nuclear Weapons in January 2003, the first country to do so in the accord's history. Six-party talks bringing together China, Russia, the U.S., Japan and the two Koreas began the same year with the aim of rolling back the north's nuclear program, but they have been stalled since December 2008.

China, North Korea's close ally, has pushed for a resumption of the talks, and although the north has said it is willing to return to the negotiating table, South Korea, the U.S. and Japan are skeptical about its commitment to bargain in good faith.

Eventual Compliance Is a Goal

In a September 2005 statement signed by all six participants in the talks, North Korea agreed to abandon all its nuclear programs in exchange for a pledge of development assistance and assurances it would not be attacked. But it later walked away from that deal, and the aim of the six-party talks is to ensure it eventually complies.

If the talks do restart, the parties could agree to invite International Atomic Energy Agency inspectors back to North Korea to monitor any denuclearization agreements. Inspectors had been in the north monitoring a nuclear freeze imposed in a 1994 agreement between Washington and Pyongyang. But they were expelled in December 2002 when that agreement broke down.

However, the prospects for new multilateral talks are dim, given that relations between the two Koreas have sunk to their lowest level in a long time. The relationship soured after last year's attack by the north on the South Korean naval

Wikimedia Commons/Kok Leng Yeo

The Arirang mass games, held in North Korea's Rungnado May Day stadium, recount the country's history in dance and gymnastics. The games feature complex gymnastics and dance routines and huge mosaics created by thousands of school children.

vessel Cheonan, sinking it, and its shelling of South Korean civilian settlements on Yeonpyeong Island in the Yellow Sea, near the maritime border between the north and the south.

North Korea has a mixed record on arms control agreements. While it joined the 1970 Nuclear Non-Proliferation Treaty and a separate accord enabling International Atomic Energy Agency inspections, it ultimately withdrew from both. It has joined pacts banning biological weapons and poisonous gases, but has shunned conventions intended to protect against the theft of nuclear materials, the use of chemical arms and exports of various weapons-related technologies and materials.

Nor has it complied with its obligations under a Security Council resolution adopted in April 2004 that required all UN members to help prevent transfers of nuclear, biological and chemical weapons and their delivery systems to terrorist organizations and other nongovernmental groups. In 2009, it signed a treaty granting nations access to outer space for peaceful purposes, but UN Security Council resolutions bar it from launching any rockets using ballistic missile technology, which includes space launch vehicles. North Korea is believed to have hundreds of ballistic missiles, some with ranges of thousands of miles.

Pyongyang has signed several antiterrorism protocols, and the U.S. State Department removed it from its list of sponsors of terrorism in 2008. Although there is no evidence of terrorist acts in over two decades, the International Criminal Court, with the cooperation of South Korea, is investigating the 2010 attacks on the vessel Cheonan and Yeonpyeong Island.

Harsh Controls on Human Rights

North Korea's closed society and secretive nature has made it difficult to assess its human rights record. But the government appears to control tightly virtually all activity inside the country. Very few North Koreans are permitted to travel abroad, and most market activities are restricted or prohibited. Large portions of society are mobilized as conscripted labor for government projects, and political dissidents face harsh punishment.

The General Assembly has adopted a resolution annually since 2005 denouncing human rights violations in North Korea, expressing serious concern over the situation and urging the government to end abuses.

The UN Human Rights Council in 2004 appointed Vitit Muntarbhorn, a Thai law professor, to investigate its record, but his term ended in 2010 without his gaining access to the country. Marzuki Darusman, the former Indonesian attorney general, has replaced Muntarbhorn and the human rights situation shows no sign of improvement.

Refugees fleeing over the Chinese border are forcibly returned home in accordance with an agreement between Beijing and Pyongyang. China considers all North Koreans entering the country illegally to be economic migrants despite international treaty obligations to permit a review of those seeking political asylum. North Korean women are vulnerable to attack and human trafficking while in China, whether they flee for political or economic reasons.

In April, a four-member delegation from the Elders, former heads of state Martti Ahtisaari of Finland, Norway's Gro Brundtland, Mary Robinson of Ireland and the American Jimmy Carter, visited North Korea to discuss human rights, among other issues. Pyongyang, while offering to discuss the question, assured the delegation that it had no problems at all in this area.

Where Does the Aid Go?

Since the 1980s, even in good years, North Korea has faced food shortages with a chronic grain deficit of 500,000 tons to 1 million tons a year. About six million people, or a fourth of the population, remain at risk of malnutrition. North Korea's relative scarcity of arable land and energy-intensive agriculture make the country ill-suited for food self-sufficiency.

Furthermore, the southwestern region, which provides most of the country's output of rice, the country's staple, is susceptible to frequent flooding during the summer rainy season. The cold winter of 2010-11 reportedly damaged some of the winter crop, and an outbreak of foot and mouth disease in late 2010 also took a heavy toll on livestock.

Regular reports that the emergency food aid sent each year to North Korea rarely reaches the country's poor and starving, but instead is used to prop up the government and military, have increasingly soured international donors. The U.S. and South Korea have long pushed for better in-country monitoring to assure food gets to those in need.

The World Food Program conducted an assessment early this year and concluded the country would face serious shortages by late spring or early summer. But South Korean critics accuse the north of exaggerating its needs in an effort to build up international food stocks in the run-up to April 15, 2012, the 100th anniversary of the birth of Kim Il Sung, who died in 1994 but is extolled as the country's "eternal president."

The government is expected to hold celebrations and provide gifts to citizens as the government sets the stage for an eventual transfer of power from his son Kim Jong-il to his grandson Kim Jong-un. ■

International Puzzle:
Ending a Decade of Afghan War
Jeffrey Laurenti

Afghanistan in 2011 marks 10 years since a series of dramatic events reawakened the interest and finally the intervention of the international community in that conflict-racked country. With President Obama's announcement of a withdrawal of a third of United States military forces by summer's end in 2012, the U.S. made clear it was decisively turning from a focus on a military-centered strategy to one centered on a political solution.

Ten years ago, the self-styled "emirate" of the Taliban opted to defy intensifying international pressures, including United Nations sanctions, against its alliance with Al Qaeda. This had been signaled early in the year by Mullah Muhammad Omar's deferring to Al Qaeda ideologues demanding the destruction of the country's outstanding Buddhist monuments at Bamiyan, over the strenuous protests of the UN Educational, Scientific and Cultural Organization.

Taliban leaders insisted on sheltering Osama bin Laden after the audacious attacks of Sept. 11, 2001, despite American warnings of forceful retaliation. The emirate regime quickly disintegrated once the U.S. allied itself with the armed remnants of the Northern Alliance, but instead of surrendering, the Taliban decamped to Pakistan. Out of a UN conference in Bonn in December 2001 emerged a fragile Afghan governing lineup led by Hamid Karzai, and promises of international assistance to support the new regime. Afghans' hopes ran high, and Americans assumed the war was won.

Ten years later, Karzai is still in Kabul, leader of a constitutional Islamic republic with an elected parliament, fitfully functioning ministries and a large army of uncertain motivation, all dependent on international largesse. The Taliban leadership remains sheltered in Pakistan, its forces resurgent since 2005 and able to strike across much of Afghanistan. The U.S. has responded to the Taliban's revival by major increases in its own force levels from 26,600 at the start of 2008 to 103,700 at the start of 2011, seeking to reverse the Taliban gains before its force levels begin dropping later in the year.

Lisbon Agreement Stems Loss of Forces

The hemorrhage of Western troop contingents defecting from the NATO-run International Security Assistance Force was stanched by NATO's agreement at Lisbon in November 2010 to fix a 2014 deadline for turning responsibility for the country's security over to the Afghan National Army. The UN, originally restricted to a "light footprint" in post-Taliban Afghanistan, has become a principal actor and referee in Afghan politics and society, repeatedly angering the presidential palace and its warlord allies by intervening to block election fraud.

This 10th anniversary year is one in which violence in the long-smoldering war has been ratcheted up to its highest levels since the Soviet Union withdrew its forces in 1989. At the same time, political leaders on the various sides of the conflict began taking seriously the exploratory talks to end it. The American stealth raid that killed Osama bin Laden in his guarded compound in Pakistan has profoundly affected the calculus of many parties about their strategic priorities. When President Obama announced the pace of his promised draw-down of force levels beginning in the summer 2011, the war-weary took heart that an Afghan endgame might at last be in sight.

The change Obama announced was not universally welcomed. The chairman of the House Intelligence Committee, Mike Rogers, Republican of Michigan, offered a telling critique: "The president is trying to find a political solution with a mili-

U.S. Army Photo/ Sgt. Ruth Pagan

An Afghan police officer holds a child at a groundbreaking ceremony for a kindergarten building in Kandahar City.

tary component, when it needs to be the other way around." But all of America's European allies with troops in Afghanistan, and much of the U.S. military itself, was already persuaded that a military solution with a political component had failed in the eight years it was applied.

Military Gains, Civilian Casualties

In Washington and at the NATO headquarters in Brussels, there had been high hopes that the heightened tempo of combat led by augmented American forces in 2010-11 could win back the seeming victory of 2001. Aggressive military campaigns apparently succeeded in driving Taliban fighters out of the Pashtun provinces in Afghanistan's south, and a new emphasis on night raids and on targeted killings of Taliban mid-level commanders and shadow governors took a heavy toll on the Taliban. But if President Karzai is to be believed, they also took a toll on the Afghan public's waning tolerance for the foreign forces in their midst.

"Civilian casualties are the main cause of worsening the relationships between Afghanistan and the United States," Karzai said in March 2011, four days before a midnight NATO strike killed the president's cousin. By May 2011, Karzai was insisting that NATO cease air attacks on Afghan homes "immediately," threatening "unilateral action" against the foreign allies-turned-occupiers if it did not.

Yet senior NATO military officers stood their ground, insisting that "without night operations we could not have achieved the progress we have achieved, because we are removing so many fighters and insurgent commanders from the battlefield."

Confirming the escalating death toll, the UN reported that Afghan civilian casualties in 2010 had risen 19 percent over 2009 levels. Insurgent attacks had caused three-quarters of the deaths—a dramatic reversal of the ratio three years before—as Taliban fighters deployed more deadly improvised explosive devices, targeted crowded public places and doubled their assassinations and executions.

In Helmand and Kandahar provinces, the epicenter of the American offensive to wrest back control of lost ground, civilian deaths soared by 588 percent and 248 percent respectively in 2010. And civilian casualties in 2011 have continued their grim rise. By May 2011 they had soared to the highest monthly toll on record in the war, the UN reported, attributing responsibility for 82 percent of the 368 conflict-related civilian deaths to attacks by antigovernment fighters.

UN Mission Itself Is an Issue

The UN mission in Afghanistan has itself become a focus of controversy in the country—not just because of Taliban hostility to its mandate to assist the country's reconstruction, but because of the Kabul power-brokers' fury at UN interventions to thwart wholesale fraud in the 2009 presidential and 2010 parliamentary elections. It is one of the few institutions in the country that still affords space to Afghans disillusioned with the warlord kleptocracy controlling much of the government machinery.

In early 2011 the Karzai government asked the UN Security Council to strip the mission of its mandates to aid the country's political institutions, which the council rebuffed. After a demented Florida fundamentalist notoriously burned a copy of the Koran, it was against the UN offices in supposedly secure Mazar-i-Sharif that Afghan fundamentalists directed their deadly fury. Someone was trying to send a message.

The UN mission may nonetheless be particularly helpful in creating a channel for participation for those in the broader society who feel shut out by palace insiders in the process of negotiating peace as an Afghan endgame approaches.

The Obama administration signaled its determination to seek a negotiated solution to the Afghan war in February 2011, when Secretary of State Hillary Clinton said: "We are launching a diplomatic surge to move this conflict toward a political outcome that shatters the alliance between the Taliban and Al Qaeda, ends the insurgency, and helps to produce not only a more stable Afghanistan but a more stable region." She subtly redefined the three preconditions that President George W. Bush had set for talking with the Taliban—that they sever ties with Al Qaeda, lay down their arms and accept the 2004 Afghan constitution—as end goals for a negotiated settlement.

Clearly some momentum for a peace settlement was under way. In 2011, through German facilitation, the U.S. took part in direct talks with Taliban representatives for the first time in 10 years, with each side seeking to determine

UN Photo/Eric Kanalstein

An Afghan National Police honor guard conducts a routine training exercise in Kabul.

Fault Lines **49**

whether the other was serious about negotiations. The Obama administration in June 2011 won Security Council revision of the sanctions regime imposed against the Taliban and Al Qaeda in 1999, treating Taliban figures separately and facilitating their removal from the sanctions blacklist.

Obama's announcement on troop levels was also expected to allow Taliban leaders to assure their most diehard fighters that entering negotiations was not a capitulation, despite their longstanding insistence they would never talk with the "occupiers" until all their troops were gone.

Tricky Negotiations Lie Ahead

Negotiating will not be easy. It is not, after all, simply or even primarily a civil war among Afghans, and the insurgency does not view the Karzai government as having either moral or military legitimacy to be its real interlocutor. They insist on dealing with the people who are running Kabul's side of the war: the Americans.

But the war is not simply an American-led venture either. The Taliban first gained power as the instrument of Pakistani security agencies to implant an allied, if not always pliant, government on their western frontier. The mujahideen militias of the Northern Alliance that had resisted the Taliban in the 1990s—many of whose warlord leaders have been grafted onto the current Kabul regime—were supplied and financed by India, Iran and Russia, which might again back them if Western forces withdraw. Japan and Europe have acquired a major stake in the outcome in Afghanistan, thanks to their investment in Afghanistan's stabilization.

A respected international task force chaired by Lakhdar Brahimi, former UN representative in Afghanistan, and Thomas R. Pickering, former U.S. under secretary of state (and chair of the United Nations Association-USA's Strategy Council), in March called for an international facilitator, ideally designated by the UN, to arrange a multi-tiered negotiation that would accommodate all involved. European governments have embraced the proposal; Washington has been cool.

Indeed, in contrast to the 2001 Bonn conference convened by the UN to cobble together the post-Taliban interim government, both Washington and Kabul have been skeptical about a UN footprint at "Bonn II," the parley that Germany will host on the 10th anniversary of the first.

This time the German hosts hope to plug the gaping hole at the first conference, the absence of the Taliban, whose resilience and resurgence 10 years later mark them, for better or worse, as an ineradicable part of the Afghan social landscape. But Afghanistan has changed profoundly in these 10 years. Can the Taliban reconcile themselves to that? ∎

Talking Points

1. A common problem in volatile global hot spots is the weak tools available to the international community to monitor and enforce diplomatic agreements. Given this, a cynic might conclude that ambitious treaties are worthless. How can the UN strengthen its verification efforts? Or would the UN do better to focus on more concrete methods of ending conflict, like aid or peacekeeping?

2. The UN Security Council can pressure nations like Iran and North Korea by imposing sanctions for their noncompliance with international demands on major peace and security issues. Should the council be doing more to put together incentive packages detailing how compliance would be rewarded, thereby offering both carrots and sticks supported by the UN's international legitimacy?

3. While the UN has committed significant resources to Iraq and Afghanistan, other regions considered less critical to the foreign policy interests of major powers, like central Africa, also struggle with significant economic, public health and peace and security challenges. Should the UN be focusing more on the latter areas, given that the major powers are more likely to expend their own blood and treasure in stabilizing regions that enhance their national interests?

4. Nongovernmental groups considered terrorist organizations have become increasingly influential in many troubled areas. Yet a lot of nations refuse to officially meet with these parties. Should the UN be doing more to encourage and manage dialogue and negotiations between member countries and moderate elements in terrorist groups? If so, how could this be done?

UN Photo/David Ohana

Ghanaian men wait outside an immigration center, stranded at the border town of Sallum in northwestern Egypt, after fleeing the uprising in Libya in March 2011.

A Change of Pace on Human Rights

54 A New Human Rights Council?
Jacques Fomerand

59 Why Are Special Human Rights Procedures So Special?
Ted Piccone

62 Iraqi Refugees: Still There
Elizabeth Ferris

66 In Support of the Complaint Procedure
Helmut Volger

69 Talking Points

A New Human Rights Council?
Jacques Fomerand

Are tectonic changes taking place at the United Nations and its Human Rights Council? Who could have predicted the council's extraordinary response to the clamor for democratization that began sweeping Africa and the Middle East late in 2010?

Most remarkable, perhaps, was the UN reaction to the brutal assault of the Libyan leader Col. Muammar el-Qaddafi on peaceful protests in his country in January.

In a resolution adopted by consensus at a Feb. 25 special session of the rights council at its home in Geneva, the top UN human rights body called upon the Libyan government to end immediately all violations of human rights, stop attacks on civilians and meet the aspirations and demands of its people.

The council also set up an inquiry into charges of human rights violations and recommended that the General Assembly suspend Libya's membership in the rights council. Just 24 hours later, the 15-nation Security Council, meeting in New York, deplored Libya's "gross and systematic violation of human rights" and called on the International Criminal Court to investigate. It also imposed an arms embargo on the country and a travel ban and asset freeze on Qaddafi's family.

Unexpected Moves on Libya

Then, on March 1, the General Assembly acted on the rights council's recommendation, suspending Libya's council membership. Two days later, the prosecutor of the International Criminal Court opened an investigation, and on March 17, the Security Council established a no-fly zone over Libya, thus giving the green light to a NATO armed intervention designed to protect the rights of Libyan civilians.

The UN response was unusually swift and decisive. Equally surprising was its grounding on the notion of a "responsibility to protect," a doctrine that until then was viewed by most observers as a fuzzy concept, of concern mainly to a clique of academics and activists. [See "Libya in Revolt: Testing the Responsibility to Protect," P. 11]

The swift pace appeared to slacken by late spring, however, as turmoil continued to roil the Arab world.

A move to condemn Syria in the Security Council over a similar drive against protesters stalled, and little enthusiasm developed for authorizing yet another military intervention. But the Human Rights Council convened another special session, where an overwhelming majority condemned the Syrian use of lethal violence against protestors and asked Navanethem Pillay, the UN High Commissioner for Human Rights, for an urgent investigation.

Shortly afterward, Damascus, under pressure from the West because of President Bashar al-Assad's repression of demonstrators, withdrew from a race for a council seat, clearing the way for the election of Kuwait, hardly a beacon for human rights, in its place.

Do these developments signal basic changes at the Human Rights Council, particularly following the General Assembly's review of its effectiveness during its first five years? And what has been the role of the Obama administration in this still unfolding drama?

While President George W. Bush had shunned council membership even after the revamping of the human rights apparatus in 2006, Obama's administration ran for, and won, a seat on the 47-nation body. Obama argued that engagement was the more effective path to reform. Did the council's high profile during the Arab Spring lend credence to Obama's arguments?

A Council in High Gear

The council has acted with unusual speed in recent months in addressing human rights violations. Beyond events in North Africa and the Middle East, the council met in special session on Dec. 23 to condemn strongly reports of rights abuses in Ivory Coast after a bitterly contested presidential election. It also set up an inquiry to investigate the charges.

In its regular sessions, the council extended the mandates of all of its special procedures investigators involved with abuses such as torture, racism and violence against women. It also added two new investigations, choosing to examine discrimination against women in law, and the right to peaceful assembly and association. Equally striking was the council's appointment of an expert to investigate rights abuses in Iran. [*See "Why Are Special Human Rights Procedures So Special?" P. 59*]

Naysayers countered that the council is indifferent to complaints about what the New York-based organization Human Rights Watch refers to as its "selectivity syndrome"— its routine turning of a blind eye to many of the world's worst rights violators.

The council did poke into a few targets like Burundi, Equatorial Guinea and the Democratic Republic of Congo. But it did not address violent clampdowns on peaceful protesters in Bahrain, Belarus and Yemen.

And it continued to devote an outsized share of its time to the long-simmering Israeli-Palestinian conflict, where its frequent scoldings of Israel regularly stir the ire of Washington, Israel's closest ally.

The council endorsed a fact-finding mission's conclusion that Israel had violated international humanitarian law in a May 2010 military operation targeting a flotilla of ships carrying humanitarian aid and construction materials to Gaza.

It also asked the Security Council to request an International Criminal Court investigation of possible war crimes in the 2008-09 Gaza war. Security Council follow-up was unlikely after the international jurist Richard Goldstone of South Africa, who led an earlier investigation, renounced his own inquiry's central finding that Israel had intentionally targeted Gaza civilians.

Polarization and Cultural Relativism

There was some irony in the rights council's recent activism. Only months before pillorying the Qaddafi regime for attacks on protesters, two dozen countries had lavishly praised Tripoli's human rights record.

Members of the UN Human Rights Council, meeting at their headquarters in Geneva in March 2011, agree to appoint a human rights investigator to monitor Iran.

Equally puzzling to the uninitiated might be the council's inaction on a joint study by two of its own investigators of "global practices in relation to secret detention in the context of counterterrorism." The study documented instances of secret detention in more than 60 nations and urged them to launch independent inquiries. (The U.S. was on the list for its "high-value detainee program," among other issues). But a number of Middle Eastern and African nations joined Russia in seeking to bar discussion of the report.

They objected that the experts had exceeded their mandate. During the debate, countries mentioned in the report remained silent or denied having any secret detention facilities within their borders.

These peculiarities were stark reminders that the council is driven by its member nations and is an eminently political body. Of its 47 members, the majority, 26, come from Asia and Africa. Only seven seats are earmarked for Western Europe, eight for Latin America and six for Eastern Europe.

Deep Cleavage Bars Consensus

In effect, the balance of power lies not with the West and its liberal vision of human rights, but with a coalition of developing nations that tends to perceive human rights accountability as, at least, a potential intrusion on their sovereignty, and, at most, an alibi for covert intervention in their domestic affairs. Most of them at the same time generally accord greater weight to economic and social rights than to civil and political rights, emphasizing the divide between developing nations and the industrialized world, although the developing bloc is often joined by Russia and China.

The cleavage runs deep and at times compels the council to abandon its preference for consensus and resort to formal voting.

Developing countries' prickly concern for their sovereignty was dramatically underlined in May 2009 when a narrow council majority led by nonaligned nations concluded that charges of violations of human rights and humanitarian law by all sides at the end of the Sri Lanka civil war were an internal matter of no concern to the UN. More recently, similar concerns emerged in council deliberations over Libya's use of force against civilians.

Another perennial focus of debates centers on whether human rights are absolute or depend to some extent on a society's traditional values and culture. It took two years of debate for the council in 2011 to finally approve a resolution affirming that a better understanding and appreciation of traditional values of dignity, freedom and responsibility contributed to promoting and protecting human rights. The vote was 24-14 with 7 abstentions.

Moscow Plays a Wild Card

The council also asked its advisory committee to prepare a study of the subject for later discussion. This Russian initiative at first created turmoil among defenders of the idea that rights were absolute, because it failed to note that "traditional values" were often invoked to justify harmful practices such as female genital mutilation. The flames were fanned when the Russian foreign ministry stated that the goal was "to change the international community's approach towards human rights."

The ministry said: "It's no secret that some cultures perceive them as a burden imposed by the Western Christian civilization. Moreover, the West has discredited the noble idea by meddling in the internal affairs of other countries under the pretence of protecting human rights and taking the idea of tolerance to absurdity. Dignity, freedom and responsibility are traditional values that are shared by mankind. An emphasis on links between traditional values and human rights will help to recognize human rights and fully understand them."

Will Washington Stick It Out?

As called for by the General Assembly in 2006, the council carried out a self-evaluation, and the review was released together with establishment of a working group in the fall of 2009. The group met in October 2010 and February 2011 in Geneva. After extensive formal and informal discussions and negotiations in and outside the UN, it agreed on a series of recommendations in March. The General Assembly adopted a package of modest council procedural reforms a few months later.

The review triggered many proposals, most of them from outside groups, aiming to address the council's structural problems. But these prescriptions got lost in the council's country-driven organizational culture, and what seemingly started as a "rational comprehensive" process slowly turned into a set of incremental adjustments of procedures and process that bears little relation to what the Obama administration had hoped for in deciding to join the council rather than steer clear of it.

In fact, the lackluster reform package prompted Washington to disassociate itself from the review's conclusions and pledge to continue to evaluate the council, session by session.

But the Obama administration also told the U.S. Congress that it would continue its "principled and pragmatic engagement." To a skeptical Republican-led House of Representatives, it argued that the U.S. could build coalitions with like-minded countries and steer the council toward a more balanced approach to human rights. It said it could still manage to press its policy priorities and focus attention on individual problem countries. Republican critics remained largely unmoved.

From their point of view, U.S. membership gave the council undeserved legitimacy while empowering human rights abusers to attack Washington. "We do not help the cause of human rights or the victims of abuses by trying to prop up the failed Human Rights Council," Rep. Ileana Ros-Lehtinen, the Florida Republican who chairs the House Committee on Foreign Affairs, said in April.

Some Seek Retreat on Rights

Despite the unprecedented activism of the council in recent months, it is difficult to ignore the indifference of so many members to the fundamental tenets of human rights. The risks of slippage are ever present and many of these members would like to turn the clock back. Their barely veiled attacks on the independence of the office of the UN High Commissioner for Human Rights are multiplying.

At the same time, the European Union has shown a limited ability to build coalitions in the council and exert leadership. Its members are often divided, lean toward consensus over dissent and are reticent to present resolutions aimed at individual countries.

In addition, it is difficult to anticipate how and to what extent the council will deal with Iran, the continuing civil strife in the Middle East, the bold Russian attack on the universality of rights or, for that matter, the tensions brewing from the brutal climax of the civil war in Sri Lanka. What follow-up will it give to the investigations that it ordered? Will it heed Pillay's plea at the opening of the council's 17th session on May 30? "Experience shows," she said, "that democratic transition is incomplete if it fails to include appropriate institutional reforms, including transitional justice processes, which are indispensable for the proper functioning of a democratic system."

Over the long term, the ad-hoc nature of the council may develop a surprising logic that takes human rights down new paths. But in this generally inhospitable environment, defenders of human rights should remain cautious. In either event, it is difficult to disagree with Susan Rice, the U.S. ambassador to the UN, who told skeptical American legislators, "I'd rather be in there and call foul." ■

Why Are Special Human Rights Procedures So Special?

Ted Piccone

There was a stretch of turbulence and hostility against the United Nations' so-called special procedures for human rights. But this system of independent experts, known at the UN as "special rapporteurs," and working groups appointed by the Human Rights Council to monitor problems around the world, now seems to have emerged from adverse times.

Indeed, supporters of an active international posture on human rights quietly but firmly seized the initiative from those opposing intervention, as measures to defend existing special rapporteurs and to set up new mandates were adopted by the Human Rights Council by persuasive majorities or even consensus. While this bodes well for the system's future, chronic lack of cooperation from governments, inadequate resources and weak implementation continue to pose major challenges.

The creation of the Human Rights Council in 2006 brought new efforts by countries leery of UN scrutiny to rein in mandates for monitoring thematic and country-specific situations and make recommendations. From a humble, almost accidental beginning in the early days of the UN's Office for Human Rights, the precursor to the UN Office of the High Commissioner, special procedures evolved into a useful way to raise awareness of compelling human rights crises in the 1970s and 80s, notably those stemming from apartheid in South Africa and the military governments of Chile and Argentina.

They were so useful that some countries started putting up roadblocks and criticizing their performance in the halls of Geneva and elsewhere. In a few cases, criticism of a particularly rambunctious special rapporteur may have been justified, but by and large these experts fulfilled their mandates with courage and finesse. In 2006-07, the early phase of the new Human Rights Council gave those who opposed the independence of the special procedures system a chance to weaken it.

New Review Program as Alternative?

Some nations insisted that country-specific rapporteurs were no longer needed in light of the new Universal Periodic Review, which assesses the human rights obligations of each UN member. While this argument has failed to gain much traction, some nations succeeded in creating a code of conduct to limit the scope of special procedures activity. A series of vitriolic attacks accusing special rapporteurs of violating the code of conduct ensued, which acted as a cover to avoid serious discussion of their findings. This perhaps marked the low point for what Secretary-General Kofi Annan once called "the crown jewel" of the UN human rights system.

The current five-year review of the council, mandated upon its creation by the General Assembly, gave both friends and opponents of the special procedures another chance to battle. After months of consultations and negotiations, the competition is so far a draw: an effort by Algeria, Pakistan and others to start a legal committee to "enforce" the code of conduct was defeated, partly by a French counterproposal to establish a code of conduct instead for countries.

Over the last two years, a group of countries led largely by the U.S. began a disciplined campaign to strengthen and expand the special procedures as a way to show the council's value by doing rather than debating. Numerous country-specific mandates were extended, for example, Myanmar, North Korea and Sudan; while 19 thematic mandates were renewed. Notably, two new mandates were established by consensus: a special rapporteur on freedom of assembly and association, an initiative led by a coalition composed of the U.S., Indonesia, Nigeria and others; and a working group to examine laws that discriminate against women.

Iran Rapporteur a Major Step

In the realm of special procedures, however, the high-water mark was probably the creation of a special rapporteur on Iran in March 2011, the first new country-specific mandate initiated since the council began. After three years of campaigning, human rights advocates in and outside Iran had persuaded key swing countries like Brazil, South Korea, Senegal and Zambia to join more predictable votes from Western and Latin American nations to adopt the resolution by a sizable margin of 22-7 with 14 abstentions.

The tide turned against Iran for a combination of reasons: deterioration in its human rights situation, continued condemnation by the Security Council for its nuclear program and bungled efforts by Tehran to burnish its international reputation. Whether Iran allows the independent expert to visit or not, the new rapporteur will be able to shine a spotlight on abuses there, even if only through interviews with exiles and activists in third countries, a tactic other rapporteurs have used when dealing with intransigent officials in North Korea and Myanmar.

The main challenge the system faces is this kind of weak or nonexistent cooperation with special rapporteurs, who have a UN mandate but are not paid employees of the organization. An 18-month study I conducted at the Brookings Institution on the impact of the special procedures on human rights at the national level found that too many governments ignore or deny the experts' findings or block access to the country or to victims.

National cooperation was particularly bad when it came to responding to written charges of violations: more than 50 percent of communications received no reply while only 18 percent generated some positive movement. Yet even when they are kept from visiting a country, these UN experts amplify the voices of a beleaguered community of human rights defenders, mobilize advocacy and publicize testimony.

Filling in a Blank Sheet

In sum, the Brookings report found persuasive evidence that the special procedures deserve recognition as unique instruments. They prompt governments to re-examine and correct actions that violate human rights across a broad range of categories. By shedding light on issues like the fate of people who have disappeared, mistreatment of political prisoners, fair access to health services and violence against women, these monitors tackle the hard issues and elevate them to the highest levels of political power. That creates a public record that some would like to hide, increasing pressure for remedies and perhaps, most important, giving a voice to victims.

Some governments respond through legislative or executive action, and often in ways that directly benefit the victims. In Cambodia, the UN's monitor intervened to obtain better treatment and ultimately freedom for a journalist accused of defamation. In Afghanistan, the UN expert persuaded authorities to release hundreds of illegally detained prisoners. In Georgia, Indonesia, Spain and Colombia, UN experts uncovered unacceptable conditions for the displaced, abused women, prisoners and innocent civilians and influenced governments to take action. Some rapporteurs conduct follow-up visits or inquiries but no formal follow-up mechanism exists.

Prospects are good that with more resources and continued exertion, the special procedures can still punch above their weight. One positive signal is the continued appointment of highly regarded experts for some of the most sensitive mandates. Maina Kiai, a human rights activist from Kenya, for the mandate on freedom of assembly; Juan Méndez, a leading expert in international human rights law and former victim of torture, for the mandate on freedom from torture; and Christof Heyns, a South African human rights law professor for the mandate on extrajudicial executions are a few examples. The selection process managed by the Human Rights Council president is more open and consultative than before, giving an opportunity for advocates of civil society to press candidacies.

Difficulties on Gaza Report

The politics of appointment, however, can get tricky, as was seen dramatically this year and last year when Richard Goldstone, a South African jurist who is Jewish, chaired a special fact-finding mission on Israel's military operation in Gaza launched in December 2008.

After a path-breaking report accusing both the Israelis and the Palestinians of major violations of human rights and humanitarian law, including deliberate targeting of civilians by Israel, Goldstone met a storm of criticism from defenders of Israel. In a bizarre twist, Goldstone rescinded the most controversial finding in April 2011 in a Washington Post op-ed article, a step he took without approval and in opposition to the conclusions of his three colleagues on the panel. While this is unlikely to result in any particular action by the council, it demonstrates the power that these mandates hold in the court of national and international public opinion. ∎

Iraqi Refugees: Still There

Elizabeth Ferris

Millions of Iraqis have fled their communities as a result of violence and insecurity in the eight years since the United States invaded Iraq. Together with most of those displaced by the Saddam Hussein regime, these Iraqis live in uncertain conditions throughout the Middle East.

The governments of the region have generally allowed them to remain but haven't recognized them as refugees nor given them formal residency rights. Not yet persuaded that it's safe to return to their country, they live in limbo. Some hope for resettlement to another country, some seek asylum in Europe.

But most are just waiting. The United Nations High Commissioner for Refugees provides some assistance to them and host governments, but agrees with the refugees that the time is not right to promote their large-scale return.

Patterns of displacement from Iraq are longstanding and complex. For years, hundreds of thousands of Iraqis fled Saddam Hussein's government as victims of persecution and violence. Most sought refuge in nearby countries, particularly Iran and Turkey, while others traveled to Europe.

UNHCR Photo/B. Heger

Iraqi refugees at a registration center of the UN High Commissioner for Refugees in Douma, a suburb of Damascus, the Syrian capital.

An Initial Surge of Hope

After the fall of Hussein, Iraqis returned in droves hoping for a safe situation. However, their return was short-lived, as violence, especially sectarian, erupted, leading many returning refugees to flee again to neighboring countries. As violence escalated, particularly after the February 2006 bombing of one of Shiite Islam's holiest shrines, al-Askari mosque in Samarra, 1.5 million more Iraqis fled, mostly to Syria and Jordan.

In addition to this outflow, two million more fled their communities but remained within Iraqi borders as internally displaced people. Both groups were driven by widespread violence and fear, recounting experiences of threats, murder of relatives and kidnappings. By 2008, 15 percent of Iraq's people had been driven from their homes, whether still in the country or fleeing to neighboring areas.

There were also sectarian and religious dimensions to the flight. The fears that Iraq was moving toward Shiite rule led many Sunnis to leave the country, and indeed 75 percent of the Iraqis in neighboring countries were Sunni.

Small religious minorities—Christians, Yazidis, Sabeans—were disproportionately represented among the refugees, and their communities have been sharply diminished in Iraq. Experiencing religious persecution in addition to the generalized violence, members of such religious minorities, which once flourished in Iraq, lost hope that their country would in the post-Saddam Hussein era be characterized by religious tolerance.

Savings Have Run Out

Most of the refugees fled to neighboring Jordan and Syria, which initially welcomed them as temporary guests. But as their numbers increased, Jordan and to a lesser extent Syria began to make it more difficult for Iraqis to enter. Neither Syria, Jordan nor Lebanon has signed the 1951 Refugee Convention, which means that the Iraqis are not acknowledged as refugees and have none of the rights that refugee status would bring in many countries, notably the right not to be forcibly returned to their countries.

The Iraqi refugees in Syria and Jordan are a heterogeneous group. Many of those who left initially were from the educated middle class, including many professionals and civil servants. They didn't arrive as empty-handed refugees, but brought savings to support themselves.

But as the years have passed, savings have been depleted and prospects for jobs are scarce. Iraqi doctors and computer engineers found that their credentials weren't recognized and they could not work in their professions.

Although many poor and unskilled Iraqis also fled, an assumption that the Iraqi refugees were wealthy, coupled with an assumption that they had supported Saddam Hussein (some had), meant that the Iraqi government had little incentive to assist them as refugees or to promote their return.

Unlike other large refugee flows, the Iraqi refugees never lived in camps, with the exception of a few thousand Palestinians who were housed in tents along the borders. Rather, they rented apartments or lived with family and friends in urban centers. While this meant that they avoided some of the problems of refugee camps, it also meant that they were largely invisible to international observers, including the UN refugee agency, which was trying to assist and protect them.

Questions on Totals Persist

The UN agency offered assistance to the refugees in the region and support to Syrian and Jordanian efforts to enable Iraqis to access public schools and health services. Cash assistance was provided to groups of the particularly vulnerable. But identifying refugees dispersed among the local population proved difficult.

The agency began to try to register the refugees, particularly as critics charged that numbers were inflated. But its efforts found only 151,000 Iraqis in Syria and 31,000 in Jordan. These numbers were far lower than most estimates, which indicated over a million Iraqis in Syria and up to 500,000 in Jordan.

Did this mean that there were many fewer refugees than first thought? Or that some of the refugees had returned home? Or that refugees were fearful of registering lest their names and contacts in a government database make it easier for them to be rounded up and sent home?

Further complicating the issue of numbers and assistance is the mobility of the Iraqi refugees, particularly those living in Syria. Iraqis routinely cross back and forth to Iraq from Syria. They return to check on property, to collect pensions, to take care of relatives and, in some cases, to work.

For all of the refugees, conditions in exile have been tough. Although tolerated by the authorities, many Iraqi families have found themselves destitute and engaging in what are euphemistically called "negative coping behaviors," including child labor, survival sex and petty crime.

What Next for the Refugees?

Traditionally, there are three solutions for refugees: voluntary return to their country of origin, local integration in a country of refuge or resettlement in a third country. In the case of Iraqis in neighboring countries, return has been slow and local integration is impossible. Resettlement in third countries has become a favored, though limited, option.

Although the security situation has improved greatly in Iraq in the past few years, few refugees have chosen to return. The High Commissioner for Refugees has not encouraged Iraqis to return although the office does provide assistance for those who choose to do so. The 100,000 or so who have returned since 2008 have largely done so because of deteriorating conditions in exile rather than confidence that life is back to normal in Iraq.

Most refugees are afraid to return, particularly those whose homes are in places in which they would be a religious minority. The lack of jobs and services in Iraq has led many refugees to decide that they are better off—even eking out a living on the margins of society—in neighboring countries than taking their chances back in Iraq.

A particular impediment to return has been many Iraqi refugees' loss of property. Their homes and businesses have been taken over by others and prospects for a timely resolution of claims are slim. Most of those who have returned have done so without assistance from either the UN refugee agency or the Iraqi government.

In fact, the Iraqi government has until recently not shown much support for the return of refugees.

In early 2011, the Iraqi Minister of Displacement and Migration did indicate that support for returnees would be increased, but there is still no indication that this announcement will result in significantly higher returns.

From the beginning, host countries have made it clear that while refugees would be tolerated, their presence would be a temporary measure. The Iraqis would not be allowed to stay permanently nor integrate into local society. This position had an economic basis: employment opportunities for national populations were already lacking, and absorbing large numbers of Iraqis into the labor force was economically and politically risky.

Moreover, experiences with Palestinian refugees almost six decades ago have also made the region wary. In both Syria and Jordan, the initial expressions of welcome for the Iraqi refugees have given way to resentment and xenophobia; Iraqi refugees are blamed for all kinds of social and economic problems.

Stay or Move On?

However, many refugees have rebuilt their lives in host countries; they have found jobs, registered children in schools and either rented or bought property. The UN refugee agency has tried to emphasize self-reliance as part of an interim solution, but this has been difficult to put into action in light of the restricted political and economic environment. Without meaningful, legal employment and without acceptance of their right to remain, refugees find prospects for sustainable local integration limited.

In this context, resettlement has emerged as a favored option. By mid-2010, over 100,000 Iraqi refugees had been accepted for resettlement, but the process of approving individual applications has been painfully slow. Onerous security checks mean that Iraqis accepted for resettlement must wait at least a year until they board a plane.

For Iraqis resettled in the U.S., the record has been mixed. Expectations of what life in the U.S. will be like are perhaps unreasonably high; given the U.S. economic climate, even Iraqi professionals will meet a challenge in finding entry-level jobs.

Iraqis have sought asylum in distant countries. They make up the largest group applying for asylum in Europe. Many have gone to Sweden, which had a tradition of welcoming Iraqi refugees from earlier eras and has a significant Iraqi resident population. But just as the welcome is wearing thin in the Iraq region, so too European governments are becoming tougher in admitting Iraqis seeking protection.

And so, Iraqi refugees continue to wait. Some will be accepted for resettlement and will have a chance to begin new lives. Most will continue to eke out an uncertain existence in nearby countries, waiting for evidence that conditions in Iraq will make return home a feasible choice. The Iraqi refugees will likely continue to be tolerated but increasingly resented in host countries. In a world beset by humanitarian crises, it is important to remember that the Iraqi refugees are still there. ■

In Support of the Complaint Procedure
Helmut Volger

The General Assembly replaced the Commission on Human Rights with the Human Rights Council in 2006 to reform the United Nations' work to protect individuals' rights. But it left it to the council to decide whether to set up a complaint procedure comparable to the commission's model.

That model was created by Economic and Social Council Resolution 1503 of May 27, 1970. The procedure established two working groups to check on the status of accusations of violations filed by people and nongovernmental organizations for admissibility, accuracy and relevance, and then present the findings to the commission in closed meetings. The commission could confine itself to announcing the names of the countries being examined or start a public procedure.

Under this confidential approach, the procedure provided, according to a 1998 report of the commission, "a valuable vehicle" for action on "serious human rights situations."

The Human Rights Council decided to use the old resolution on a working basis as a complaint procedure "to address consistent patterns of gross and reliably attested violations of human rights and all fundamental freedoms." With some modifications on time frame and status updates, the council took over the handling of complaints.

Nine Bodies Monitor the Treaties

But is there still a need for such a time-consuming procedure? The UN human rights protection system embraces nine human rights bodies monitoring the work of the treaties. In addition, the council has more than 40 "special procedures"—special rapporteurs, independent experts and working groups in the field working under thematic and country mandates and reporting to the council.

Yet it is vital to keep this mechanism. The procedure applies to all countries and can therefore be used to address complaints against countries that have not ratified human rights treaties. It can also be used not only by the victims, but by other people or groups (including nongovernmental organizations) with direct and reliable knowledge of the violations.

Its combination of carefully checked proofs of gross human rights violations and confidentiality, with its ability to name offending countries that have a bad record, makes it still valuable for placing subtle but effective political pressure on offending governments, who can redress the violations without losing face.

Evidence of its usefulness is in the numbers. In recent years, an average of 30,000 communications annually, representing 100 cases, have been processed under the procedure. And the response rate of governments named in the complaints is high: more than 90 percent provide comments, according to the High Commissioner for Human Rights.

All in all, countries with poor records could not avoid being put on the agenda: up to 2003, human rights situations in 84 countries had been discussed under the complaint procedure, according to figures from the same source.

It Is, After All, a Last Resort

But it is clear that the complaint procedure should serve only as a last resort for those who cannot access special rapporteurs or the treaty bodies of human rights treaties. The procedure has severe limitations: it does not offer direct relief for victims; the person making the complaint must first exhaust the domestic legal remedies; the mechanism generally takes more than a year, and the secrecy of the proceedings often works to the advantage of the country in question.

Yet the procedure's political relevance is grounded in its ability to draw worldwide attention to gross violations and to exert pressure on offending countries. This may appear to be of little consolation, but for those concerned it is a lot.

In this context, politicians and nongovernmental organizations striving to protect human rights should increase their efforts to keep the complaint procedure intact: in the report documenting the council's five-year review, the procedure is not mentioned at all, evidence of heavy opposition from member countries to any reform of the mechanism.

Another problem is that the two working groups are not currently presenting any cases to the council under the complaint procedure, as the Hungarian ambassador to the UN, speaking for the European Union, critically remarked in June 2011. Since the whole procedure is confidential, one can only speculate on the reasons—perhaps there is political disagreement in the working group on situations.

Be that as it may, this underlines the complaint procedure's need for more political support than ever. ■

UN Photo/Jean-Marc Ferré

Navanethem Pillay (right), the UN High Commissioner for Human Rights, speaks to Chérif Bassiouni, chairman of a commission created by the UN Human Rights Council in June 2011 to investigate allegations of human rights violations in Libya.

Talking Points

1. UN members have long been divided over whether human rights are universal or whether culture and tradition should be taken into account in defining them. Genital circumcision, for example, is deemed cruel by Western nations but seen as a vital tradition to many non-Western societies. Is it right for decisions on such matters to be decided by a vote of a political body? If not, on what basis should such decisions be made?

2. Does the flurry of recent action undertaken by the Human Rights Council in response to developments of the Arab Spring represent a long-term shift in its efforts to protect human rights from oppressive regimes? Or is it merely a calculated reaction to remain relevant and potent amid massive popular uprisings for freedom against tyrannical governments?

3. Special rapporteurs—individuals appointed by the Human Rights Council to monitor specific countries or certain human rights concerns—often face major obstacles in fulfilling their mandates from nations that block them from entering their country, deny their findings or fail to take seriously their proposals for reform. These countries often argue that international human rights initiatives violate their national sovereignty. Should the UN emphasize universal human rights over concerns of individual countries and their sovereignty? How could the UN improve its human rights monitoring, encourage compliance with the missions of its special rapporteurs and better encourage proposed reforms in a way that was not deemed intrusive by the countries in question?

4. The international community currently shares unevenly the burdens of caring for people forced to flee their homes by a conflict or natural disaster. How could the responsibility be more fairly divided among the refugees' home country, nations voluntarily or involuntarily offering temporary refuge, and the overall international community? How much should this responsibility depend on factors like whether the crisis was a natural disaster or a conflict, the relative wealth of the home country and the temporary hosts, a refugee's ability to pay, or whether a nation had signed the 1951 international convention that defines what a refugee is, what are their rights and what are the legal obligations of host countries?

UNHCR Photo/Glenna Gordon

Refugees from Ivory Coast walk along a forest track in eastern Liberia in March 2011. More than 100,000 Ivorians crossed into Liberia to escape violent outbreaks following Ivory Coast's disputed presidential elections.

Building Peace and Keeping It

72 **The False Promise of 'Free and Fair Elections'**
     Mike McGovern

76 **South Sudan: The Path Forward**
     Amir Osman

80 **UN Intervention Rescues Ivory Coast by a Hair's Breadth**
     Richard Gowan

84 **Margot Wallström: UN Watchdog on Sexual Abuse in War**
     Barbara Crossette

87 **Somalia's Life as a Piracy Center**
     Evelyn Leopold

91 **Talking Points**

The False Promise of 'Free and Fair Elections'
Mike McGovern

Institutions including the United Nations could do a better job of supporting democracies in Africa. The experience of Guinea between 2008 and 2011 is an example.

Guinea is a rich country whose people are poor: it has the world's biggest reserves of bauxite, from which aluminum is made, as well as major reserves of iron, gold, diamonds, petroleum, and even uranium. It has rich soil, and most of West Africa's rivers begin in Guinea. Yet the UN Human Development Index currently ranks it as 156th of the 169 countries evaluated in 2010.

Many Guineans, like many analysts, attribute this poverty in large part to poor governance. On Guinea's 50th anniversary of independence in 2008, the country was still ruled by its second president, Gen. Lansana Conté. By the end of that year he died in office, and was succeeded in a mostly bloodless coup d'état.

What happened in the next year is still a sad memory for most Guineans, with an increasingly erratic Capt. Moussa Dadis Camara making it clear that he meant to cling to power, rather than to prepare elections and withdraw, as he had promised at the time of the coup. His men ended up killing almost 200 Guinean civilians and in the recriminations that followed, Camara was shot in the head by his aide de camp.

As painful and embarrassing as this all was, it did lead the way to open presidential elections in 2010. The elections were hotly contested and the loser, former Prime Minister Cellou Dalein Diallo, challenged the results. However, international observers agreed that they were credible and the loser eventually bowed to the results for the sake of national peace.

The winner was Alpha Condé, a graduate of the Paris Institute of Political Studies who holds a doctorate in public law from the University of Paris. Condé was Guinea's "historic opponent," having been beaten, arrested and imprisoned for fighting to bring multiparty democracy to Guinea in the 1990s.

An Illusion of a Successful Cycle

For some, this was the end of the story. Guinea, and the international actors who had supported it, had "dodged a bullet," something half miraculous and difficult to explain. Most international participants interested in pushing Guinea in the right direction were happy to take some credit.

The dramatic and dangerous period seemed to have come to a close. It had been difficult enough to squeeze post-financial crisis money from donors by predicting the possibility of civil war or regional destabilization. Now every institution involved could enter Guinea in the success column. By comparison, the implosion of the situation in Ivory Coast after elections showed that the Guinean success was really an achievement.

The problem is that with the presidential elections, Guinea was just beginning the long process of working out of the deep hole its leaders had dug. This was the moment that international actors needed to ramp up their engagement with

Guinea, to support legislative elections, judicial reform, security sector reform, professionalization of the civil service, training the press to be less partisan and more professional, and many other tasks, too.

Sticking strictly to the area of democratization, it should be clear even to a casual observer that a credible process leading to new leadership in one arm of government—in this case the executive—is unlikely to lead to medium-term improvements in democratic practice if the other parts of government are atrophied. As one observer noted, a winner-takes-all presidential election in a system where the executive effectively exercises imperial powers over the other parts of government is just a coup d'état by another name.

Given Guinea's long and difficult history with authoritarian rule, this was always the most likely outcome of the presidential elections. Guinean politicians envision exercising the untrammeled prerogatives of an imperial presidency, whether for good or for ill.

Because it is a presidential system, the executive is less answerable to the legislature than in a parliamentary system, such as Britain's. Guineans understand that an overly strong executive does not serve the best interests of most citizens, but the average citizen doesn't have much experience with identifying, prioritizing and putting in place the mechanisms that help to guard against a slide toward authoritarianism.

Indeed, looking back to 2008, when Lansana Conté died, the main reason the Guinean population initially accepted the Camara coup d'état as the least bad outcome was because the person constitutionally designated to act as interim head of state, the National Assembly president, Aboubacar Somparé, was a veteran of both the authoritarian Conté regime and that of his authoritarian predecessor, Ahmed Sékou Touré.

Somparé was trusted neither by ordinary Guineans nor by the rest of the political class. The near-unanimous mantra in Conakry in early 2009 was that if the president of the National Assembly had held power, he would have rigged elections to make himself president for life. Moreover, he headed a legislature most Guineans considered a farce, a product of rigged elections in 2002 that were boycotted by most of the opposition parties.

New Elections Due Since 2006

New legislative elections had been due since 2006, but pressure for and interest in these elections by international observers has been tepid at best. Had the head of a credible legislative body been available to serve as interim president and organizer of new elections, Guinea might have been spared hundreds of civilian deaths and the pillaging of hundreds of millions of dollars by the junta.

It is easy to say that elections do not a democracy make. Everyone agrees, yet all the institutions with the power to do otherwise continue to act as if they thought elections and democracy were synonymous. The reasons for this are partly obvious. Electoral specialists, of whom there are now many, have developed formidable skills. The UN Development Program, the African Union, the Carter Center or the European Union can send teams who can make new electoral lists, train the national press corps for a constructive role, monitor and audit elections and spot major irregularities with a high level of accuracy. Donors can feel assured that the costs of such interventions are relatively predictable one-time-only investments.

Except when they are not, as in the case of Ivory Coast, where everyone agreed that incumbent Laurent Gbagbo, who had tenaciously clung to power since 2000, had lost the elections and needed to go. Everyone, that is, except for Gbagbo and his supporters, who did after all constitute 46 percent of the population and the majority in Abidjan, the country's commercial capital.

Here the successful technocratic intervention ran up against the reality of politics. For this is the real allure of the focus on elections. International actors can present themselves as simply making technocratic interventions, adding transparency and fairness to the process and leveling the playing field. Who could object to that?

Well, the people who lose transparent and fair elections, for starters. And this becomes an especially acute problem when the losers do not lose by much, when the national political setting is already polarized, when the security forces are undisciplined, or partisan civilian militias have been armed.

When all these elements are combined, and the loser is the incumbent, the result is rather predictable. This has been seen recently in Ivory Coast, Kenya and Zimbabwe. Politics rears its head again, except now the losers are bellicose, the winners are locked out of the presidential palace and their supporters handed a genuine grievance, and the international community is called upon to choose a side.

Alternative Approaches

So what alternative approaches are available? Two seem to me to be of particular importance.

First, applying election expertise not so much to presidential as to legislative elections. As Guineans like to say, despots are not born, but made. Certifying one or another lifelong politician as the duly elected head of state, rewarding him or her with new donor financing for having replaced an autocrat, and then walking away is a reliable way to turn a politician into a despot. Insisting that legislative elections be as fair, transparent and timely as the presidential elections can give the losers in executive elections a sense that they still have a role to play. Their parties can counterbalance authoritarian, nepotistic or otherwise irresponsible tendencies of their president.

As already noted, in case of a vacancy of power in the executive, a legitimately elected legislature is a far better source of interim rule than a military takeover. Observing presidential elections and certifying the ascent of the candidate who becomes president may become the price of entry for also observing legislative elections, but both donors and institutions can make it clear that the legislatives are the main show.

Second, it is possible that what is holding democracy back in some African countries is not poor elections, but a lack of term limits. This is not a problem particular to African countries: the last two mayors of New York City have attempted (one of them successfully) to extend the number of terms they could serve. Most New Yorkers think that both attempts were ill-considered.

We can assume that those in power would almost always prefer to stay in power rather than leave. History suggests this is a universal phenomenon. History also suggests that only a tiny fraction of those who rule longer than a decade or so become better at what they do. One needn't elaborate on this discouraging process here.

Chinua Achebe's "Anthills of the Savannah" is perhaps the most arresting narrative we have of such a process. It depicts three brilliant school friends who have reached the pinnacles of their chosen fields. One is the military leader of the country, another his cabinet minister and the third the fiery editor of the state newspaper. As the president becomes increasingly deluded and despotic, encouraged by the sycophants around him, all three enter a spiral of destruction.

International and African institutions could join to educate voters about the risks inherent in extending term limits: they have often turned well-liked presidents into presidents-for-life, and they open the door for later presidents, liked or not, to cling to power.

These are just two of several elements that could support the development of thriving democracies in Africa. Such initiatives can and should be led by Africans, as nations like Ghana have as much to show as most rich countries when it comes to exemplary democratic practice in the past few decades.

Doing less than this may seem cost-effective in the shortest of short-term perspectives. But given the ways that poor governance has led to stalled development, poor health and education, and even wars and flows of refugees, the medium-term costs of myopic efforts toward democratic support are far greater than the cost of taking a broader view of what constitutes democracy. ■

Joe Penney

Guinea is rich in bauxite, iron, gold and diamonds, but its people are poor and all business is done in cash. Due to extremely high inflation, the millions of Guinean francs seen here are worth less than $2,000.

South Sudan: The Path Forward
Amir Osman

The signing in January 2005 of the comprehensive peace agreement between the government of Sudan in Khartoum and the rebels known as the Sudan People's Liberation Movement brought an end to more than 20 years of civil war. It is considered the most significant political achievement in Sudan's history.

The peace agreement set out a map for peace with key requirements for the two parties to share wealth and power, and establish a new "government of national unity" and a semiautonomous "government of South Sudan." The agreement provided for a transition of six years, when Sudan would enact democratic reforms to "make unity attractive." At the end of this period, southerners would vote whether to remain part of Sudan or become independent.

As it happened, the unity government failed on democratic reforms and unity was not attractive to southerners. In the referendum in January they voted overwhelmingly for independence. Consequently, the world's newest country, the Republic of South Sudan, was born on July 9.

A Major List of Challenges Ahead

The splitting of Sudan could turn out to be a success story if the international community adopts a comprehensive and coherent approach to its support and if the primary beneficiaries of that support are the people of Sudan and not the two governments. A lasting peace in Sudan is possible only when the Sudanese enjoy freedom and democracy. For this to come about, northern and southern Sudan as well as the international community will need to overcome many challenges.

South Sudan will not prosper absent a stable north, and vice versa. The two countries' governments need to work on internal nation-building tasks while resolving outstanding provisions of the peace agreement, such as oil-sharing, defining borders, citizenship requirements, security arrangements and the status of the Abyei region, which to date has proven the most critical issue.

Both sides claim Abyei, which lies between the two Sudans, and disagree over who is eligible to vote to determine its status. This referendum was scheduled for earlier this year but never took place. The Abyei dispute resulted in the invasion of Abyei by Sudan's army, and brought the sides to the verge of a resumption of war.

Peace between the two countries is possible only if both are viable. It also requires engagement from the international community.

In the south, the key challenges are severe underdevelopment, corruption and instability caused by militias fighting for representation and equal development and grievances against the ruling party. There is also the possibility of a return to war with the north if the relationship is not carefully handled.

In the north, the challenges are also enormous. The ruling National Congress Party, with a long history of political manipulation, has not carried out envisioned reforms to promote democracy, good governance and respect for human rights. In addition to adopting a new constitution, the government faces potential conflicts in marginalized areas in addition to a separate eight-year conflict in Darfur in western Sudan, unrest in southern Kordofan's Nuba Mountains, the Abyei dispute and serious grievances among the people of eastern Sudan.

The crimes in Darfur ascribed to the government in the north led the International Criminal Court to issue a warrant for President Omar al-Bashir charging war crimes, crimes against humanity and genocide. Since the failed Darfur peace agreement in 2005, the international community has tried vainly to settle the conflict through negotiations between the Khartoum government and the armed movements of Darfur.

The north, which had relied on exploiting resources from the south, will suffer economically from the south's independence. It will lose significant oil revenue and has agreed to assume all the country's debt of $38 billion, adding more burdens to economic growth.

Meanwhile, it is widely speculated that the international community is limiting its support to the north after July 2011. The political situation in the north is already fragile and further economic shortfalls will contribute to more frustration. This could be a recipe for war, not only between the north and the south but also with other marginalized groups in the north.

Like the south, the north remains vulnerable without continued support from donor countries. But any continued support should be conditioned on actions by the government in Khartoum to bring a lasting peace to Darfur, end political repression and commit to democratic government under a new national constitution.

The South's Internal Challenges

After the Republic of South Sudan raised its flag on July 9, the world rushed to recognize the new nation. A visit by the United Nations Security Council to both parts of the country in May 2011 made it clear that the new republic would be welcomed by the international community. The UN and donor countries appear disposed to help South Sudan overcome the development and security challenges but there is a need for better coordination.

After Sudan's April 2010 general elections, insecurity increased when several candidates took up arms against the southern army in protest. The elections consolidated power in the hands of the ruling Sudan People's Liberation Movement, dominated by the majority Dinka tribe, to the displeasure of other ethnic groups.

In addition to those who took up arms after elections, some of the familiar warlords from the civil war have resurfaced in South Sudan and are also fighting the government and its armed forces. Deaths in the first three and a half months of 2011 reached 800, and more than 94,000 were driven from their homes, according to figures from Lise Grande, the UN humanitarian coordinator for Sudan. On the eve of independence, ethnic divisions became the major source of conflict in South Sudan. The international community must take urgent steps to open a dialogue amongst the groups.

Violence was not in evidence in 2005, at the beginning of the transitional period, when the people of southern Sudan were unified against the common enemy:

the ruling National Congress Party in the north.

South Sudan's new government should deal with the minority groups and political protests nonviolently, through political means. An inclusive political process to adopt a new constitution upholding human rights and democracy would serve as an opening for dialogue among southern Sudanese.

Assistance to the south should be conditioned on adoption of a constitution that meets the aspirations of the people of South Sudan.

Security Forces of Dubious Effectiveness

As in other postwar situations, ex-combatants constitute the vast majority of a bloated security sector. The south's police, army and other security forces lack basic training and often face shortages of basic equipment. This poses yet another threat to the stability of South Sudan. Not only are these forces unable to protect civilians, they are themselves often responsible for human-rights violations.

The new government needs to form a professional army and police force and professionalize its military with an understandable recruitment process that gives southern citizens the opportunity to serve.

But the reality on the ground has made it difficult for the new government and the UN to disarm former combatants and reintegrate them into civilian life. Efforts by the UN and donor countries to reform the security sector should focus on training forces to provide effective security.

Meanwhile, to ensure civilians are protected, the Security Council should ensure that the new peacekeeping mission in South Sudan is better equipped and has a stronger mandate to protect civilians than its predecessor, the United Nations Mission in Sudan. The earlier force lacked sufficient troops to prevent violence, had limited mobility and fell short of helping the parties make the shift to real democracy as specified in the peace agreement.

The long-term goal of the new mission should be to enable peaceful relations between the two new countries. But from the start, the mission must be fully prepared to help the new government in the south protect its citizens until the day the new government can assume that responsibility.

Oil Royalties Eaten by Security Needs

The civil war pitting Sudan's south against Khartoum raged for all but a few years from 1955 to 2005, killing two million people, devastating the lives of millions more and leaving the south with little infrastructure. In 2005, when the peace accord was signed, southern Sudan had few schools, hospitals, paved roads or civil and governmental institutions. Under the agreement, the south started directly receiving its share of money from the country's oil sales and invited investors from the Gulf, Europe, Asia and neighboring countries. But the oil money has had little impact on development as most of the budget goes to security. Corruption also remains a factor slowing development.

While UN agencies and donor countries have been contributing to development for six years and appear committed to continue, these efforts will fail unless the new government improves the way it spends money and the international community does a better job of coordinating assistance. A primary focus should be on human development to help the people of South Sudan run their country's affairs properly. The new government should also tap the expertise of its many well-educated people who fled to other countries during the war.

For South Sudan to succeed, its government agencies must operate more effectively, conquer corruption and better harness international aid. ■

UN Photo/Eskinder Debebe

The mood is jubilant in Juba on July 9, 2011, as the Republic of South Sudan celebrates its independence. Six days later, South Sudan became the 193rd member of the United Nations.

UN Intervention Rescues Ivory Coast by a Hair's Breadth

Richard Gowan

For over four months after presidential elections in November 2010, Ivory Coast stood on the brink of renewed civil war. The United Nations peacekeeping force there appeared unable to halt fighting between supporters of the internationally recognized election winner, Alassane Ouattara, and his opponent, Laurent Gbagbo. The peacekeepers became targets for Gbagbo's supporters. Yet in April, bolstered by a new mandate and joined by France, the UN force conducted offensive operations to protect civilians as violence peaked.

These operations have been hailed as a successful exercise of the Responsibility to Protect, the international community's framework to prevent genocide, war crimes, ethnic cleansing and crimes against humanity. Secretary-General Ban Ki-moon was praised for making a tough defense of the election results. The UN intervention, while it may not have generated the same level of interest as an earlier international foray in Libya, was no less remarkable.

Nonetheless, the UN only very narrowly averted disaster and the country's stability is still uncertain.

The UN has a troubled history in Ivory Coast. In September 2002, after almost a decade of political instability, the former French colony fell into all-out civil war. This stemmed from tensions within the military—which had seized power in 1999-2000—and political divisions between the Muslim north and Christian south. Gbagbo, the incumbent president, who won national elections in 2000, called on the Economic Community of West African States and France to send peacekeepers.

Peace terms were hammered out in January 2003, and the UN sent a small political mission with military observers to help carry out the accord. In spite of efforts by Gbagbo to build a government of national unity, the political process stalled and the country remained in a state of war.

Replacement of Peacekeepers Authorized

In February 2004, the Security Council authorized a UN force to replace the peacekeepers from the Economic Community of West African States. Both the UN soldiers and the separate French military presence, dubbed Operation Licorne, were nominally impartial. But in late 2004, an Ivorian air force plane bombed a French base in mysterious circumstances, killing nine soldiers. The French destroyed the Ivorian air force, sparking major riots during which protestors threatened UN personnel.

In 2005, talks hosted by South Africa resulted in a final peace agreement, which stipulated that national elections should be held as early as fall that year. This did not guarantee stability. In 2006, rioters launched attacks on the UN peacekeeping mission, development officials and the French. There was also a loss of trust between the UN and Gbagbo, who increasingly portrayed the UN and French operations as favoring his opponents. These strains grew as the elections were repeatedly postponed.

When Gbagbo finally called elections in 2010, it was widely expected that he would be victorious. His main rivals were Ouattara, a former prime minister and International Monetary Fund official, and Henry Konan Bédié, a former president. In line with the 2005 agreement, the special representative of the secretary-general, Choi Young-jin, was given the task of certifying the election results.

Voters Have Their Say

A first round of voting in October went smoothly, with Gbagbo in the lead but Ouattara not far behind. Reflecting the divisions left from the civil war, Ouattara enjoyed majority support in the north; Gbagbo led in the south. Bédié then endorsed Ouattara, and a run-off vote was held in the last week of November.

The aftermath of the second round was confused, but the Independent Electoral Commission, an Ivorian body, announced in early December that Ouattara had won with nearly 55 percent of the vote. Gbagbo's camp refused to accept the result, contending that its candidate had scored a narrow victory. However, Choi Young-jin certified the results confirming Ouattara's victory, and the secretary-general called on Gbagbo to accept this decision.

The situation deteriorated quickly as Gbagbo ignored outside pressure to resign. In Abidjan, the commercial capital, a battalion of Bangladeshi peacekeepers protected Ouattara in a hotel while Gbagbo supporters went on a rampage. There were soon reports of hundreds of fatalities in Abidjan alone. UN units were also severely harassed as they struggled to monitor the violence.

All the main UN political organs engaged with the crisis in December. The Security Council followed Ban's lead in calling for Gbagbo to respect the election results, although it was initially delayed by Russian objections to interfering. On Dec. 20, the council authorized the UN mission to remain in place six months more, in spite of calls from Gbagbo for the departure of peacekeepers and Operation Licorne. As the situation deteriorated, the General Assembly gave its unanimous support to Ouattara's victory, while the Human Rights Council demanded an end to violence.

West African Bloc Is Also Heard

The Economic Community of West African States also threw its weight behind Ouattara, and gave serious consideration to sending in military forces. The regional dimension of the crisis was underlined by a huge flow of refugees from Ivory Coast—it is estimated that 450,000 left by early March—and reports that young men in neighboring Liberia planned to join the conflict as mercenaries. While Nigeria and some other West African countries favored a military solution, others, including Ivory Coast's neighbor Ghana, thought the risks were too high, especially as the Ivorian security forces remained loyal to Gbagbo, who paid them.

Efforts to mediate began with a visit by the former South African president, Thabo Mbeki, to Abidjan on behalf of the African Union. Mbeki, having hosted the 2005 peace talks, believed that the level of pressure on Gbagbo was counter-productive, but his visit offered no way out of the crisis. Nonetheless, the African Union continued to give top priority to finding a mediated solution, appointing a panel of the leaders of Burkina Faso, Chad, Mauritania, South Africa and Tanzania to direct the diplomatic effort in January.

After the initial rush of international efforts to resolve the Ivorian crisis, there was a loss of momentum in the first quarter of 2011. This reflected both divisions between the African Union's insistence on mediation (a stance promoted by South Africa with Russian support at the UN) and a shift of attention toward events in Tunisia and Egypt.

Meanwhile, Gbagbo's supporters continued to harass UN peacekeepers while Operation Licorne—reduced from 4,000 troops in 2003 to fewer than 1,000 by early 2011—also avoided confrontations. In January, the Security Council approved the temporary transfer of 2,000 peacekeepers from Liberia to Ivory Coast, bringing the mission's strength to roughly 11,000 military and police personnel. But officials at UN headquarters feared that the force's leaders were being too risk-averse, and the mission provided poor reporting on events on the ground. There were even press reports that some Ivorian UN staff had assisted Gbagbo's thugs.

President's Support Crumbles

Gbagbo's position was not as strong as it appeared, however. Targeted sanctions imposed by the European Union and U.S. in December 2010 were gradually weakening his powerbase; the European Union's position was critical, as France remained Ivory Coast's main trading partner.

Meanwhile, the African Union panel came to the view that Ouattara's right to the presidency must be upheld. On March 10, the African Union endorsed the panel's conclusions that the original election results were correct and that Ouattara should be allowed to put together a national unity government within weeks to end the standoff.

Most decisively, however, forces from northern Ivory Coast loyal to Ouattara launched a fast-moving and highly effective offensive in late March, quickly capturing towns in the west of the country. This advance was marred by reports of large-scale killings of civilians, but the level of general violence and attacks on peacekeepers by Gbagbo loyalists in Abidjan also spiked.

On March 30 the Security Council authorized the UN peacekeepers to use all necessary means to protect civilians from attacks by heavy weapons. The council also announced new sanctions on Gbagbo, while France readied its forces for action.

The collapse of Gbagbo's position was sudden and complete. Ouattara's supporters were in Abidjan in the first week of April, while French and UN helicopters attacked Gbagbo's security forces. This sparked immediate controversy over whether the peacekeepers had switched from impartiality to fighting on Ouattara's behalf, but the UN defended its actions in terms of protecting civilians and its own forces. Gbagbo was captured on April 11 and put under house arrest. There have since been credible reports of continuing attacks on his supporters.

Violence Draws Attention of the Court

Ouattara was finally inaugurated on May 20. Prior to this he had launched a truth commission to review the violence of the post-elections crisis. In late June, the prosecutor of the International Criminal Court announced his intention to investigate war crimes by both Gbagbo and Ouattara supporters, involving 3,000 deaths.

Security remains a concern, and at the end of June the Security Council decided to keep the UN mission at its crisis-level strength of 11,000. The mission launched a program to boost security in the west of the country, where the level of violence had been especially high.

It will now be necessary for the UN to reinforce Ivory Coast's comparative stability, to ensure that those now in power seek real justice rather than revenge in dealing with Gbagbo's supporters, and that the Ivorian economy fully recovers.

It is true that the UN ultimately played a significant part in resolving the crisis, but it is worth underlining how slow and uncertain international action proved —hundreds or thousands of lives were lost while the UN, African Union and Economic Community of West African States searched for a consensus on what to do.

Had Ouattara's supporters not been able to mount a decisive offensive in March and April, the crisis could have dragged on considerably longer. The resolution of the Ivorian crisis was a success for the UN. But it had come very close to a disaster.

UN Photo/Aristide Bodegla

Laurent Gbagbo, Ivory Coast's former president, in an Abidjan hotel in April 2011 after surrendering to forces backing Alassane Ouattara, who defeated Gbagbo in November 2010 elections.

Building Peace and Keeping It **83**

Margot Wallström: UN Watchdog on Sexual Abuse in War

Barbara Crossette

In 2009, when the UN Security Council had all but despaired of seeing serious action taken against sexual abuse in conflict zones, the council asked Secretary-General Ban Ki-moon to appoint a watchdog. He chose Margot Wallström of Sweden, a former government minister and a vice president of the European Commission, and gave her an internationally recognized panel of experts to advise her. She began her mission in 2010.

It was not the best of times, however, to interrupt the cycle of abuse in conflict areas. The UN was in the midst of yet another self-examination about how rape on a large scale could be occurring in the eastern Democratic Republic of Congo, where the UN has one of its largest peacekeeping missions.

This time, however, she said in New York in an interview in her new role, the UN not only acknowledged its shortcomings and pledged to do better, but also agreed to go beyond promises to work harder on prevention and start behaving more like cops.

Yet despite the pledges, the peacekeeping mission, working in the most extreme conditions, has been unable to exert more control or influence over various armed militias and gangs operating in eastern Congo, the secretary-general said in a report to the Security Council in mid-2011, as renewal of the UN mission was discussed.

"There were continued attacks against civilians, including acts of sexual violence, by foreign and Congolese armed groups and some FARDC [Congo army] elements," his report said, adding that "in Orientale Province ... the Lord's Resistance Army continued to attack and abduct civilians." But it noted "an encouraging development" in the Congolese army, which had put on trial some officers accused of human rights violations in South Kivu province.

Rape a Factor in Political Disputes, Too

Globally, sexual abuse is not confined to conflict areas, Wallström said. It is a tactic that has entered political disputes—in Kyrgyzstan and Guinea last year—and in the economic exploitation of resources, a significant part of the problem in Congo, she said.

Indeed, Wallström wrote an opinion article in The Guardian of London on the direct links between the exploitation of precious metals or minerals and war, mentioning coltan, a rare ore used in making mobile phones.

"Although it is complicated to track conflict minerals, this cannot become an excuse for not trying," she wrote. "After all, neither American nor European consumers want their MP3 players and mobile phones to be funding gang rape in Africa." She praised the Obama administration for including a provision in the finance bill passed by the U.S. Congress demanding the labeling of "conflict minerals" on the market.

Margot Wallström, the UN secretary-general's special representative on sexual violence in conflict.

In the interview, she said that sexual assault is a phenomenon that "is planned, it's systematic, and it's carried out to control the territory, to instill fear, to terrorize the population."

"If you as a child have seen, maybe, your mother being raped in front of the whole village, do you ever feel safe again?" she said. "This [fear] is often carried over from generation to generation, and this is why it is such an impediment to restoring peace and security in a country."

"We must go after the perpetrators, because if you think that we have only one spotlight, the UN system—were they slow, all those relevant questions—[then] the spotlight turns on the UN," she said. "Meanwhile, we allow the perpetrators to walk free. Where are they now? They go to the next village and continue to rape and loot and pillage. We have to prosecute them, because otherwise the whole talk about ending impunity means nothing. We have to start being serious about how we go after them."

Some Way to Restore Dignity

Wallström said she believed in the wisdom of listening to women in disturbed areas, assuring them the UN was there to hear and help and asking for advice. She spoke about victimized women in Congo discussing reparations who suggested "bringing something back to the village"—not money but a community project, perhaps, that would restore their dignity among villagers.

For example, in Afghanistan, she said, female UN police officers assigned to patrolling back streets or quieter neighborhoods, where their presence gives a psychological lift to local women, are also able to collect intelligence as they get to know people.

She related a story told to her by one officer: "Women would come up to them when they saw that they were women police, and would report about a big wedding taking place on the next day or on the weekend," Wallström said. "They could tell them that there were 600 guests arriving from all over. This was not told to the police patrolling the main streets because [they would have thought] it was not important. [But] it's a security issue. That's very valuable information women could obtain by engaging with other women."

Wallström said she welcomed reports of abuse or security threats from any quarter, including the media and nongovernmental organizations closest to the scene, because these could set off quicker investigations and more rapid responses, possibly allowing troops to chase down perpetrators before they disappear into the bush or urban neighborhoods. The UN, she said, needs better monitoring systems everywhere and all help is appreciated.

Born in 1954 and married with two children, Wallström was elected to the Swedish Parliament while still in her 20s. She later served in three ministerial positions for civil affairs, culture and social affairs, respectively, before becoming executive vice president of Worldview Global Media, an organization based in Sri Lanka. She joined the European Commission in 1999, and in 2004 was appointed its vice president for inter-institutional relations and communication. Through her years on the commission, she followed the UN's efforts to counter sexual abuse as she also promoted women's rights and political inclusion in Europe.

Victims Who Are Not Women

In tackling how to better understand the nature of sexual violence—or what taboos in some places keep it from happening—Wallström said she was aware that men and boys are also targets, because rape can be intended as the ultimate humiliation.

"We know this, that it is not exclusively women that are targeted," she said. "Boys are also raped and sexually abused. It is important to understand that phenomenon as well, unfortunately. Maybe this is a way to mobilize more sensitivity, because some could argue that people are being tortured, their limbs being chopped off, and here you talk about rape. They try to play it down by comparing it with other atrocities. I think if we explain that this happens not only exclusively to women, maybe we can also mobilize a deeper understanding and sympathy."

"Sexual abuse is not cultural," Wallström said. "It isn't even sexual. It's criminal. And that's how we have to treat these things. Can you think of any other human rights violation where we would conclude that it is inevitable? It's collateral damage? This is what we have to change: the whole attitude to the problem."

The world has focused on rapes in African conflicts partly because of repeated reports from places such as Congo, Sudan, Liberia and Sierra Leone. But the problem knows few boundaries, Wallström said. "We had it in the Balkans—a horrible expression of this is that there were rape camps for ethnic cleansing. We cannot say that it is cultural. It is not African or any other culture. It exists, unfortunately, everywhere." ∎

[A version of this article appeared in The InterDependent, a UNA-USA publication (www.theinterdependent.com), on Sept. 20, 2010.]

Somalia's Life as a Piracy Center
Evelyn Leopold

The golden age of piracy is back. More than 2,500 pirates are pursuing anything that floats in the Indian Ocean and the Gulf of Aden, turning much of Somalia into an economy of corruption.

They don't wear romantic eye patches. But they give interviews, try to act like Robin Hood and have even opened a sort of stock exchange.

Few captives have been killed but torture is not unknown and sailors have been used as human shields against military intervention.

Since the vast majority of pirates captured by foreign navies around the Horn of Africa are eventually released, the United Nations is looking into creating proper courts and prisons in the Somali region of Puntland along the Indian Ocean and in Somaliland itself, bordering the Gulf of Aden. But there is no quick fix.

Expressing frustration, U.S. Secretary of State Hillary Clinton told a Senate committee in March: "I'm fed up with it. We need to do more, and make it clear that the entire world better get behind what we do and get this scourge resolved."

No Functioning Government for 20 Years

Somalia has been without a functioning central government since the 1991 ouster of the dictator Mohamed Siad Barre, resulting in a civil war that has yet to subside. The internationally recognized Transitional Federal Government controls only a part of Mogadishu, the capital, while the Islamic Al Shabab group (which says it wants close ties to Al Qaeda) controls swathes of southern and central Somalia.

The piracy arose as a response by local fishermen to intrusion by foreign trawlers and over time became a profitable occupation. The 2004 tsunami fueled its growth, demolishing Somali fishing fleets and washing ashore rusting containers of toxic waste from European vessels.

The pirates' impact is appalling and gets worse every month. Estimates of the annual cost range from $7 billion to $12 billion in captured vessels, ransom, insurance premiums, naval patrols, prosecutions, damage to local fishing fleets and lost tourism. Unhampered, it is projected to increase to as much as $15 billion by 2014.

In 2010, pirates seized a record 53 ships and 1,181 crew members worldwide, most of them off the Somalia coast, according to the International Maritime Bureau in London. That's a 10 percent increase over 2009. In the first quarter of 2011, there were 97 attacks off Somalia recorded, up from 35 in the same period last year. International Maritime Bureau figures showed that on March 31, Somali pirates were holding 596 crew members aboard 28 ships.

A Vast Area for Naval Patrols

In a June report to the UN Security Council, Secretary-General Ban Ki-moon said that as of May 2011, the geographical area of the attacks stretched to 2.8 million square miles, an area difficult for naval forces to patrol.

With Somalia's economy in shambles (although inventive businessmen have devised a thriving, inexpensive and cutting-edge cellphone system), piracy appeals to young men. According to some sources it provides annual income of $80,000 if you are not caught. That is a fortune in Somalia compared with the average annual wage of $500 and worth the risk unless you are imprisoned or killed.

According to the UN report, there are 50 principal pirate leaders, 300 leaders of attack groups and 2,500 ordinary sailors. Financing is provided by 10 to 20 individuals. There are also armed people guarding captured ships as well as ransom negotiators. So ransoms have to be huge to pay all these people.

The big money goes to those running the show. Kenya has complained about a spurt in housing prices as Somalis buy property there and in Dubai.

And yet in the south, Somalia is experiencing the worst humanitarian situation in 10 years because of drought, food shortages, soaring food prices and warfare, UN agencies reported in June.

A pirate stock exchange was set up in 2009 in Xarardheere, 250 miles northeast of Mogadishu in the region of Galmudug. Statistics are hard to come by but Reuters has given the most credible account, suggesting that over 70 entities are listed on the exchange, a sort of cooperative venture. When a pirate operation is successful, it pays investors a share. According to a former pirate who spoke to Reuters, "The shares are open to all and everybody can take part, whether personally at sea or on land by providing cash, weapons or useful materials."

"We've made piracy a community activity," he was quoted as saying, indicating many shared in the spoils. Xaradheere's exchange is open 24 hours a day and serves as a bustling focal point for the town's economy.

Plowing the Profits Back In

In good Robin Hood fashion, the area has profited from piracy, according to a local security officer, who says the pirates give the district a cut of the profits for schools, hospitals and charities. The ransom buys bigger and better pirate vessels with sophisticated navigation and Global Positioning System equipment, according to Jack Lang, a former French culture minister and a UN legal adviser on piracy.

"There is a race between the pirates and the rest of the world," Lang said. Piracy has taken on an industrial scope, he said at a news conference in January. The big ransom demands, the use of advanced technologies and a talent for money-laundering invites comparisons to the mafia. "There's machinery behind this and it functions quite well," he said.

However, he added, common forensic and police methods used against the mafia have not been employed. Bank note serial numbers, for example, are not tracked, and fingerprints and DNA evidence is not gathered.

And while the pirates chat easily about the funds they provide to the community, some experts point to a growing use of violence.

In February, four Americans who had been taken from their yacht in the Indian Ocean were shot dead in a botched rescue by U.S. naval forces. Two pirates were killed and 15 detained. But unlike this event most of piracy's victims are from developing nations and are often held under ghastly conditions, according to a report underwritten by the One Earth Future Foundation of Louisville, Colo.

That report found that worldwide, a total of 4,185 seafarers were attacked with firearms and rocket-propelled grenades in 2010; 342 were locked in ship security rooms, and 516 were used as human shields to ward off attacks.

Called The Human Cost of Somali Piracy, the report said sailors were sometimes locked in freezers, hung from meat hooks or had their genitals attached to electric wires. Worse yet, pirates have called the families of captive sailors by cellphone and then beat them within earshot.

Some of this was in revenge after U.S. forces killed three Somali pirates in April 2009 to secure the release of a captured American ship captain. One pirate, speaking to Reuters, said: "I lost the money I invested and my comrades. No forgiveness for the Americans. Revenge. Our business will go on."

A Prison for 1,000

So the question remains: what has to be done to discourage people from joining the lucrative piracy business?

Lang suggested setting up proper courts and prisons in Puntland and Somaliland where tribal elders were increasingly uncomfortable with piracy and where

U.S. Navy Photo/Specialist 2nd Class Jason R. Zalasky

Suspected pirates in the Gulf of Aden off Somalia keep their hands in the air after being caught by the U.S. Navy trying to hijack a commercial ship.

Building Peace and Keeping It **89**

militant Islamists were not taking up arms. Kenya and the Seychelles, for example, are no longer willing to prosecute or imprison those captured in its waters.

The UN Security Council asked the secretary-general to investigate, and Patricia O'Brien, the under secretary-general for legal affairs, briefed the council on her findings in June.

Two agencies, the UN Development Program and the UN Office on Drugs and Crime, are already trying to set up courts in Somaliland and Puntland, she said. A prison for 1,000 inmates is also needed. The agencies estimated the project would take three years and cost $24 million.

Another proposal was to use the court complex set up for the International Criminal Tribunal for Rwanda, in Arusha, Tanzania, once the genocide trials there end. Tanzania was willing but Somali leaders prefer the courts at home, and are not happy about international jurists taking part, diplomats said.

"Achieving international standards will be a critical step because it will open the way for naval states to be able to enter into arrangements with Somali authorities for the transfer of piracy suspects apprehended at sea," O'Brien said.

Council diplomats listening to the report were somewhat skeptical that enough evidence could be provided by seafarers, most of them legally inexperienced, to hold up in a trial. They questioned the impact of the courts, a sensible but big-ticket item, noting that judges and other legal staff would have to be trained. In addition, legislation would have to be adopted by a barely functioning central government. But the court plans will probably be supported.

To change the dynamic, however, many actions are needed. For one, banks processing the piracy funds from London to Dubai have to be investigated. And shippers need to take sensible precautions rather than just adding the price of a ransom into their running costs.

"One of our big problems is that a lot of major shipping companies in the world think it's the price of doing business," Secretary Clinton said. "They pay a ransom and they just go on their merry way. That has been a huge problem."

Basically, the entire country has to be rebuilt along with its economy, with schools and enterprises that give young people hope. It's a long-term incremental process, and like most realities involving poverty, it won't be as sexy as a pirate in an eye patch. ∎

Talking Points

1. In situations requiring peacekeepers, a conflict's root causes typically have political underpinnings. Should the UN try to always remain neutral by strictly adhering to the nonpolitical mandate of protecting vulnerable citizens? Or should peacekeepers engage in more aggressive offensive operations that might save more lives, even if that could give the impression of taking sides?

2. "Free and fair elections" can have unintended consequences in fragile states, including undesirable election results, economic instability as factions wrestle over assets, or large-scale political violence stemming from a lack of experience with peaceful transitions of power. Do political freedoms lead to economic and social progress, or is the international community better off working to ensure economic and social stability before holding democratic elections?

3. Sexual abuse, targeted acts of violence and deliberate subjugation of women are major concerns in conflict zones; long-term strategies for changing these deeply embedded behaviors are ultimately needed. Given the international community's short attention span, how can the UN ensure that women's rights are respected long after peacekeepers leave?

4. Somali pirates are a huge and costly problem, and under international law, any nation can try pirates it captures on the high seas. Why, then, are the vast majority of the pirates captured by foreign navies let free? Can Somali authorities be entrusted to create a competent judicial and penal system addressing piracy, given their lack of a functioning government?

UN Photo/David Ohana

UN Secretary-General Ban Ki-moon and U.S. leader Barack Obama confer outside a Group of Eight summit in Deauville, France, in May 2011.

UN Perspectives

94 **Washington and Turtle Bay: Hop on the Roller Coaster**
James Traub

98 **People and Ideas for the Next Secretary-General**
Thomas G. Weiss

102 **Picking the UN Leader Should Be More of a Contest**
Simon Minching

105 **Touching the Lives of Half the World**
Barbara Crossette

110 **Help Wanted for Work That Makes a Difference**
Gus Feissel

114 **Why UN Reform Remains an Elusive Goal**
Minh-Thu Pham

117 **What the United Nations Loses to Academic Indifference**
Helmut Volger

121 **Talking Points**

Washington and Turtle Bay: Hop on the Roller Coaster

James Traub

As a presidential candidate, Barack Obama would tell audiences, "I want to go before the United Nations and say, 'America's back!' " His listeners didn't need to be told where America had been under George W. Bush—on a bender of unilateralism and bellicosity, or so Democrats argued.

Obama proposed to re-engage the world; and to do so through multilateral institutions, above all the UN. Upon taking office, Obama made good his vow by appointing Susan Rice, one of his senior foreign policy advisers, as UN ambassador; by joining the Human Rights Council, which the Bush administration had scorned; and by repaying, without conditions, the roughly $1 billion in arrears run up under President Bush.

The United States is indeed "back" at the UN. The agony of the debate over war in Iraq, the sustained verbal barrage from John Bolton when he was the chief U.S. delegate—they're all memories. Nick Birnback, now with UN peacekeeping in Somalia but at the time chief spokesman for the peacekeeping department, says that he and his colleagues were astonished when, during his first General Assembly meeting in 2009, Obama arranged to chair a session of current and potential troop contributors for peacekeeping missions—an unprecedented act. "Compared to every other administration," he says, "they're on a different planet."

President Obama took office at a fortunate moment for U.S. engagement. The UN was not rocked either by scandal or by deeply divisive political issues like Iraq or Security Council reform, and Secretary-General Ban Ki-moon was staunchly pro-American. President Bill Clinton endured a bruising battle to deny a second term to Boutros Boutros-Ghali, an unpopular figure in the U.S. Ban, by contrast, seems to hew instinctively to the American line on all major subjects, and has provided no ammunition to conservative critics of the UN. As Robert Orr, one of Ban's senior advisers, notes, "The administration and the secretary-general have worked hard to get the UN out of the gunsights, and they've largely succeeded."

A Consonance of Hopes and Ideas

But it's not simply a matter of good fortune. In its 2010 National Security Strategy document, the Obama White House listed "promoting a just and sustainable international order" as among America's core interests. "In a world of transnational challenges," the report said, "the United States will need to invest in strengthening the international system, working from inside international institutions and frameworks to face their imperfections head on and to mobilize transnational cooperation." The decision to join the Human Rights Council, widely derided as a tool to protect rather than confront autocrats, constituted a down payment on that commitment.

The UN also fits into Obama's strategy of strengthening relations with the world's emerging powers. Bruce Jones, director of the New York University Center on International Cooperation, contends that the White House "is not thinking about the UN in a narrow institutional sense," but is using it as a forum to deepen relations with countries like India and Brazil, as well as to explore areas of cooperation with Russia and China. Obama has gone beyond vague promises to support "Security Council reform" by endorsing India's candidacy for permanent membership in the Council. The tangled politics of reform, however, ensure that India will have to bide its time for a number, perhaps a very large number, of years.

While the Bush administration, at least in its final years, supported a wide range of UN peacekeeping missions as well as the global campaign against AIDS, the U.S. now seeks to play an active role on a range of transnational issues, including climate change, public health, food security and economic development, which Obama views as core national security concerns. The president has formally endorsed the UN's Millennium Development Goals as the framework for U.S. development efforts. "That's a big deal rhetorically," Orr says.

Of course the central mission of the UN for any American administration is the adjudication of high politics through the Security Council. In his first year in office, Obama built on the Bush administration's efforts to use the council to keep pressure on Iran; his singular achievement in this regard was persuading Russia and China not to veto sanctions designed to halt Iran's nuclear program. Here the administration's larger program of "engagement," at least with Russia, fed into its activism at the UN.

'Leadership From Behind'

In recent months, the U.S. has adopted a self-effacing posture in the Security Council offering a startling comparison to the Bush administration's aggressive brand of leadership. The U.S. Mission did not use its presidency of the Security Council in December 2010 to focus attention on major issues, as it has in the past, and offered a muted response to widespread charges of electoral fraud in Ivory Coast. During the long debate over intervention in Libya, the White House relinquished council leadership to France and Britain, which strongly advocated the establishment of a no-fly zone.

Deeply sensitive to anti-American feeling in the Arab world, Obama refused to move forward until the Arab League had endorsed a no-fly zone. Even then, the U.S. Mission operated quietly to toughen the language of the resolution and to press Russia and China to let it through. The administration was criticized for an abdication of leadership; others, however, saw in this quiet strategy a new model of "leadership from behind" suitable to a world that the U.S. no longer dominates as it long has.

The debate over Libya brought up a larger critique of Obama and the policy of engagement: the U.S. has become diffident on human rights. One official of a nongovernmental group who closely tracks human rights policy says the U.S. has frittered away too much energy in the Human Rights Council fighting the Goldstone Report, which described alleged war crimes by Israel (as well as by Hamas) in the Gaza war, and has shown little penchant for leadership. (Both Israel and Washington dismissed the report as flawed and biased.) U.S. officials did lead a successful effort to get Libya suspended from the council, and to prevent Syria from joining. Nevertheless, this official says, "They could play a strong role, but they are at maybe 10 percent of potential."

Philippe Bolopion, UN director for the organization Human Rights Watch, points out that the U.S. "did little" to force the Sri Lankan issue onto the Security Council's agenda while thousands of civilians were slaughtered in an army drive to quash the Tamil Tiger separatist revolt in the spring of 2009. And, he said, it has made only a tepid effort to back calls for an international commission of inquiry into the killings. (Few other major states showed a serious appetite either to stop or to investigate them.) Obama has embraced the "responsibility to protect," the UN-endorsed principle that stipulates that nations must act to stop mass atrocities; but his rhetoric has outstripped his actual commitments.

Copters Possibly, but Not Troops

Indeed, the administration's rhetoric on the international order invites skeptical scrutiny. Little has come of the administration's promises of UN reform, as Republicans have been quick to observe. Others criticize Rice for spending more time in Washington than many of her predecessors. And there is somewhat less than meets the eye to the president's activism on peacekeeping. "They're willing to pick up the phone when we come to them with specific asks," says Birnback, the peacekeeping spokesman, noting as an example, helicopters for Darfur or to urge India to keep its gunships in the Democratic Republic of Congo.

The administration, however, has declined to contribute combat troops to peacekeeping missions (though it has deployed some police officers and other specialists), and has proved reluctant to supply logistical or airlift assets when the UN has asked.

For its first two years in office, the Obama administration was able to operate at the UN with little regard for domestic politics, but the election of 2010 gave Republicans a majority in the House of Representatives and reduced the Democratic edge in the Senate. The Clinton administration suffered a similar defeat in 1994, and the UN felt the impact in onerous demands and unpaid dues. Since that time, thanks to acrimony over the lack of UN support for the 2003 U.S.-led invasion of Iraq and the oil-for-food scandal, the UN has become even more of a bugbear among conservatives than in the 1990s.

Use of Surpluses Won't Always Work

The chairman of the House Foreign Affairs Committee, Ileana Ros-Lehtinen, Republican of Florida, is an inveterate critic of the UN and skeptic of multilateralism. She recently wrote, "We should not be afraid to stand up for our values and interests, even if that means standing alone." In 2007, Ros-Lehtinen introduced legislation that would have made all U.S. contributions to the UN voluntary, thus permitting the UN's largest dues-payer to starve those UN agencies of which it did not approve.

UN Photo/Ky Chung

Barack Obama arrives at UN headquarters in New York in September 2010 to address the General Assembly. Escorting the U.S. leader is Desmond Parker, the UN chief of protocol.

For the 2011 budget, Ros-Lehtinen and other members of the House leadership proposed deep cuts in U.S. contributions to peacekeeping operations as well as both UN dues and voluntary contributions. The Obama administration will be able to use existing surplus to compensate for such cuts; but Republicans are likely to suggest yet deeper reductions for 2012.

This Democratic White House thus finds itself in the same predicament that the last one did. Just as Richard Holbrooke, UN ambassador in 1999-2000, struggled to persuade conservative congressmen that the UN was a bargain for a superpower that could not afford to police the globe alone, so Susan Rice now delivers speeches pointing out that "each UN peacekeeper costs a fraction of what it would cost to field a U.S. soldier to do the same job."

As Holbrooke once described the UN as "flawed but indispensable," so Rice concedes that the institution "isn't perfect—far from it," but deserves dependable U.S. support. The administration, says one U.S. official, is deeply worried about the 2012 budget, for sharp cuts could bring an abrupt end to the era of good feeling at the UN that Obama's election ushered in.

The fight over funding is a reminder of American ambivalence toward the UN. Beyond the divide on the subject between Democrats and Republicans, the U.S. is bound to resist constraints on its behavior, even as it seeks to use the UN to advance its own interests. UN advocates, in and out of the U.S., might wish it otherwise; but it has always been so, and probably always will be. ■

People and Ideas for the Next Secretary-General
Thomas G. Weiss

Jan. 1, 2012, marks the start of a new term for United Nations Secretary-General Ban Ki-moon. Such a moment usually provokes the question Lenin famously posed in 1901, "What is to be done?"

A lightning bolt might simultaneously knock all 193 UN members off their horses. But short of that, it is unlikely the UN will tackle the most crucial shortcoming in contemporary international relations: the gap between efforts to meet the increasing number of threats to human existence (climate change, terrorism, nuclear proliferation) and the stubborn insistence on narrowly defined national interests as the only basis for international decision-making.

The secretary-general, starting on the first day of the new term, should relentlessly pursue two strategies: speaking out often and energetically, and recruiting truly independent staff members and giving them leeway to succeed or fail.

Neither requires permission of the countries whose dues pay the UN's bills. Indeed, both were pursued to varying degrees by predecessors, in particular by Dag Hammarskjöld, the second secretary-general.

The UN's strength lies in its universality and perceived legitimacy. These give it credibility and power in formulating global norms and principles, which matter because people—ordinary citizens as well as politicians and government officials—care what others think about them. This is why approbation and its opposite, shaming, can modify behavior. It is also why, at their finest moments, UN secretaries-general are seen as "secular popes" who can use the prestige and visibility of their office to exert global leadership.

It is often asked, "Is the UN headed by a 'secretary' or a 'general'?" Actually, the answer is "neither," but he (not yet she) has more capacities than pundits commonly believe. The UN's ideas and moral voice can be very powerful, and have been used by secretaries-general to set the agenda even at the price of irritating powers big and small.

Taking a stand and voicing it before major powers and regional organizations have spoken should be in bold-faced print in job descriptions on First Avenue. Visibility is an asset; finessing controversy is not.

The second task, an independent staff, would in many ways involve moving back to the future. The secretary-general must hire and promote world-class staff and give them the freedom to mount their own pulpits and take the lead in pursuing new thinking.

Ideas and concepts are a crucial force in human progress, and 12 years of research by the independent UN Intellectual History Project, of which I was co-director, lead to the conclusion that the UN's major contribution since its birth in 1945 may well have been its role in framing the world's intellectual agenda.

The next secretary-general's legacy could be ensured by reinvigorating the UN staff and boosting its morale. We urgently need to revive the notion of an autonomous international civil service, Dag Hammarskjöld's passion. Competence and integrity should outweigh nationality, gender and cronyism, which have unfortunately become widely applied criteria for recruitment, retention and promotion. In fact, Hammarskjöld championed an ideal that harks back to what the Carnegie Endowment for International Peace during World War II called the "great experiment" of the League of Nations.

'Munich of International Cooperation'

Hammarskjöld spelled out the importance of a first-rate independent staff in a speech in May 1961 at Oxford University shortly before his death. An erosion or abandonment of the international civil service "might, if accepted by the member nations, well prove to be the Munich of international cooperation," he asserted. Historical analogies often are misleading, but the sinking quality, morale and output of the contemporary UN civil service all but fulfills Hammarskjöld's prophecy.

Setting aside senior UN positions for officials nominated and approved by their home countries belies integrity. Governments seek to use such appointments to protect their interests and even to spy. From the outset, the Security Council's five permanent members—Britain, China, France, Russia and the United States—have reserved the right to designate nationals to fill the key posts in the secretary-general's cabinet.

The influx of former colonies into the UN in the 1950s and 1960s led to a clamor for a fair share of patronage opportunities, following the bad example set by older countries. As a result, competence was played down while geographic distribution became an obsession, and national origins were enshrined as the main criterion for recruitment and promotion. All positions above the director level, and often at every level, became the object of government lobbying.

The UN should rediscover the idealistic roots of the international civil service, make room for creative idea-mongers, and mark out career development paths for a 21st-century Secretariat staff that is younger and more versatile. There are ways to attract candidates with integrity and talent, including turnover, fewer permanent contracts, and supplementing or replacing national quotas with regional or linguistic allotments.

Ban Ki-moon has said he wants the UN to be a "powerhouse of ideas." This should be a top priority for a newly re-energized staff: to formulate and promote the ideas that have characterized the best of the UN over six and a half decades.

The system should provide more intellectual leadership to deal with the changed nature of crucial problems and their solutions. It should seek to bridge the deepening gap between scientific knowledge and political decision-making. Because policy research and ideas matter, the UN should enhance its ability to produce and nurture world-class public intellectuals, thinkers and planners.

UN officials are typically considered inferior to their counterparts from the Washington-based international financial institutions. This notion reflects, in part, the resources spent on research in these institutions as well as their respective cultures and the attention paid them by the media.

The reality has often been different. Nine people with substantial experience within the UN and its policy discussions have won the Nobel Prize in the economic sciences—Jan Tinbergen, Wassily Leontief, Gunnar Myrdal, James Meade, W. Arthur Lewis, Theodore W. Schultz, Lawrence R. Klein, Richard Stone and Amartya Sen—while only one from the World Bank, Joseph Stiglitz, has done so. But he later resigned from the bank in protest and is now associated with UN policy work.

Then there are the individual Nobel Peace Prize winners who worked for years as UN staff members: Ralph Bunche, Dag Hammarskjöld, Kofi Annan, Mohamed ElBaradei and Martti Ahtisaari. In addition, 15 organizations and individuals associated with the UN have also won Nobel Peace Prizes. No other organization comes even close to being such a center of excellence, something often overlooked by those looking for answers to global problems.

Untapped Potential

For the UN staff and its ideas to be taken more seriously, the secretary-general should put a greater focus on steps to improve research, analysis and policy work. He should facilitate staff exchanges with universities and think tanks for original and synthetic research, create space within the UN system for truly independent research and analysis, and increase collaboration between the UN economic and social entities and the analytical staff of the Bretton Woods institutions—the World Bank and International Monetary Fund.

He should do more to promote UN economic and social research to reach larger audiences and have more impact on decisions of economic and finance ministers around the world. He should transform the UN human resources strategy to exert intellectual leadership.

Despite a rich tradition of contributions from UN agencies and organizations, the system's full potential for policy research and analysis has scarcely been tapped. Cross-agency collaboration is too rare; researchers in different parts of the system seldom venture beyond their silos. Regular mandatory gatherings for sharing research and ideas could reduce parochialism. A new research council could expand collaboration, and reduce functional overlap.

The UN should seek as many alliances as possible with centers of expertise and excellence around the world—in academia, think tanks, government policy units and corporate research centers. Human resources practices should do more to foster creative thinking, penetrating analysis and policy-focused research of a top caliber.

The model of the Intergovernmental Panel on Climate Change could be replicated for other pressing issues. Intellectual firepower is essential but will depend on better staff recruitment, appointment and promotion. These nuts-and-bolts issues affect directly the quality of the work done across the UN system.

By definition, to pursue bold and forward-looking ideas, the UN cannot possibly please all UN members all of the time. Challenging conventional or "politically correct" wisdom requires longer-term financing because the exploration of ideas, while vital, is not cheap and must be shielded from outside interference.

Ideally donors should provide multi-year financing for research and analysis, with no strings attached, through assessed contributions. But voluntary financing is more likely, so conversations should begin about the systemwide need for such policy autonomy.

Without first-rate people and adequate money, messages are typically watered down to satisfy the lowest common intergovernmental denominator. Yet we have learned since 1990 from the predictable howls greeting the annual Human Development Reports that intellectual independence can not only be tolerated but also be healthy.

This experience suggests that researchers should be freed from a need to check analyses with boards or donors before publication. We need islands or safety zones within which serious and independent analysis can take place, protected from government threats to block publication or cut off funds. The tolerance for controversy should be far higher; academic freedom should not be an alien concept for UN researchers working on 21st-century intellectual and policy challenges.

We can legitimately debate a broad range of desirable qualifications for a secretary-general, but two are fundamental: tolerance for differences in views and a willingness to withstand predictable flak from UN members. ■

UN Photo/Mark Garten

Secretary-General Ban Ki-moon engages in some telephone diplomacy.

Picking the UN Leader Should Be More of a Contest
Simon Minching

Ban Ki-moon, a South Korean, nailed down a second five-year term as secretary-general of the United Nations before the end of the first half of 2011; his new term starts in January. That gives the UN membership another five years to make the selection process more transparent and deliberative, so as to maximize the odds that it can identify and install the most qualified leader.

Sensible methods for achieving these goals have been put forward from time to time, but to date, the suggestions have been politically difficult. Maybe 2016 will be different.

An Opaque and Exclusive Process

At its very first session in 1946, the General Assembly—where every UN member has a vote and no one has veto power—quickly set out the method for selecting the secretary-general. Most significantly, it explicitly delegated the lead role in this process to the Security Council. A General Assembly resolution instructed the council to present it with a single name, provided that person was supported by at least 9 of the council's 15 members, including its five permanent members—Britain, China, France, Russia and the United States.

The 1946 resolution required only a majority vote of the assembly to confirm the council's choice, "unless the General Assembly itself decides that a two-thirds majority is called for." It also delineated a five-year term of office with the possibility for a second appointment, and put a confidentiality requirement on the discussion and decision-making in both the Security Council and the assembly.

While these ground rules might have seemed agreeable enough at first blush, they have led over time to a process that is opaque and insider-driven.

For example, the requirement that any candidate presented to the assembly must have the support of at least nine council members, including every permanent member, might seem aimed at ensuring candidates with broad support. But this also hands to each permanent member the power to block what might otherwise be a legitimate candidate.

Straw Poll Move Proves an Impediment

Then, in 1981, the council shifted from official meetings to informal straw polls to gauge members' leanings on particular candidates. Ten years later, color-coded secret ballots came into use, differentiating between straw votes from permanent and nonpermanent members.

These moves—reminiscent of the colored smoke signals displayed during the selection of a new pope—had the practical effect of significantly decreasing transparency.

By switching to straw polls, UN members were now able to flout information standards required by the Provisional Rules of Procedure for all official meetings.

Colored ballots made it easier for permanent members to cover indications of "discouragement" of a contender they disliked. Casting an anonymous red ballot meant the permanent member could informally impede or derail a candidature without showing its hand, rather than cast a veto in a formal council meeting.

After the council forwards its candidate of choice to the assembly for consideration, the appointment has typically been confirmed by consensus, although it is within the assembly's right to hold an up-or-down vote. Only once, in 1950, has the latter ever occurred, when the assembly voted 46 to 5 to extend the Norwegian Trygve Lie's term of office.

Such passivity by the General Assembly in the process has been institutionally promoted from the beginning. The 1946 resolution setting out the selection framework states, "it would be desirable for the Security Council to proffer one candidate only for consideration ... and for debate on the nomination in the General Assembly to be avoided." Such rubber-stamping would be undeniably more acceptable if a candidate for secretary-general had first undergone an open, inclusive and vigorous vetting.

Instead the process has become an exercise in fulfilling the bidding of the elite club of Security Council permanent members, to the overall detriment of the organization.

Obstacles and Prospects for Reform

The shortcomings of the selection process are only partly a result of these structural impediments. There are also the UN's immutable traditions, including the

UN Photo/Evan Schneider

Over the years, a secretary-general has never been elected from Eastern Europe. Africa has successfully put forward Kofi Annan of Ghana, shown here, and Boutros Boutros-Ghali of Egypt.

uncodified, yet widely accepted principle of regional rotation, and the institution's deeply embedded preference for the tidiness of consensus.

Under the regional rotation tradition, each successive secretary-general must come from a different part of the world according to an informally agreed-upon ordering.

But over the years, a secretary-general has been elected from only four of the five major regional groupings, leaving Eastern Europe to the side of the road. The four successful regional blocs have been Africa (Kofi Annan of Ghana and Boutros Boutros-Ghali of Egypt), Asia (U Thant of Myanmar and Ban Ki-moon of South Korea), Latin America and the Caribbean (Javier Perez de Cuellar of Peru), and the "Western European and others" grouping (Trygve Lie of Norway, Dag Hammarskjöld of Sweden and Kurt Waldheim of Austria).

Due to regional politicking and neighborhood rivalries, strong candidates who cause even minimal controversy never seem to get their foot in the door, because consensus reigns supreme. Such is the reason for the UN never having an Eastern European candidate thus far—Russian intransigence has not allowed for it.

Some Feasible Proposals

The UN is certainly not alone in shunning change. Resistance to significant reform is common in large institutions and can take a variety of forms. Disparate or conflicting interests, coordination problems and the appeal of holding out for improvements at a later date—when the cast of characters might be different—all contribute to brutally slow rates of transformation.

Many reasonable reforms have nonetheless been put forward, including a 2006 call by the United Nations Association-USA for at least two candidates to be submitted to the assembly. UNA-USA also recommended a reassessment of the regional rotation principle and greater transparency through extensive consultations between prospective candidates, top UN officials and the UN membership.

The common denominator in these reform proposals is that they target a narrow set of key issues, avoid linkage to parallel Security Council reform efforts (which would make for needless complexity), and resist the appeal to propose such transformative change that would require an amendment of the UN Charter. The bar has been correctly set quite high for such amendments. They come into force only after approval by a two-thirds vote of the General Assembly and ratification by two-thirds of all UN members, including all five permanent members of the Security Council.

This helps account for the vague and piecemeal attempts taken to date to improve the flawed secretary-general selection process. Overly ambitious reforms stand little to no chance of adoption.

Nevertheless, reforms that lie within achievable bounds must be undertaken. Otherwise, the secretary-general selection process will continue to be opaque, needlessly restrictive in its candidate pool, and driven by the interests of a select few.

That is a recipe for lackluster nominations at a time when the UN's success inexorably depends on an articulate, inspiring and dexterous leader capable of navigating the challenges of a loosely defined office in an increasingly complex world. ■

Touching the Lives of Half the World
Barbara Crossette

UN Women, the United Nations' newest agency, will bring to the 66th General Assembly in 2011-12 a strategic plan for action that is strong on women's political participation, economic opportunity and access to law and justice. It is a bold agenda for an agency whose creation was the subject of long and intense negotiations among UN members, a number of whom did not favor a more powerful voice for women in the organization and its work.

UN Women, led by Michelle Bachelet as executive director, a former president of Chile, is still struggling to meet a goal of $500 million in voluntary donations to begin and sustain field work over the next two years.

UN Women is officially titled the Entity for Gender Equality and the Empowerment of Women. "Entity" was chosen as a vague designation when there was no agreement to construct it formally as either a full-fledged independent agency or a department of the UN Secretariat, as many women's organizations had hoped. The organization, however, has its own executive board, and Bachelet holds the rank of UN under secretary-general with cabinet rank.

Michelle Bachelet, the executive director of UN Women, at a panel discussion at UN headquarters in New York.

UN Photo/Paulo Filgueiras

If UN Women is to succeed in making its presence felt globally, it will need significant funds to support activities in the field and not be seen as just another office in New York. From its creation, UN Women was expected to operate on a biennial budget of about $1 billion. (The agency's strategic plan for 2011-13 published in late June calls for $1.2 billion.) About half of the agency's expenses—for such things as office space and salaries—will come from regular UN assessed funds. The rest is expected to be raised from voluntary country donations.

Pledges Are Coming Slowly

Yet almost a year after its founding by the General Assembly in July 2010, UN Women had received only $104.5 million in pledges, of which $38.5 million had actually been paid by July 1. The largest potential donor was Spain, with a $25.4 million pledge. Canada has pledged and paid more than $10 million. Other contributors pledging and/or paying $4 million or more are Norway, Australia, the Netherlands, Sweden, the United States and Finland.

Britain had not yet pledged or contributed funds by mid-2011. The U.S. announced in late June that it would commit $6 million in 2011, with perhaps more to come in 2012. UN Women's performance over the coming year is likely to be watched closely by member nations who have not yet stepped up to help financially, as well as by those who have been first to pay and will be asked to continue their support.

The new agency will also have on show in the coming year its first major report: Progress of the World's Women: In Pursuit of Justice, published in July. The report provides a comprehensive survey of the legal status of the world's women, and the distance still to go before laws mean anything to many if not most of half the global population.

"Although equality between women and men is guaranteed in the constitutions of 139 countries and territories," the report says, "inadequate laws and implementation gaps make these guarantees hollow promises, having little impact on the day-to-day lives of women." As an example, the report shows domestic violence persists virtually everywhere despite its being outlawed in 125 countries. Indeed, 127 countries do not criminalize rape within marriage.

Level Playing Field

The report advocates putting more women into law enforcement, training judges to overcome biases and giving women more access to courts and truth commissions during and after conflict. It argues for quotas for women in national legislatures, a controversial subject even among advocates for women's rights, many of whom would prefer to expand opportunities for women to enter politics on their own. In some countries it has become evident that quota systems are too easily manipulated by powerful politicians and parties to insure that known loyalists and not independent women get seats.

Bachelet, aware of this, said at a Women's Foreign Policy Group event in New York in April that "increasing the numbers of women in leadership positions is a sign of their empowerment, not a substitute for it." She called on governments to provide a level playing field for women to compete politically. She listed as goals "the elimination of discriminatory legal provisions . . . in family codes, electoral codes, penal codes, and the provision of a basic level of physical and social security."

To underline the report's findings—and the amount of work to be done around the world—a survey at about the same time by the Thomson Reuters Foundation, through its TrustLaw global center for news, information and free legal assistance, identified the five most dangerous countries in the world to be a woman. Not all of them were predictable.

Using a basket of indicators from health care and economic status to human rights, trafficking of women and girls, feticide and infanticide, the survey listed the five worst countries (in descending order) as Afghanistan, the Democratic Republic of Congo, Pakistan, India and Somalia. Numerically, this makes South Asia, not Africa, the least safe place to be born female—if born at all because of sex-selective abortions, a growing (and illegal) practice that helped pull down India's reputation in the survey.

A Vast Task Before a New Agency

The scope of the job ahead of UN Women is obviously large, and Bachelet is hoping to have a visible presence for the agency in the field as soon as possible. But the agency's mandate, the product of a divided General Assembly, limits the deployment of specialists and support programs to countries requesting them. That makes persuasion a priority not far behind fundraising. She has said that she plans to raise both issues in talks with governments.

The agency's strategic plan for 2011-13 takes as its starting point the mounting evidence that gender equality is good not only for women and the societies in which they live but also for a nation's economic growth. "Against this backdrop, governments are increasingly recognizing that they cannot develop and prosper without engaging one-half of their population," the plan says. Until now UN offices dealing with the advancement of women have had "insufficient authority and resources for the organizations and programs intended to lead the way to gender equality," it continues.

Most immediately ambitious in the plan may be the aim of building a more coordinated, effective and efficient approach to gender equality throughout the UN system and its agencies in the field. When UN Women was formed, four existing bodies dealing with issues of importance to women were scrapped. These four—underfinanced, sometimes competitive and often having little impact globally—were the Office of the Special Adviser on Gender Issues and Advancement of Women, the Division for the Advancement of Women, the UN Development Fund for Women and the UN International Research and Training Institute for the Advancement of Women.

An Education in Repression

In Bachelet, Secretary-General Ban Ki-moon found a uniquely qualified candidate to organize and administer a new agency to replace the chaos and jealousies of a fragmented system, if it was a system at all. Advisers to Ban say that he persisted over weeks and in repeated meetings to persuade Bachelet, still a political player in Chile, to move to New York and take on the job of executive director.

Bachelet, a Socialist, was imprisoned and tortured under the Chilean military dictator Augusto Pinochet; her father, an air force general, died in the regime's custody. She and her mother were forced into exile. All of these tragedies experienced as a young woman became part of an early education in political repression and personal dislocation, which describes the plight of untold numbers of women in the world today.

She returned to Chile in 1979 and after the fall of Pinochet became a rising political star. By then she had been trained as a physician and surgeon, and was turning to an interest in military affairs, studying at the Inter-American Defense College in Washington in the mid-1990s. She later served Chile as health minister and defense minister before being elected president in 2006. Her four-year term ended in March 2010; Chile's constitution limits a president to only one term, but does not bar another term after a break from office. Bachelet became available for a UN assignment at a propitious moment.

Advocates and organizations for women were relieved and delighted when she agreed to head UN Women. There was, however, some grumbling in developing nations where hopes were high that the position would go to someone from the developing world. Chile is now a member of the Organization for Economic Cooperation and Development and more a developed than developing country. In an interview at the time, Bachelet said this was not a problem for her. The problems women face, and the hopes they have, are universal, she said. They want security, equality and dignity, and protection against persistent vulnerabilities.

Traveling to Build Bridges

In June, to emphasize the agency's global nature, Bachelet announced a team of senior appointees from Norway, Spain, Egypt, India, Turkey and Burundi. While seeking to establish an international presence for the new agency, she also traveled widely in her first six months in office, to Africa, Latin America, Europe and Asia.

Everywhere she goes, she emphasizes to varied audiences inside the UN and among the general public that she is counting on working closely with many partners apart from governments. She includes in the strategic plan the media, private sector, foundations, academic institutions, religious and traditional leaders as well as "men and boys whose attitudes and behaviors are an essential determinant of the lives women and girls lead."

Bachelet's greatest challenge may prove to be the passive resistance in the UN Secretariat and in key ministries of member countries that sign all the appropriate international conventions and action plans for women but then do little to carry out pledges or set aside enough money for the job. A small army of special representatives past and present working on human rights and violence against women, including ending rape as a weapon of war or a means of intimidation and suppression in civilian life, have discovered that changing behavior is not easy.

The Gender Equality Architecture Reform campaign, the most influential of nongovernmental coalitions that lobbied for the creation of UN Women, has urged the agency to remain strong on two important points. The campaign groups more than 300 human rights, justice and women's organizations around the world and reflects a wide range of women's voices in many cultures.

The campaign urged her to keep human rights at the forefront of the agency's work, and to listen to the voices of women at the grassroots level—something that is not often done in the UN, where officials work mostly with governments. "Ensure that women, who are often marginalized, whether on the basis of race, class, ethnicity, culture, sexuality, age or other factors, are incorporated into the design, programming and development of UN Women's plans and operations at all levels," the coalition said.

To bolster the new agency's work, the coalition recommends establishing formal nongovernmental structures such as advisory councils and utilizing the knowledge, experience and political savvy of local organizations in planning programs and setting priorities. When it comes to dealing with lax or recalcitrant governments, the campaign is effectively saying: "Take us with you. We can help." ■

UN Photo/Staton Winter

Young Liberians peer into a room where Michelle Bachelet, the executive director of UN Women, confers with a group of women in the central Liberian town of Totota.

Help Wanted for Work That Makes a Difference
Gus Feissel

Wanted: men and women of integrity who are impartial, independent, dedicated to the global goals and principles of the United Nations, who are above being influenced by national (and personal) interests and who seek nothing less than the betterment of the world and all its inhabitants.

This might well be the philosophical bent of a job description for a UN civil servant and certainly for the secretary-general as the guiding figure of the Secretariat.

The mandate for the UN civil service is set out in Article 97 of the UN Charter, which says that the "Secretariat shall comprise a Secretary-General and such staff that the Organization shall require." The international civil service is the main vehicle through which the secretary-general carries out the range of political, economic, human rights, social, legal and administrative policies and programs entrusted to him by the Charter and the various principal organs. The Charter does not give a job description either for the secretary-general or his supporting civil servants. Article 101 simply says the "paramount consideration in the employment of the staff is the necessity of securing the highest standards of efficiency, competence and integrity."

Article 100 emphasizes the independent and impartial character of the civil service, saying that "in the performance of their duties, the secretary-general and the staff shall not seek or receive instructions from any government or from any other authority external to the organization." Through decisions made by the General Assembly and other UN organs, member countries act as a whole, not as individual nations. Decisions by those bodies provide direction for the Secretariat and define its duties. Article 100 calls on member countries to respect the exclusive international character of the civil service and to refrain from trying to influence that service in its work.

Defining Roles as the System Developed

The role of the civil service, as of the UN itself, had to be defined on the job. The process of establishing an independent and impartial civil service was not easy. Serious differences emerged from the outset about the role of the secretary-general and the civil service. A major point of disagreement was whether the secretary-general and the Secretariat should be limited to administrative functions or whether their mandate included political functions as well.

Dag Hammarskjöld, the secretary-general from April 1953 until his death in September 1961, believed that the charter entrusted the secretary-general and the staff with responsibilities in both political and administrative areas. He was also adamant that, as the charter laid out, the secretary-general and the civil service must be independent and impartial. He warned of serious consequences for the future of the organization should this concept be undermined.

UN Photo

Dag Hammarskjöld, the UN secretary-general from 1953 until his death in a plane crash in 1961, delivered a speech at Oxford University in May 1961 that remains today the definition of a UN civil servant.

Hammarskjöld's speech, "The International Civil Servant in Law and in Fact," delivered at Oxford University on May 30, 1961, remains the definition of a UN civil servant. His perseverance, integrity and philosophical guidance in those formative years built the basis for the stature and respect the UN enjoys today. Kofi Annan, the seventh secretary-general, said in a speech marking the 40th anniversary of Hammarskjöld's death: "His words and his actions have done more to shape public expectations of the office and indeed of the organization than those of any other man or woman in its history."

Over the years, the secretary-general and the civil service have become more involved in political issues brought before the UN. Ralph Bunche, who performed a crucial role at the world body in its first 25 years, moved the Hammarskjöld philosophy forward, playing a major part in the UN's emerging role in conflict resolution. He won the Nobel Peace Prize for his role as mediator of the Arab-Israeli conflict of 1948-49 and was a highly effective negotiator in the Suez and Congo crises. The former UN Under Secretary-General Sir Brian Urquhart, in his book "Ralph Bunche: An American Life," describes him as the central figure in the first generation of UN staff members, setting the benchmarks for later generations. Secretary-General U Thant, in his memoirs, described Bunche as an international civil servant in the truest sense of the term.

Enhancing Civil Servants' Roles

In my 35-year career at the UN, I was fortunate to work for two iconic civil servants: Sir Brian and Philippe de Seynes. Their presence left an indelible mark on the organization and had a major influence in ensuring the continuation and development of the principles guiding civil servants.

Sir Brian's career at the UN spanned 40 years. He worked closely with the first five secretaries-general. He was heavily influenced by Hammarskjöld and worked closely with Bunche, succeeding him as under secretary-general for special political affairs, a position he held for 14 years until his retirement in 1986. Sir Brian was a key architect of UN peacekeeping, being intimately involved in shaping and carrying out the 13 UN peacekeeping operations during the organization's first 40 years and establishing the basis for the many that followed. Having served as a director in his office for the two years before his retirement, I witnessed that Sir Brian personified the high ideals and philosophical grounding of the best of the UN's dedicated international civil servants.

De Seynes, who was the under secretary-general for Economic and Social Affairs from 1955 to 1975, has been described as an intellectual giant and a true prototype of the international civil servant. He expanded the role of the UN into several major economic areas, notably the establishment of the UN Conference on Trade and Development, the UN Industrial Development Organization, the UN Environment Program and the UN Population Fund.

As I saw firsthand as his special assistant for the five years before his retirement, his independent attributes and grasp of a wide range of international economic and social issues were widely recognized and respected. Written by de Seynes himself, his annual speeches to the Second Committee of the General Assembly guaranteed a full house. As a tribute upon his retirement, his close associates gave him a four-inch-thick, two-volume collection of his speeches and notes spanning his 20 years at the UN.

Where Ideas Are Valued

These extraordinary people helped the UN grow and mature into a forum for discourse and concerted action in all fields of international endeavor. Most of us do not cast such long shadows as de Seynes, Sir Brian, Hammarskjöld and Bunche.

Not all ideas change the role of the UN itself. Yet ideas at every level are a valued commodity. Thus people of vision, practical suggestions and expertise in a variety of fields are in demand. Given the breadth of activities covered by the organization, the UN offers both a stimulating and varied career as well as the chance to contribute tangibly to a better world.

For junior positions competition is keen. Advanced degrees are normally required, willingness to serve in distant places may be necessary and some opportunities may at times be restricted because of the need to allot positions among member countries, given that the international civil servants are drawn from a broad array of countries.

Opportunities extend to the numerous organizations of the UN family as well. The Web site http://careers.un.org provides comprehensive information about working at the UN as well as job openings.

Recruitment Is Different Now

The recruitment procedure has totally changed from when I was hired. There were no exams, and I was hired through a series of interviews. Moving from one position to another was initiated primarily by the head of the office seeking to fill the position; this process is more formal today.

Being an international civil servant is a special experience: it means working with a chosen few who have an unusual outlook on life—that of a citizen of the world. It often means working in one's own niche with specific goals, or possibly in some challenging circumstance of disaster or conflict, or in a post where one encounters health issues, poverty and great need on a daily basis.

Whatever that niche is, the UN staffers spend their working years not pursuing any national interest or agenda, no personal gain or fame, but seeking, as our fanciful opening job description suggested, nothing less than the betterment of the world. It is a career of honor, and when the working years end, each of the men and women can look back and know that theirs was a different path, one that gave significant meaning to their lives.

My 35 years at the UN offer a good example of the stimulating milieu, of the interesting people and the variety of worthy causes one serves. My career took me from entry-level professional to being in charge of the UN operation in Cyprus as assistant secretary-general, with responsibilities spanning a spectrum, from administering technical assistance projects; being the assistant to the person in charge of all economic and social activities; serving as secretary of the committee that established a major intergovernmental commission and a department in the Secretariat (UN Center on Transnational Corporations); developing and directing a program to assist developing countries in their dealings with multinational corporations; directing the monitoring and analysis of geographic areas of concern to the secretary-general; and finally, being intimately involved in peacekeeping activities and conflict resolution negotiations. I can't imagine having spent my life so satisfactorily in any other career. ▪

Why UN Reform Remains an Elusive Goal
Minh-Thu Pham

Calls to reform the vast United Nations bureaucracy to make it more efficient and effective are constantly heard among those who follow the UN and from its critics. Attempts to strengthen it date nearly from the UN's beginnings. In 1954, less than 10 years after the UN's founding, Secretary-General Dag Hammarskjöld sought to review the UN's workload and reform the role of the secretary-general.

With agreement on the need for fundamental reform and so many attempts, why has change been so difficult to achieve?

Reform at any large bureaucratic institution must be a process and not an event. The adoption of a resolution is not reform, though it may be a start. At the UN, changes involve many parties: the secretary-general, to propose needed changes; the member nations, to debate proposals and pay for them when adopted; and the secretary-general and his staff, to carry them forward. It is a repetitive process that can take years, and as a result, it is often seen as tinkering rather than fundamental overhaul.

Policymakers need to understand what reform actually means. To U.S. legislators, such reform often means forcing the UN to do what they want. Some of the measures they advocate would weaken the institution, for example, confining it to being financed by voluntary contributions only rather than through the existing system of assessed national dues. For others reform is improving the UN's basic operations and accountability, while still others see it as slashing the budget, or increasing it substantially so that the UN can do all that is demanded of it.

U.S. Ideas May Arouse Suspicions

Some past U.S. efforts have backfired. Many countries routinely oppose U.S. proposals because they suspect that in the long run, the measures will weaken the UN and enhance U.S. influence over it, to their own detriment.

Some U.S. reform drives have accompanied threats from Congress to withhold financing, as well as criticism that is often unfair and untrue. These send a message that Washington is more interested in tearing down the UN than making it stronger.

John Bolton, the U.S. ambassador to the UN in 2005-06, famously said that if the UN lost 10 of its floors, "it wouldn't make a bit of difference," and this played directly into the suspicions of countries cynical about U.S. objectives. Many have argued that his approach doomed bold changes at the 2005 UN Summit, despite considerable pressure for reform generated by mismanagement in the oil-for-food program in Iraq. While the summit made some important changes, diplomats widely charged that ham-handed U.S. tactics doomed other key proposals.

The UN's internal structures have also distorted motivations for achieving reform. The Security Council's five veto-wielding permanent members—Britain, China, France, Russia and the U.S.—enjoy outsized influence at the UN with their considerable power in matters ranging from creating peacekeeping missions to imposing sanctions.

As a result, countries that feel they lack sufficient sway over Security Council matters find ways to leverage what authority they do have. For example, the General Assembly's management and budget committee, formally known as the Fifth Committee, gives an equal vote to all 193 UN members and enjoys great influence over the budget, UN staffing and administrative matters. This enables the Group of 77, a voting bloc of 131 developing countries, to leverage its influence over UN spending, programs, staffing and even the secretary-general.

It's no wonder then that efforts to reform the budget, the dues structure, UN management and other basic operations are so challenging. Expanding the Security Council, or at least serious reform of its working methods to include

UN Photo/Paulo Filgueiras

Secretary-General Ban Ki-moon addresses a General Assembly debate on UN management reform in April 2008.

the views of other countries, would go a long way toward alleviating this. But it's well known that governments that already have a coveted seat and a veto carefully guard what they have.

No Public Outcry

Another obstacle to reform is the lack of public fervor around the world for management matters. National delegations are unlikely to be called to account for their votes. Spending and administrative questions are often so technical that even the delegates have trouble keeping up.

But the UN operates primarily in countries heavily dependent on outside help, so they stand to benefit the most from a reformed UN. Yet it's often those same countries that erect barriers to reform, whether out of mistrust of the big powers or because they seek to preserve jobs for their nationals or to be a good sport in the Group of 77.

The world is more integrated now than ever, with global threats posing far greater challenges than any one country could tackle alone. Yet while we should be embracing greater multilateral cooperation and stronger international institutions, narrow political concerns bar the way. In most countries, it is simply unpopular to support a stronger UN.

In the U.S., support for international institutions like the UN is often seen as weak, anti-American and a threat to national sovereignty. Elsewhere in the world, the UN is seen as too easily influenced by the Western powers.

Constructive U.S. leadership is essential to genuine reform. While there was a marked shift at the start of the Obama administration on top-level issues, changes were slow to filter down, and it took nearly two years to put in place an ambassador for management and reform. Even so, the Obama administration has pursued reform, mostly behind the scenes, and rebuilt critical relationships with countries whose support it needs.

The goodwill generated thus far has yielded some positive results, notably in the Human Rights Council and in the efficiency of peacekeeping operations. Secretary-General Ban Ki-moon's second term, which many hope will free him to make bolder moves, and a renewed high-level U.S. focus on management, could help achieve more significant change.

However, the world's crises won't wait. Every day, the demands placed on the UN are greater. Until Washington is able to persuade the American people that an effective UN serves U.S. interests and until leaders around the world can make the case to their people, the dynamics at the UN will be hard to change.

But they must change. The UN can seem at times like the dumping ground for the world's most difficult problems, asked to step in only when no one else can resolve them. But when the UN fails, where do we turn? Will we have to wait for another world war or other cataclysmic crisis to persuade governments to make our international institutions more effective? By then it may be too late. ■

What the United Nations Loses To Academic Indifference

Helmut Volger

The United Nations is trying to cope with such major problems as civil wars, suppression of human rights and a strained environment. And to a significant extent academia is working on helping the UN understand and manage these issues.

But the academic world also passes up many opportunities to help develop legal and political tools and institutional structures to do this work and evaluate the results. Using my experience as a UN researcher since the mid-1980s, plus an e-mail survey I recently conducted among UN researchers in Europe and the United States, I've found strong and weak points in UN-related studies.

This research is carried out in most of the member countries by only a handful of people: scholars of international law, political science and economics, mostly as a hobby and occasionally with the help of grants. The documents flowing out of this work convey often interesting information, but their usual audience is other UN experts, not academics in general, and by no means the public.

The e-mail survey asked six questions about the structure and goals of the scholars' work. The responses described their work as generally not coordinated, neither within a single academic discipline nor among disciplines or departments. This makes the scholars of the UN small islands in a large sea of indifference, with little way to build bridges to the outside world. Given the excellent quality of most studies of the UN, it is a loss that its strengths and weaknesses are not discussed on a wider level.

Regionally, the differences are worth noting. In the U.S., Canada and Scandinavia, private foundations and nongovernmental organizations since the mid-1980s have developed institutions that fuel nongovernmental political initiatives —such as disarmament and environmental protection—with empirical findings. In Germany, however, the task of examining the UN still falls predominantly on academic institutions.

In this difficult environment, a small number of committed UN associations and international academic research networks, such as the Academic Council on the UN System, seek to foster coordination and public awareness through conferences and books.

UN Research Units

In their work, UN scholars are supported by the research branches established by the UN since the mid-60s. Above all, the UN University, founded in 1973, supervises the study of 12 thematic institutes that work with academic institutions in 10 member countries.

The UN University is complemented by other institutes that explore the efficiency of the organization's operations and train its officials (the Institute for

Training and Research); social development (the Research Institute for Social Development); disarmament (the Institute for Disarmament Research) and the advancement of women (the International Research and Training Institute for the Advancement of Women). This latter organization has now been integrated into the newly established UN Women.

All these publish papers and books in their field, dealing with topics such as gender and development and democracy or governance and human rights; international nonproliferation movements; and overarching themes like the future of international environmental law or climate change and sustainability. Yet they all suffer from understaffing and scarce resources. Their findings are not promoted enough nor noted widely.

Academic indifference toward the UN has two main causes. First, there is a lack of pressure from students. For most students of international law, economics, international relations and political science, the UN does not offer enough attractive career prospects, so there is little cry for area focuses or classes on UN issues; universities see no reason to expand their small UN curriculums. Second, government bodies seldom seek academic advice in formulating their UN policies and—even more important—rarely commission studies on UN matters, thus damping the market for services of universities and research institutions.

Linking Academics to Action

As one UN expert described in his reply to the survey, academia and foreign policy officials rarely interact, and even when they do, it's on a small scale. These contacts come either in routine meetings of scientific advisory boards to ministries, providing hardly any concrete policy recommendations, or on an ad hoc basis at the request of individual UN scholars who are trying to persuade government officials of the value of continuous substantial advice.

Some noteworthy exceptions prove what research on the UN can achieve. For instance, broad-based studies on climate problems in many countries came under serious discussion after the 1992 Rio de Janeiro conference on environment and development. UN-related research provided grist for later negotiations.

Switzerland, which joined the UN only in 2002, has grasped the usefulness of coordinated UN research. In 2007 its Federal Department of Foreign Affairs created with Swiss universities a nationwide academic network called UNO Academia, now known as the Academic Platform Switzerland UN. Other UN members could follow this model by starting similar networks or specialized institutes.

What Are the Implications?

Why is it important to assess the state of research on the UN?

Without institutional memory of the UN's achievements recorded by historians and social scientists, member countries cannot evaluate its ups and downs. Such knowledge would demonstrate the success rate of the UN in many areas and provide illustrative material for young UN officials.

Without a systematic scholarly analysis of UN structures, debates over reform lack consistency and benchmarks needed for political and economic efficiency.

UN Photo/Eskinder Debebe

Students in Hiroshima, Japan, listen as UN Secretary-General Ban Ki-moon speaks at their high school in August 2010. Few schools around the world teach their students about the UN.

The debate on reform of the Security Council at the time of the 2005 World Summit offered ample proof: as long as the country groups lack sufficient reliable research data on the council's functioning, informal working methods, communication and decision-making structures, the debate remains chaotic and futile.

Concerning global problems—where the UN pays the most attention—organized research would give politicians well-defined alternatives to present instead of off-the-cuff instant agreements in times of difficulty, like the current talks over what to do after expiration of the Kyoto Protocol on UN climate protection.

Thorough studies of the UN would also help to dispel the myths of simple causes and simple remedies and could help politicians grasp that world problems are difficult and need a lot of time and money. Research would show the UN's political benefit, underlining that it cannot be replaced and showing how its extensive development work and continuing debates on financial regulation complement other bodies like the Group of 20.

The lackluster attention academics and politicians give to researching the UN has another consequence—a dearth of UN teaching. Fortunately, the Model United Nations programs, which are simulations carried out by students taking over the roles of national delegations, are a strongly motivating experience, arousing a lasting interest in the UN and political affairs among the young people and inspiring them to strive for jobs as UN officials. The United Nations Association-USA's Global Classrooms is one such program.

Without knowing more about the UN, political decision-makers in member countries are hardly able to grasp what the UN needs to do, what it can do and what it needs to carry forward. Equally important, as long as the media and the public do not share in this knowledge, governments will not get the consent of their people to support the UN more consistently. ■

[A version of this article appeared in The InterDependent, a UNA-USA publication (www.theinterdependent.com), on March 16, 2011]

Talking Points

1. Improving the UN workforce is a reform that all member countries agree on, but how to do so is often a point of contention. Is it more important to strengthen the national quota framework, so that the Secretariat can look at problems from a broad international perspective? Or should UN hiring be based on merit alone, improving overall quality but risking offending some nations or excluding their point of view?

2. The character of the U.S.-UN relationship is defined by a range of considerations, including what Washington thinks it can achieve unilaterally or through other arrangements, the UN secretary-general's own priorities, and diplomats' tolerance for America's foreign policy agenda. Considering the current relationship, how would you rate the Obama administration's policy of UN "re-engagement"?

3. The General Assembly's sole formal criterion for picking a new secretary-general is "possessing and displaying, inter alia, commitment to the purposes and principles of the Charter of the United Nations, extensive leadership, and administrative and diplomatic experience." Should the UN membership write a more explicit set of qualifications for its top position? If so, what should such a list entail?

4. UN Women, the newest UN agency, is dedicated to gender equality and empowering women. Since many other UN agencies pursue these same goals, among their other responsibilities, should they quickly transfer these activities—and the resources needed to carry them out—to UN Women, to maximize its effectiveness? Or should UN Women have to prove itself before becoming the de facto umbrella agency for all UN gender-related endeavors?

UN Photo/Evan Schneider

Secretary-General Ban Ki-moon helps test a communal water pump at the Mwandama Millennium Village in Malawi in 2010. National seed and fertilizer subsidies have enabled Malawi to donate crops to the World Food Program and sell surplus corn to other countries.

Global Aid: Questions of Supply and Demand

124 Planet Earth: Serving Billions Each Day
Abigail Somma

129 Which Path to Food Security?
Nathanial Gronewold

134 After the Millennium Development Goals: What Next?
Hélène Gandois

137 The Changing World of International Aid
Alexander Shakow

141 Talking Points

Planet Earth: Serving Billions Each Day
Abigail Somma

It took countless millennia for the world population to reach a billion, in 1804. About 40 years from now, in 2050, that number is expected to reach 9.3 billion. And it could get significantly higher.

Yet, with the meter nearing seven billion, we are already stretching earth's limits. Climate change provokes environmental havoc while natural resources dwindle. Our increasing consumption eats up fisheries, destroys forests, dries up water tables and taxes the globe in countless other ways.

What's an overburdened planet to do?

In a 2004 interview with the U.S. Public Broadcasting Service, the population expert Lester Brown said rising food prices "may be the first global economic indicator to signal serious trouble in the relationship between us now, 6.3 billion, and the earth's natural system and resources on which we depend."

Brown seems right. In 2008, global food prices shot up dramatically and riots flared around the world, hitting Kenya, Haiti, Bangladesh and Egypt, among others. After a brief dip, food prices are now back up, with the United Nations Food and Agriculture Organization reporting prices soared to records for three months beginning last December before falling back slightly in March.

Unfortunately, riots also came back. In January, Algeria saw four days of violent protests sparked by unemployment and climbing food prices, after the cost of flour and cooking oil doubled in a few months.

An Old Warning 200 Years Later

For a few years, the name Thomas Malthus has been resurfacing in the media and among policy experts. Malthus predicted in 1798 that the world would starve because of too many people and too little food.

Two hundred years ago, he was off the mark: the industrial revolution led the world down a more auspicious path. But his concerns linger. Will population growth outstrip food supply? Can our planet accommodate so many people with growing needs, desires and purchasing power?

The economist and long-time UN adviser Jeffrey Sachs recently invoked Malthus at a University of Toronto conference. "In a way we think we've beaten the Malthusian challenge for the last two centuries, but Malthus still has a specter hanging over us," he said. "What we've not proved is that we can feed the entire planet on a sustainable basis for the long term."

The latest figures from the UN Population Division, released in May, predict the world population will reach 9.3 billion in 2050 and 10.1 billion in 2100. The 2050 figure adds 156 million more people to previous projections from 2008. While the increase in sheer numbers is not enormous, the revision reflects a worrisome trend.

For example, the population of Africa, which surpassed a billion in 2009, is projected to double by 2050. Hania Zlotnik, the division's director, has said that without further decreases in fertility, Africa's population could triple by 2050.

That a significant portion of growth will be in low-income, high-fertility countries creates a major problem for the UN and aid agencies trying to feed the world's hungry and manage its disasters. Organizations squeezed by financial constraints are already expected to do more with less; a growing population will compound the pressure.

Managing Extra People

To understand the challenges of two billion additional people, it is necessary to understand the nature of the growth and its concurrent trends. It's not just that there will be more people. Each demographic trend requires its own consideration.

First, the overwhelming majority of growth is expected in developing countries. According to an article in Foreign Affairs magazine in February 2010, over 70 percent of growth between now and 2050 will come in 24 countries, all classified by the World Bank as low-income or lower-middle-income, with average per capita annual earnings under $3,855 in 2008. These are the same countries most likely to suffer the effects of climate change and confront shortages of water and food. They are also least equipped to manage extra people.

Furthermore, unlike any other time in history, nearly all population growth will take place in urban centers. By 2050, the UN predicts that 70 percent of the world population will be urban, as opposed to about half today. In 1800, a mere 3 percent of the world's population lived in cities.

The number of megacities is also proliferating. In 1900, only 12 cities had one million or more inhabitants. As of 2008, there were more than 400 cities with more than a million. By 2009, there were 21 megacities with more than 10 million inhabitants. In September 2010, Foreign Policy magazine predicted that by 2050, "China alone would have 15 supercities, each with an average population of 25 million (Europe will have none)."

City governments will have to meet demands for housing, energy, water, sanitation and other infrastructure and services, while the population growth is centered in urban poverty.

Young Nations With Special Needs

Another trend requiring special attention is the "youth bulge" in a number of developing countries. This spike in people aged 15 to 29 requires a focus on education and jobs, to drive growth and avoid chaos.

While young populations can be dynamic, they are prone to conflict. Paul Hewett of the Population Council noted in a 2004 interview with the Public Broadcasting Service that 18 of the 25 youngest countries had had conflicts since 1995. "If you want to know where the world's future conflicts will be, look at the youthful countries," he said.

The Washington-based organization Population Action International reports that between 1970 and 1999, 80 percent of civil conflicts occurred in countries where 60 percent or more of the population were under the age of 30. Some media assessments ascribe the 2011 uprisings that brought down a handful of North African and Middle Eastern dictators in large part to the youth bulge. About 60 percent of the region's population is under 30.

Countries Aging Too Fast to Manage

Meanwhile, in the developed world, there is a very different demographic trajectory. If not for migration, the developed world would actually lose population by 2050. Furthermore, with falling birth rates and increasing longevity, most developed countries are aging rapidly, another new trend in history. For example, in Japan, 44 percent of the population will be over 60 in 2050. A number of other countries—South Korea, Italy and Germany— aren't far behind. This population curve will have a major impact on their economies, pension systems, health care and work-force composition.

But it's not just wealthy countries that are aging. Fertility is falling around the globe—from nearly 5 children per woman in the 1960s to 2.6 children per woman today—putting many developing countries into the aging column. The needs of such societies, including workers, may induce increased migration as labor supply follows demand.

Ironically, even at a time when the world is confronting the strain of feeding more people, governments of wealthy countries are promoting childbearing to bring workers into the population. A number of developed countries offer tax benefits and generous leave time to new parents, while some, like Japan and Singapore, sponsor dating services.

Juggling All Those Needs at Once

One thing is certain: keeping up is a constant challenge. And that brings us back to Malthus, and ensuring that he is never vindicated. How can the world of 2050 do this?

In policy circles, this is often phrased as the question, "How do we achieve sustainable development?" This means we must allow for wealth creation, economic growth and evolution without sacrificing the integrity of the earth or the vast number of life forms on it.

More simply: how do we make room for all the people without destroying the planet?

Sustainable development requires changing our way of life on many fronts, from food and water supply to energy and transport. It means reducing greenhouse gas emissions, harnessing renewable energy and putting into place climate-change adaptation measures. It means significantly more investment in agriculture, and advancing technology and innovation, from expanding plant varieties to utilizing no-till soil and no-drip irrigation.

It means creating environmentally intelligent buildings, modes of transport and public spaces. It also means modifying consumption habits, which many argue are just as dangerous to sustainability as a growing population. As we continue to feel the effects of our current ways of life, people all over the world will have to grasp the true cost of a daily hamburger.

Possibly Not a Global Problem

But while all these steps are necessary, will they be sufficient?

To accommodate nine billion people by 2050, the Food and Agriculture Organization predicts a need to increase food production by 70 percent. But not just more food is needed. We have the food right now and we're already missing the mark. Despite a world where plenty of food is produced, 925 million people go to bed hungry because of a lack of earning opportunities and social safety nets.

This raises another disturbing point. Perhaps the main issue isn't that Malthus was ahead of time. Is the real issue that the current Malthusian challenge isn't global, but regional?

While some parts of the world will have a very difficult time feeding their growing populations in 2050, it seems unlikely that the aging populations of wealthy countries are in any real danger. By contrast, in sub-Saharan Africa, which has the world's highest population growth, a third of the people are already malnourished. Take Niger: its population is expected to quadruple from 15 million to 55 million by 2050, yet it already faces increasing loss of land to desert, rapid urbanization and food shortages.

UN Photo/Jean-Marc Ferré

UN members gather in Doha, Qatar, in 2008 to discuss ways to improve development assistance. A similar conference in Monterrey, Mexico, in 2002 was meant to significantly increase aid flows, but wealthy countries have fallen far short of their commitments.

Global Aid: Questions of Supply and Demand **127**

So is the answer another "green revolution" like the one that pulled many Asian and Latin American families out of poverty in the last century? In part, yes. But it also requires a look at the other side of the coin: fewer people. A reduction in human fertility, which is associated with higher income levels and lower maternal and child mortality, would help. In Niger, the average woman bears nearly eight children. And while lower fertility won't happen overnight, it's not impossible.

A number of developing countries have had remarkable success with reducing fertility levels in a relatively short time. Iran brought down its fertility level from 6.6 per woman in 1980 to 1.9 in 2006. Thailand, Bangladesh and a number of other developing countries achieved similar declines, even if not quite so extreme.

Two Big Items for Rio Conference

Reducing fertility requires access to family planning and reproductive health information. However, another effective solution is increasing access to education. According to UN surveys between 1994 and 2008 in 22 sub-Saharan African countries, contraceptive use was four times higher among women with a secondary education than among those with no education. Not surprisingly, a number of studies indicate men's education can also have a significant impact.

Sustainability requires addressing food production and population levels while reducing our environmental footprint. And all sectors have to play a role: governments, business and ordinary people at the national and local levels. Additionally, sound guidance is needed at the international level.

At the moment, the UN is preparing for the Conference on Sustainable Development in Rio de Janeiro next year, which promises to garner significant attention.

What will come out of it is anyone's guess, but the original Earth Summit, in Rio in 1992, established important international agreements, including conventions on climate change, biodiversity and deserts. The parley next year, Rio+20, has two themes: green economy and sustainable development governance.

The problems are evident. But so is the need for direction. It will take leadership, collective will and some sacrifice to make sustainability a reality. It will take all of that and more to put the vision of Thomas Malthus to bed for good. ■

Which Path to Food Security?
Nathanial Gronewold

Picture a field-worker in sub-Saharan Africa researching the deficiencies of agriculture in the poorest countries in the world for a large international organization. Her mission is to interview small-holder farmers to determine their needs, and then report what they tell her to headquarters.

Of course, anyone with a fleeting knowledge of the way food is grown in the developing world can imagine what those farmers will most likely say. Their plots are rain-fed, and no rain means no food, so they'll explain that they need irrigation (only 4 percent of farmland is irrigated in sub-Saharan Africa). Help purchasing fertilizers will also be necessary. They'll mention that a third of their produce rots before it reaches the market, thus dry, off-the-ground storage would help a lot, along with better rural roads and perhaps money for fuel so they can get crops to market quickly, earning more cash and investing in better production the next year.

The bosses read this, and later tell the aid worker to pass on this piece of advice from the top: "Try to buy rain index futures."

It's perplexing, but that is exactly the advice that the World Bank's president, Robert Zoellick, offers farmers in a sleek new video designed to highlight the bank's actions in response to the latest global food price spike.

In the clip the World Bank chief is asked by an unidentified man from India why the rich world has yet to keep promises made in 2007 and 2008 to help poor nations become self-sufficient in food. The question encompassed irrigation, fertilizers and drought-resistant genetically modified crops. In response, Zoellick prescribes weather derivative contracts.

"What that means is the so-called derivatives will say 'if rain doesn't reach a certain level, which would likely mean a poor crop year, then they'll get a payment that will go to the government,'" Zoellick explains in the public relations video. "It's a form of insurance policy."

World Bank representatives declined an opportunity to explain why derivatives may be useful to farmers who lack basic farm implements. Nevertheless, Zoellick's answer, "buy rain index futures," is strong evidence that experts there and elsewhere don't truly intend to make greater food production a top priority in development policy moving forward. Record food prices that sparked rioting and trade restrictions in 2008 have returned as a dominant theme of geopolitics in 2011, but the world leaders given the task of meeting the problem seem no more prepared to respond now than they were at the outset of the food price crisis four years ago.

Were the hypothetical aid worker to actually pass on this bit of advice to Third World farmers, they would no doubt be perfectly baffled. But what the head of the World Bank is saying largely echoes the conclusions reached by many others in the aid world.

Same Response

These groups say this in a report released on June 2, a policy prospectus requested by the Group of 20 in November 2010. In that report a coalition of government aid agencies, including the Food and Agriculture Organization, the World Bank, the International Fund for Agricultural Development, the International Monetary Fund and the UN Conference on Trade and Development, highly recommend insurance, derivatives and other complex hedging tools, access to which they promise they can help facilitate.

And what does this report say about direct spending on farmers' food production tools such as machinery, irrigation and fertilizers? "Most of the investment, both in primary agriculture and downstream sectors, will have to come from private sources, primarily farmers themselves purchasing implements and machinery, improving soil fertility, etc.," is the response in this new report, titled "Price Volatility in Food and Agricultural Markets: Policy Responses."

Or to put it another way: don't spend too much public money on direct productivity inputs, but do spend more on complicated risk-management financial products.

For students of foreign aid, it shouldn't come as any big surprise that the agencies would reach such a conclusion. Mainly run by economists more comfortable with mathematical modeling than they are with practical mechanisms, the official aid industry tends to see the current run-up in food prices as primarily a market problem that requires market solutions—like derivatives—as suggested by the multi-agency report. Though they pledged earlier to end their neglect of agriculture in a round of food security summits, the support they are now offering, as outlined in the June 2 paper, is along the lines they are familiar with—establishing market mechanisms, special emergency funds, lending for large infrastructure projects and the like.

In its food crisis response Web page, the World Bank lists an array of funds it has established, which appear mainly designed to help governments finance emergency food procurements and "food for work" projects. Financing for seed and fertilizer procurement is mentioned, yes, but is clearly not a priority. A $1.2 billion rapid financing facility primarily consists of loans on offer, and risk management tools and crop insurance rank high on the list of options. The multi-agency report says public funding for research and development and some infrastructure enhancements are acceptable, but the international aid agencies continue to shun direct support to farmers—a common form of subsidy in wealthy nations.

The sequence of events that led to a repeat of the 2007-08 commodity price spike in 2010-11 isn't difficult to follow. Yet the 10 aid agencies studying the problem seem to have drawn no greater lessons this time.

Search for Stability Brings Volatility

Beginning around 2006, commodities exchanges decided to open trading in agriculture and energy futures contracts to more sectors, especially speculators who have no intention of taking final delivery of products, on the assumption that more liquid markets are less volatile. In 2007, computer-based platforms replaced open out-cry as the main forum for commodities trading, expanding the field further.

Instead of encouraging stability, the markets became more volatile. With the stock market flat, investors quickly shifted their attention to commodities, thus setting in motion a rapid escalation in food and fuel prices that culminated in $145-per-barrel crude oil prices in the summer of 2008—all while oil company executives kept insisting there was plenty of crude to supply the market.

Agricultural commodities rode the bubble in tandem, and the Food and Agriculture Organization's global index soared to all-time highs. Strong demand from China and India and bad weather took the blame.

If any good came out of it, it was that the 2007-08 round of food price inflation exposed the failure of five decades of international development theory and the dangerous over-reliance of poor nations on food imports from the rich world. Developing world governments were largely unprepared, leaving them scrambling for quick fixes to calm their furious populations.

Rich nations ultimately promised to change course and pledged $6.6 billion toward helping the poorest countries become self-sufficient in food production

UN Photo/Martine Perret

The rice fields in Baucau, Timor-Leste, may look lush, but many developing nations are in great need of fertilizers, irrigation systems and better distribution methods to increase their food productivity.

at a gathering at Food and Agriculture Organization headquarters in Rome in the summer of 2008. Then months later the collapse of the Western financial system sent commodities prices tumbling, temporarily eliminating any sense of urgency as attention was diverted to propping up faltering banks instead.

Three years later, through fits and starts, a repeat of bad weather in major food-exporting nations, perceived strong demand for food in emerging economies, increased crop diversion to biofuels production, and commodity price speculation—likely much more important to the equation than many market-minded development experts would care to admit—has brought us back to the peak of the 2008 situation in terms of food prices. Crude oil prices are again around $100 a barrel, despite strong oil inventories and lighter gasoline demand. This March the food price index reached a new record high and has been on a plateau since.

Just as the 2008 price inflation exposed decades of failure of aid spending ($4.6 trillion spent in total from 1960 to 2008, measured in constant 2007 dollars, according to the New York University economics professor and aid critic William Easterly), the 2011 situation has exposed how so little was accomplished in the interim.

Last year officials at the International Food Policy Research Institute said that they had seen no evidence that the food aid and development community had fundamentally shifted in philosophy—away from supporting structural adjustment-type lending programs that favored cash crops and industry toward encouraging food self-sufficiency.

The June 2 document suggests that holds true today. More blame is attributed to climate change this time, even though Food and Agriculture Organization officials acknowledged in May that more food is lost to waste and spoilage than adverse weather. That agency—now known more for its statistical acumen than its ability to grow food—should be commended for innovations in urban agricultural programs and smaller-scale efforts, but it deserves criticism for failing to promote strongly an alternative to status-quo approaches.

There is one clear example of how a truly "food first" approach can work that the Food and Agriculture Organization, World Bank and other aid organizations can seize upon.

Tired of begging for food handouts to stave off periodic famines, in 2005 the government of Malawi—a tiny landlocked sub-Saharan country of almost 16 million and an annual per capita Gross Domestic Product of $800—launched a $55 million seed and fertilizer subsidy program, delivered directly to farmers. Rather predictably, Britain's Department for International Development and the World Bank protested, the latter warning that the nation would lose access to new loans.

Malawi Donates to Others

But it was arguably the most successful single economic development program ever attempted, accomplished not by any international institution but by one of the world's least developed countries. By 2006, Malawi's corn crop had doubled. By 2007—in time for the first food price crisis—Malawi actually donated crops to the World Food Program and pulled in $120 million selling surplus corn to

Zimbabwe and other neighboring countries, more than doubling its original $55 million investment.

The initiative even improved governance, a key focus of UN aid agencies hoping to stamp out corruption.

"The subsidy program also helped expand Malawi's nascent democracy into the countryside," Roger Thurow and Scott Kilman wrote in their critical account, "Enough: Why the World's Poorest Starve in an Age of Plenty."

"As it crafted the procedure for distributing the fertilizer and seeds, the government for the first time consulted with farmer organizations and the agricultural private sector," Thurow and Kilman, two reporters for The Wall Street Journal, wrote. "And it brought the rural areas into development discussions."

Unfortunately, Malawi's well-publicized success story isn't mentioned at all in the new multi-agency report. But Malawi was given credit in the report for experimenting with weather index insurance in 2008.

Luckily, the violence and rioting that characterized much of the food price panics of 2008 haven't recurred so far, though some Mideast experts assert that higher costs of staples contributed to the 2011 Arab Spring sparked in Tunisia. The 2010 harvest in much of Africa was better than anticipated. And where it wasn't, the World Food Program planned ahead for emergencies after most market analysts warned that the world should expect a return to high commodity prices soon.

The Malawi example shows that rapidly boosting agricultural productivity in many of the poorest countries on earth can be accomplished along the lines laid out in that hypothetical field-worker's survey—spending on irrigation, fertilizers, seeds, storage and rural roads, directed first and foremost at the farmer. Do the world's most sophisticated aid organizations accept this?

It appears not.

The policy report issued by 10 aid agencies this summer lists six recommendations for strengthening the "productivity, sustainability and resilience of food and agriculture world-wide." The first two recommendations repeat themselves, encouraging more spending on research and development. Another recommends adapting to climate change.

The final three will sound familiar: calls for more spending on large infrastructure projects, developing "comprehensive national food security strategies," and finally offering farmers market incentives to spend their own money—what they may have—on the inputs needed to grow more food.

The message to struggling small-holder farmers in Africa and elsewhere is clear: you're still on your own. ■

After the Millennium Development Goals: What Next?

Hélène Gandois

The Millennium Development Goals, adopted by world leaders at a UN summit in New York in September 2000, set eight targets to be achieved by 2015. But the 2015 deadline is fast approaching and the goals will not be met.

So, what comes next? Is it already too late to come up with a new set of development goals? As yet, little thinking has been done beyond 2015 and it appears unlikely anything groundbreaking will come out of the UN community.

The goals represent human needs and basic rights that every person around the world should be able to enjoy [See a complete text of the goals on P. 236]. The UN decided in September 2010 that a follow-up development agenda should be created for the years beyond 2015, but so far only preliminary internal discussions have taken place. The UN, however, is expected to prepare recommendations for a new framework by 2013, when the membership is next due to review progress.

So What, if Anything, Should Follow?

In official UN circles, discussion about what might happen after 2015 is still damped so as not to distract from any final push to meet the deadline. As one senior official put it, "This is not the time to question the validity of the goals themselves, but rather a time to roll up our sleeves and do what is necessary to attain them, and beyond that, to look at the question of ensuring that they are sustainable after 2015."

But fulfilling this initial commitment looks like a long shot right now as the global economic crisis and rising food, commodity and energy prices have dramatically stymied progress in the last few years.

More people are hungry or malnourished today than three years ago. While there has been some progress toward the goal of universal access to education, there has been less luck on some health-related goals, with the least progress in reducing maternal mortality. For many African countries that were already off-track a few years ago, the picture is simply much worse today.

Seeking a Broader Measure?

The recent setbacks have encouraged development activists to rethink the post-2015 era. They recognize that the Millennium Development Goals provide a moral compass and a set of yardsticks for measuring progress and have inspired increased investment in certain areas, like health. But they criticize the goals for failing to take sufficient account of the vast disparity between different countries' starting points. For example, as development expert Todd Moss has noted, "it took the United States from 1800 to 1905 to take school enrollment from 40 per cent . . . to universal access." Expecting countries like Mali to do the same in just 15 years "seems utterly unworkable," he wrote in his 2010 article, "What Next for the Millennium Development Goals?"

Others criticize the goals for overselling what aid can achieve. Pouring money into poor countries does not guarantee their development. The goals may measure such yardsticks as income, hunger, school enrollment and whether women have equal rights. What they do not measure is the extent to which individuals have decent work that enables them to rise out of poverty, are safe from violence or are able to decide their own fate, as the Oxford Poverty and Human Development Initiative attempts to do.

Eleven nations—Afghanistan, Albania, Azerbaijan, Benin, Bhutan, Cambodia, the Cook Islands, Kenya, Kosovo, Mongolia and Vietnam—have joined to signal their agreement that the goals are too narrowly cast. They have called for adding a ninth goal that measures risk and vulnerability. Can a nation be on the path toward development if its people can see their livelihoods shattered overnight by conflict or an environmental disaster?

Many Voices on the Issues

In fact, a number of groups are pushing for a radical rethinking of how to achieve and measure development. But they are having a hard time speaking in one voice.

For instance, Greenpeace International calls for an "energy revolution" while Oxfam International focuses on the "need to address volatility and build resilience for vulnerable people facing environmental or other shocks." So while all may be pushing for broader development goals, they are not pushing in the same direction.

Amidst this cacophony of voices, it is unlikely that the UN membership will be able to agree on a new direction before 2015. The world has changed since the Millennium Development Goals were formulated and signed.

The Millennium Declaration that spelled them out was signed during a relatively stable and fiscally buoyant period. With the current economic crisis, rich countries are less willing to spend their limited resources on pulling other countries out of poverty. Promoting development may not be at the top of their agenda, and coming up with a new definition of development and a new set of goals may rank even lower on their list of priorities.

But simply letting 2015 pass without getting a new development framework in place is not something the UN is ready to accept. There are currently three options for a post-2015 framework:
•More of the same, with an extension of the deadline;
•A radically new definition of development, or
•A timid update of the previous set of goals, along with a new deadline.

The third option seems the most realistic at this point. But time is running short. It took about 10 years of international conferences to get the UN membership to agree to the initial goals. While some new elements will likely be added—whether to cope with the effects of climate change, mount a campaign against noncommunicable diseases or battle governmental corruption and mismanagement—it is unlikely that consensus can be reached in just four years on a radically new idea.

Discussion has started, however. And whatever their name, the new set of goals will still be at the core of development for years after the UN's 2015 line in the sand has been crossed. ■

WFP Photo/Amjad Jamal

The World Food Program distributes wheat flour and other necessities to Pakistanis in Punjab Province following torrential floods in 2010. The UN program remains the first responder in international food crises.

The Changing World of International Aid
Alexander Shakow

The last decade has seen enormous changes in the way aid resources have moved to developing countries. While traditional flows remain important, new forms of aid have shown extraordinary growth and have had a major impact on the global development architecture.

The 2002 United Nations International Conference on Financing for Development in Monterrey, Mexico, convened by Kofi Annan when he was secretary-general, produced extensive commitments, including most prominently major increases in official aid flows. In fact, since 2004 these have gone up 37 percent in real terms; the Development Assistance Committee of the Organization for Economic Cooperation and Development reports that they reached their highest level ever in 2010—$128.7 billion, or about 0.32 percent of member countries' combined gross national income.

But performance on the Monterrey commitments, reinforced by the Group of 7 industrialized nations (Britain, Canada, France, Germany, Italy, Japan and the United States) at their 2005 Gleneagles summit, has still fallen far short—about $19 billion less than the $50 billion objective—and aid to Africa has increased by $11 billion rather than the $25 billion promised.

Furthermore, the Development Assistance Committee predicts much slower official aid growth. In other ways, however, the aid world has seen some remarkable changes since 2000.

In a major shift, aid donors began a decade ago to create vehicles focused on a very limited number of problems—known as "vertical" funds—rather than rely upon existing multilateral institutions and their "horizontal" programs, which take a broader sector, or countrywide, approach.

Vertical Funds Rise in Appeal

Vertical funds are prominent in the health area; the Global Alliance for Vaccines and Immunization, which now calls itself the Gavi Alliance, and the Global Fund to Fight AIDS, Tuberculosis and Malaria are the largest, but more than a hundred such funds of varying size are believed to be operating, a reflection of their appeal to political leaders and sector specialists.

Other longer-term priorities, such as strengthening health delivery systems, offer less immediate and visible impact, and so three-fourths of increases for health financing in recent years has gone to these global funds. Moreover, there are now over 20 such funds in the burgeoning area of climate problems, with more to come in other sectors as well, despite pressures on donors to think twice before creating yet more new institutions.

New donors beyond the two dozen or so wealthy nations that make up the club of traditional aid donors are now an important feature of the aid world, reflecting in particular the growing strength of the emerging-market countries. China, South Korea, countries in the Middle East and elsewhere now donate $13 billion in official development assistance a year, and these donors promise to be an ever-increasing share of total aid flows.

A few international nongovernmental aid groups such as Save the Children and Oxfam International are now larger than a half dozen national donors. Save the Children, for example, gets 80 percent of its funds from private sources, and only 20 percent from governments—the reverse of a decade ago—and thus offers a significant competitive challenge to such UN agencies as the UN Children's Fund Unicef.

The Internet and the rise of social networking sites have spawned new forms of charitable ventures with the capacity to generate private contributions quickly and effectively, linking donors directly to individual recipients in poor countries. For example, Kiva, a nonprofit Internet-based antipoverty group, has in just under six years been able to make $217 million in small loans this way, based on the Internet fund-raising approach used in the Obama presidential campaign three years ago.

Private foundations and firms now make available over $50 billion a year in various forms of aid. The Bill and Melinda Gates Foundation is but one of the new leaders in this area. And if the billionaire executives Bill Gates and Warren Buffett are successful in encouraging other super-wealthy individuals around the world to dedicate a significant share of their wealth to charitable activities, this number could climb rapidly, even if corporate giving slows.

Development aid is of course also supplemented by a steady growth in foreign private investment and trade, particularly in middle-income countries but now increasingly even in sub-Saharan Africa.

Are New Tobacco Taxes Next?

Innovative financing ideas are being considered. UnitAid, a new international organization that seeks to bring down the cost of treating HIV/AIDS and other diseases by buying drugs in bulk, is underwritten by a small obligatory tax on airline tickets in France and a number of other countries. MassiveGood, a charity also focused on global health, is drawing on voluntary contributions linked to travel expenditures of all kinds. Other ideas are being discussed, including taxes on tobacco sales.

The competition for official financing has intensified recently as a result of anxiety about the climate. Negotiators at UN conferences in Copenhagen and Cancún agreed to create a green climate fund intended to reach $100 billion annually by 2020, but the source of such money is uncertain.

It is clear that grants and subsidized loans will be insufficient. Private industry must be a major player, and the global carbon emissions market, estimated at $121 billion in 2010, might also be a resource for mitigation and adaptation work. Fundamental questions remain, including which institution might manage such large and diverse resources and which system of governance would be acceptable.

This growing demand for resources and competition with domestic financing needs contribute to greater interest by donors (and their publics) in more visible and quicker results. This is another major feature of the changing landscape, despite the inherent difficulties of meeting expectations, especially in the 40 poorest and most fragile countries.

Over the past decade more attention has been paid to aid harmonization and greater alignment with country priorities. Eyeing these and related objectives, the 2005 Paris Declaration and the 2008 Accra Agenda for Action—endorsed by aid recipients and donors—aimed at increased development effectiveness, with mixed results.

For instance, while donors enthusiastically support efforts to "put countries in the driver's seat," they also want global funds created that are often based on top-down priorities chosen by donors, the opposite of the Paris and Accra principles. There is an urgent need to reduce such inconsistencies and to build upon the relevant strengths of both approaches.

Despite advances, much remains undone. Studies show that although most individual projects are deemed "successful" in a narrow sense, put together they do not lead to an overall reduction in the billion poor and hungry people in the world. Moreover, reliable estimates suggest that half of official development aid is lost to inefficiency or failed projects.

Another concern is that almost 100,000 aid-supported development projects are now under way—two and a half times as many as a decade ago. This number is rising even as the average project size is shrinking, resulting in even more fragmentation. It is evident that better ways to "scale up" are needed to achieve a more significant impact on poor people's lives. This task has not been made easier by the proliferation of aid sources and the resulting increase in the management burden on recipient countries.

Another aspect of the changing development terrain is that 75 percent of the world's poor are now found in middle-income countries, and 25 percent in the poorest countries. Twenty years ago, 93 percent were in low-income countries. This suggests that the focus of policy must be on poor people and not just poor countries, and on the growing disparity of incomes within countries.

Implications for the UN

The UN plays many important roles, but with few exceptions it has not been instrumental in shaping the development architecture in the past decade. As a truly universal body the UN can help encourage coordinated global action.

Perhaps the best example in this decade is the universally endorsed Millennium Development Goals initiative *[See P. 236]*. Championed by the UN, the goals have provided valuable guidance for aid donors and recipients alike. They establish a broad framework of development priorities to be achieved by 2015, and they probably generated increased aid flows, although this is difficult to prove.

While some of the poorest countries still lag far behind, two-thirds of developing countries are on track—or close—to meeting the goals' key targets for tackling extreme poverty and hunger. Work has already begun on post-2015 priorities, building on successes and failures of the eight initial goals *[See "After the Millennium Development Goals: What Next?" P. 134]*.

Certain UN agencies—particularly the UN Children's Fund and the World Food Program—stand out as key sources for humanitarian and disaster assistance. Other UN agencies and programs are less effective at delivering services, but more important for building consensus on global standards and in developing negotiating processes for global public goods, such as addressing climate change.

On the negative side, in the absence of a Security Council-style global decision-maker for international economic and financial policy, certain UN intergovernmental bodies such as the Economic and Social Council have attempted to fill the gap by convening giant meetings often marked by posturing and little substance. These sessions provide little value and seem often driven by a desire to compete with, and assert authority over, the World Bank and International Monetary Fund.

In part this reflects the dominance at the UN of foreign ministry representatives, while finance ministries play the central role at the World Bank and International Monetary Fund. As the main sources of funds appear to have little confidence in the UN to raise and manage resources, this is an area where the UN system could productively reduce its profile, focusing instead on enhancing and better coordinating major contributions by its secretariats and agencies while reducing the strain on weak developing-country governments.

The next two years promise to be eventful as these and other new elements of the aid architecture interact and, with any luck, coalesce in support of more effective development. A forum on aid effectiveness scheduled for Busan, South Korea, Nov. 29 through Dec. 1, offers an important opportunity to enhance the impact of these various sources of aid.

The Brookings Institution scholars Homi Kharas and Noam Unger have argued persuasively that this widely representative conference should "pave the way for a broad, inclusive development partnership—a global development compact … to signal a renewed political resolve that major countries will take development seriously and position aid as one of several instruments for development effectiveness … and … to forge a better delivery model at the country level."

Donor schizophrenia can be reduced by drawing out and strengthening the best aspects of both vertical and horizontal aid programs. Enhancing the volume and quality of aid from both new and traditional donors will be of great importance. And agreements at Busan and elsewhere could help promote greater partnership and bring order to the structure and focus of the new climate funds. ■

Talking Points

1. As the 2015 deadline nears for the UN's Millennium Development Goals and widespread success in meeting the goals seems unlikely, a reassessment of current priorities, new issues and measurement tools will be addressed in a post-2015 framework. Given the vast differences among countries' baselines and resources, should the international community continue its "top-down" approach in setting new goals or allow a more collaborative "bottom-up" approach that enables individual countries to define their own targets and deadlines?

2. The market-oriented development solutions proposed by the World Bank and International Monetary Fund may well stem from their being Western-led organizations focused on economic and financial aspects of international development. But if the leadership of these organizations were changed to better reflect the growth of developing countries, how would the international bodies' recommendations on food security policy shift? Would it be better to reform other institutions or to create new bodies dedicated to providing direct support to farmers?

3. Is consolidating the vast number of aid projects worldwide helpful because doing so would eliminate overlap and duplication, or does the current development system work because fragmentation promotes innovation, versatility and efficiency through competition for donor funding? What role can the UN play in clarifying the direction of nongovernmental aid efforts worldwide?

4. Proposals for sustainable development often push both supply- and demand-side approaches: better productivity will increase the supply of goods and raise standards of living; reducing the demand for goods and services with environmentally harmful side effects will lessen the stress on our ecosystem. But increases in household wealth that come from greater productivity are often linked to more demand for modern technologies, which leave a larger environmental footprint. How can the international community juggle these two conflicting forces to support a global population estimated to reach 9.3 billion people by 2050?

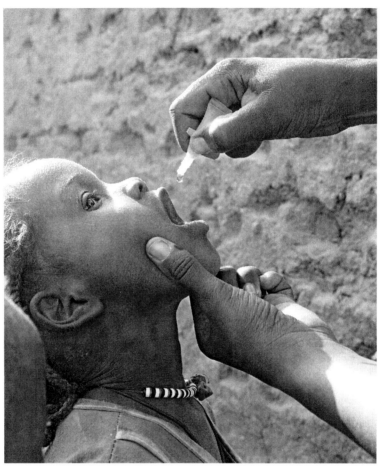

UN Photo/Olivier Chassot

A child receives a dose of polio vaccine in Darfur, western Sudan, in March. The campaign was organized by the Sudanese Ministry of Health with help from the World Health Organization and the UN Children's Fund Unicef.

Pulling Together and Crossing Borders to Improve Health

144 Polio Comeback: A Sad Lesson From Nigeria
Betsy Pisik

150 Health: From an International Concern to a Global One
A. Edward Elmendorf

154 Saving Women's Lives in Pregnancy and Childbirth
Adrienne Germain

157 Talking Points

Polio Comeback: A Sad Lesson From Nigeria
Betsy Pisik

Saidiku Ali is as buff and sculptured as any athlete. His neck is large and corded with tendons. His shoulders gleam in the harsh morning light as the 25-year-old's muscled arms flex and churn like an oiled machine. But the picture is incomplete. Those beautiful arms end in dirty calloused hands, which are stuffed into cheap plastic sandals. Ali's handsome face is overshadowed by narrowed eyes that are hard and angry and very old. And his legs are carelessly folded, like cloth, beneath a solid torso.

Ali had polio when he was a child and his legs are paralyzed and flaccid, unable to bear his weight. He is one of scores of young men who propel themselves through Nigeria's Kano City traffic on crude wooden skateboards.

His worthless limbs have limited every aspect of the life Ali wanted to lead. Instead of starting a business, the young man sells phone cards in traffic. Instead of becoming a decorated soldier, he drags his body between the cars and motorcycles honking and lurching down congested Murtala Mohammed Road. He dreams of starting a family, but for now he keeps uneasy company with a community of polio victims who take refuge on the same concrete traffic island.

"This life is an affront to my dignity," he says. "I don't want to do this. I want to hire boys to sell phone cards for me, but I need money . . . to start a business."

The Capital City of a Scourge

Northern Nigeria is home to tens of thousands of polio victims, and Kano City is their capital. The south and central parts of this sprawling, chaotic country have long complied with inoculation efforts, and are all but free of the dreaded virus. But the conservative north has willfully lagged behind, at its own painful cost.

In the early 2000s, many Muslim and community leaders in northern Nigeria began warning that the polio vaccine was so unsafe that it could be "un-Islamic." Just one dose of three bitter drops could lead to sterilization or cause HIV/AIDS, they said. Religious and then secular officials mulled whether the drops might be part of a Western plot to limit Muslim births—a theory fed in part by the U.S.-led invasions of Afghanistan and Iraq. The fear also played to the often-violent friction between Nigeria's Muslim and Christian communities. Local newspaper editorials warned the oral vaccine could "wipe out a whole generation."

In this environment, the governor of Kano State in 2003 officially halted polio vaccinations, saying the community lacked confidence in the drops. To the horror of public health officials and the polio community, vaccinations were suspended for nearly a year. A local campaign by religious leaders discredited not just the vaccine, but the aid organizations that distributed it.

"People used to yell at us on the street, and they would throw rocks at us in traffic," said one Nigerian who worked for the UN Children's Fund Unicef in Kano in

2003. "It was very tense. We talked about painting the [car] doors white." Unicef teams were blocked as they tried to enter villages and settlements, often by men waving sticks. Today, she said, it is "very painful" to see so many crippled children in areas where the vaccines had once been used to effect.

The damage was catastrophic: over the next few years, 3,372 children were crippled or killed by polio in Kano alone, according to detailed World Health Organization records.

And between 2003 and 2007, 20 previously polio-free countries were reinfected with polio viruses originating from northern Nigeria, exposing just how fragile the shell of immunity really is. The global cleanup of the Kano strain of polio has cost hundreds of millions of dollars.

"This was awful, just awful to watch," said Tayo Oeofineade, who coordinates Rotary International's Nigeria campaign to route polio. Rotary established its Polio-Plus program, aimed at eradicating the disease, in 1985, and has been especially active in underwriting small vaccine efforts in Nigeria and other poor countries.

Joe Penney

Kano State governor Mallam Ibrahim Shekarau in Kano, Nigeria, in April. He suspended polio vaccinations for a year in 2003, saying the community lacked confidence in the drops. Over the next few years, 3,372 children were crippled or killed by polio in Kano alone.

Heartbreaking Consequences

It wasn't supposed to go this way. The World Health Organization's Geneva-based polio office declared in 2002 that the virus had been beaten back to three remaining stronghold countries (Pakistan, India and Nigeria) and said polio could soon join smallpox in extinction. Months later, five predominantly Muslim states in northern Nigeria halted their vaccination programs. Four of the five soon resumed vaccinating. But Kano state's suspension of a year brought swift damage, as heartbreaking as it was predictable.

"The Islamic faith is very fundamental to the affairs of the people . . . and their opinion influences a lot of things in the community," said the Kano State governor, Ibrahim Shekarau, who formally suspended the inoculations in mid-2003, in part because the people had become so afraid of it. "We had to choose the evil of total rejection forever or the evil of temporarily stopping the program to convince the people" that the vaccine was safe enough to accept. Shekarau has since been re-elected, and even waged a credible campaign for president.

"I wouldn't want to say I was under a pressure, it was rather a pleasure to excercise the responsibility of the mandate given to me," said Shekarau, who does not regret his decision. "Even if it's [fatal to] just one of 10 million people, we felt we needed to be sure."

That decision was met with anguish by the vast polio-battling community, which brought exceptional pressure to bear from diplomatic, political and medical circles. But most important was an unprecedented rebuke from the King of Saudi Arabia, who banned Nigerian Muslims from Mecca unless they took the vaccine at the airport.

In 2011 the World Health Organization called Nigeria "one of the most entrenched reservoirs of wild polio virus." Nonetheless, the government has committed to an aggressive strategy, and new infections have dropped 95 percent, with 21 in 2010, compared with 388 cases reported in 2009, according to the World Health Organization.

Caused by a Highly Infectious Virus

Poliomyelitis is a highly infectious virus that lives in the digestive tract and attacks the nervous system, causing paralysis in hours or days in one of every 200 children infected. It is marked by a severe and sustained high fever, muscle weakness and severe constipation. The child is highly infectious at this stage, and has, unknowingly, been so for days before the symptoms. The virus is easily transmitted through feces, dirty water and direct contact.

There are two vaccines, oral and injected. They were developed by competing American virologists Albert Sabin and Jonas Salk in the 1950s-60s. Both were miraculous advances in public health: the injected Salk vaccine, which is largely used in the United States, where polio has been eradicated; and the oral Sabin vaccine, which is easier and faster to administer but will be effective only if it is kept cold. Refrigeration is a problem in the world's poorest communities, where electricity is unreliable.

Vaccination campaigns look about the same around the world: young women volunteer to be eradicators in their own neighborhoods. They are trained to overcome family objections, administer the vaccine and collect the detailed information required of every single house. Sometimes vaccination stations are set up near schools or wells, but mostly the eradicators visit the mud-walled huts and tiny cinderblock rooms that shelter the fortunate poor around the world. Each vaccinated child is identified with a black mark on his or her finger.

The UN estimates that nearly 20 million volunteers around the world have vaccinated 2.5 billion infants and toddlers in the last 20 years. In 2011, there are only six endemic countries, but experts quietly admit that more than a dozen countries could develop new cases as immunization campaigns soften.

That's why the virus must be eliminated, rather than isolated in unreachable areas. The World Health Organization's polio chief, Bruce Aylward, warned this year that the idea of merely controlling the virus was a "seductive mistake."

Unicef/Christine Nesbitt

Hafisa Salisu, a 16-year-old Nigerian girl with polio, washes her hands outside a school in Bungudu, northern Nigeria. Hand-washing stations and latrines designed to accommodate disabled children were built at the school with the help of the UN Children's Fund Unicef.

The eradication plan, drawn up by the Global Polio Eradication Initiative, was developed with redundancy, yet there are significant weaknesses in the system. The young vaccinators are too likely to take no for an answer, leaving unvaccinated children vulnerable to the disease and as infectors of others as well. The information collected from every house is often incomplete or inaccurate, making it impossible for experts to predict an outbreak or plan its response. And the oral vaccine itself is fragile, requiring constant refrigeration.

Legs 'Taken by Spirits'

The reticence of her vaccinators exasperates Unicef's Josephine Kamara, the stalwart consultant from Sierra Leone who oversees social outreach and data collection for much of Kano.

"Data collection and analysis is really an issue here," Kamara sighed in an October 2010 interview after a daily statistics meeting. She estimates that more than half of the Kano data are inaccurate, either because the vaccinators don't know how to fill out the forms properly, or fudge them to hide missing information.

Written records are the foundation of epidemiology and without them, it will be impossible to achieve complete protection against a disease, experts from the U.S. Agency for International Development and Unicef say.

The world's poorest communities are a petri dish for ravaging childhood diseases. Poor sanitation means that street gutters overflow with trash, human waste and fetid green-scummed water so noxious it is also breeding cholera, typhoid, malaria, hepatitis and deadly diarrhea. Clean water is so scarce that washing—whether of hands, clothing or dishes—is difficult. Add to this women's restricted role in society and limited health care and the social and environmental factors click into place. Health conditions are so ghastly that many mothers refuse repeated attempts to inoculate against polio because they want to see a similar effort on killers like malaria and measles.

But ignorance and superstition can be as lethal as contaminated drinking water. In some isolated and uneducated pockets of northern Nigeria, victims' legs are "taken by spirits" or withered by a punishing god. Little can challenge those beliefs.

Helping the Victims Get Around

Aminu Ahmed Tudunwada is chairman of the Polio Victims Association, which trains crippled men to build hand-cranked bikes and modified motorcycles to help them get around. The metal shop is largely underwritten by international donors; while these vehicles typically cost less than $150, few can come up with such a sum.

Association members also go out on polio vaccination days with local eradicators to urge parents to accept the oral vaccine. There are so many victims, he said, that the stigma has worn off.

"I tell them to look at me—don't let your son be like this," says the remarkably agile Tudunwada, who gets around by swinging his body forward using "crutches" consisting of wooden blocks about three inches high. "I tell them, 'You are standing while I am on the ground.'"

By far the most powerful influence in northern Nigeria is the sultan of Sokoto, the revered leader who presides informally over 70 million Muslims. After the philanthropist Bill Gates and other figures prevailed upon him, the sultan vaccinated a niece in public to prove its safety. The powerful emir of Kano did the same, well after the crisis. But neither spoke out against the 2003 vaccine ban.

Although resistance to the polio vaccine began to soften in some communities, the Global Polio Eradication Initiative and other groups were concerned about seemingly half-hearted efforts by the national and regional leaders. Bill Gates—by now the rock star of polio—drew huge crowds during a visit to Abuja, Kano and other Nigerian cities.

But little changed. And none of this is cheap.

Many Work at This Task

The initiative, founded in 1988, spends about half a billion dollars annually to fight the virus around the world. The Gates Foundation pledged more than $300 million in 2010, and Gates has promised the foundation will continue its support for years to come. Other money comes from Rotary International, the U.S. Centers for Disease Control and Prevention, the U.S. Agency for International Development, the UN Foundation, the European Development Fund and the World Health Organization. Unicef is most often the power on the ground, training locals to administer the polio drops to children in their own villages.

Others wonder, however, whether polio can ever be overcome.

Children do—albeit rarely—contract polio from the vaccine. The infected are often capable of spreading the disease before they show symptoms. And so many countries said to be polio-free are in fact vulnerable if the virus surfaces in under-vaccinated areas, although in many cases, polio will briefly flare but not spread.

Take those 20 countries that were reinfected by the Kano strain. How could the virus catch hold anew if the vaccinations were properly administered? If so many countries have such a thin veneer of protection, how many more are vulnerable? In 2010 the Democratic Republic of Congo and Tajikistan unexpectedly exploded with polio. Should epidemiologists be concerned about epidemics during the Hadj, or any large, dense gathering? For that matter, what about the U.S.—free of infectious polio since the late 1970s—where very well-to-do families now refuse to vaccinate their children out of health concerns?

"The child that is paralyzed cannot play soccer or go to school without help," said Dr. Muhammad Ali Pate, Nigeria's executive director for primary healthcare development. "Even if he is educated he cannot achieve his full potential. You cannot help but hope it will be eradicated from this world." ■

[*Pisik reported from Nigeria on a grant from the Washington-based International Reporting Project*]

Health: From an International Concern to a Global One

A. Edward Elmendorf

A generation ago, tending to health problems fell to developing countries and their partners in wealthy nations, and the United Nations was not a significant player.

What was then widely known as "international health" was largely a technical concern of bilateral donors, big nongovernmental organizations like CARE and World Vision, academic institutions and a few UN agencies including the World Health Organization, the UN Population Fund and the UN Children's Fund Unicef.

It seemed at the time that the institutional landscape was crowded, at least in comparison with other sectors, and that developing countries had many partners.

Over the past generation, however, international health has become "global health," a change in terminology that, while not yet universal, reflects a profound change in perspective. No longer can countries and institutions see health on a map of national borders, as they often did in the past.

Indeed, global health concerns have grown important enough to draw in, at one end, the UN, and at the other, citizen activists, who have been able to a remarkable extent to shape public policy and spending priorities, both international and domestic, in the United States and elsewhere.

HIV/AIDS was the pivot in turning health into a truly global issue. The poorly understood nature of a disease that was spreading rapidly through rich and poor countries, a perception that the World Health Organization couldn't cope with the growing threat, and a rapidly expanding citizens movement driven by people with HIV/AIDS and others created an environment that by the 1990s required new action from the international community.

Movement in Many Forums

The response was vast. The umbrella group UNAIDS was launched in 1996, the Security Council devoted a session to the subject in 2000, world leaders in 2000 adopted the Millennium Development Goals seeking to halt the spread of HIV/AIDS, and the General Assembly in 2001 held its first special session devoted to a single disease. The Global Fund to Fight AIDS, Tuberculosis and Malaria was begun in 2002.

Other recent health threats, such as Severe Acute Respiratory Syndrome and a 2009 flu pandemic, have also had global impact and have contributed to increasing acceptance that health issues are no longer the province of a technically oriented cadre of health workers. Global health has become a concern to all: policy makers, financiers, diplomats, health service providers, activists, an array of non-profit interest groups and citizens around the world, as well as the UN.

Global health's institutional landscape has also changed in recent years. UNAIDS, a jointly sponsored program of 10 UN agencies, was the first major global health agency created since the UN Population Fund in the 1960s.

Public-private partnerships for specific health purposes, such as the Global Fund, are also proliferating. The Bill and Melinda Gates Foundation, fueled by the success of the Microsoft Corporation, has assumed an importance in global health that is greater than that of many bilateral donors. Now the world's largest private foundation, it has committed nearly $10 billion in global health grants since its formation in 1994.

Other Alliances Develop

Other relatively recent entries include the Gavi Alliance, until recently the Global Alliance for Vaccines and Immunization, which has committed $4 billion in funds through the end of 2015, the Clinton Foundation, launched after Bill Clinton left the presidency in 2001, and UnitAid, founded in 2006 to make bulk purchases of HIV/AIDS, tuberculosis and malaria drugs to reduce costs and extend availability.

In the 1990s, the World Health Organization was widely seen as weak and ineffective despite its mandate to direct and coordinate the international response to health problems. The World Bank began filling the leadership and policy vacuum. By 1997 it had become the largest international source of financial support for health programs in developing countries.

By 2007, however, the World Bank had taken a step back from the wide vision of its 1997 health strategy, with relatively lower financial commitments and somewhat greater focus on health systems. Yet global programs and public-private partnerships remain an important part of the World Bank's overall engagement in health and in the institutional landscape. The World Health Organization re-emerged as a major player under the leadership of Dr. Gro Harlem Brundtland, its director-general from 1998 to 2003. More recently, however, it seems to have lost some donor confidence, and its World Health Assembly of 2011 revealed the organization faces a financial crisis and need for major redefinition.

The UN, the World Bank and other World Health Organization partners will need to be careful to avoid the temptation to take on World Health Organization roles. Instead, they should help the agency identify essential complementary roles for all as global health becomes more crowded and complex.

Despite the World Health Organization's continuing woes, global health financing has undergone extraordinary growth over a generation, pointing indirectly to potential areas for UN engagement. Even when adjusted for inflation, development assistance for health quadrupled from 1990 to 2007, reaching nearly $22 billion that year. By 2010 official development assistance for health was $26 billion.

The proportion of health assistance channeled through multilateral institutions dropped, even though multilateral aid is more likely to be responsive to the concerns of recipients than assistance channeled through individual nations, foundations or private organizations. By 2007, private philanthropy had grown to account for over a quarter of development assistance aimed at health concerns, while overseas spending by nongovernmental groups made up nearly another quarter as of 2006, the latest year for which figures are available.

Challenges at Every Level

Thanks to infusions from the Global Fund, the Gavi Alliance and the American President's Emergency Plan for AIDS Relief, financing for health in developing countries has tended to shift from health as a general need to particular illnesses. This has made more challenging the work of developing-country policymakers, whose job is to ensure balance among diseases, to spur development of national health systems and local health institutions and to focus on their specific priorities. The greater the political and financial imperatives and incentives created by global consensus, especially on HIV/AIDS, the more important management becomes at the country level.

What do these shifts mean for the UN and developing countries? Global problems demand increasingly global responses, and health is a main area of global concern. With this in mind, the UN has largely moved from being a bystander to becoming a forum and a major policy player. The UN may engage at three levels: through its intergovernmental organs, through leadership by the secretary-general and at the level of individual developing countries.

Concentrating on its comparative advantage as an intergovernmental forum, the UN has done much to help put health issues before policymakers and public officials around the world in ways few could have imagined a generation ago.

The Millennium Development Goals, adopted in 2000, set out specific milestones for progress by 2015 on maternal health, HIV/AIDS, malaria and other major diseases. The General Assembly Special Session on HIV/AIDS convened the next year. In 2009, the Economic and Social Council held its own meeting on how to achieve shared international health goals.

At the level of the Secretariat, Secretary-General Kofi Annan played a crucial role in establishing the Global Fund, and his successor, Ban Ki-moon, has regularly led efforts to raise money for it. In 2010, Ban expanded the UN's agenda by teaming up with Bill and Melinda Gates to focus on maternal and child health, building support for a Global Strategy for Women's and Children's Health created at that year's follow-up UN summit on the Millennium Development Goals.

And Now, Diseases of Life Choices

With health problems linked to unhealthy lifestyles a growing global concern, the UN has also begun girding for battle against noncommunicable problems such as diabetes, cancer and heart disease, acting at both the intergovernmental level and through the Secretariat. Speaking at the World Economic Forum in January 2011, Secretary-General Ban said such diseases merited as much attention as HIV/AIDS. At the initiative of Caribbean countries, the General Assembly has called world leaders and their top health officials to New York in September to look for ways to prevent and control noncommunicable diseases on a global scale.

Thus it is clear that the UN can facilitate policy formulation and institutional reform on health issues at the global level without dominating them, an approach that may be needed even more today.

At this point it is critical that the UN do all it can, around the world, to ensure that both national and local officials translate rhetoric into public health action that reaches people and communities. Support for health systems and stronger, coordinated management of donor-supported programs at the country level are keys. No one should assume this will happen by itself, and this situation creates new opportunities for the UN to engage in at the operational level.

Multiple partners—global, regional, national, local, public, private, nonprofit and corporate—must work in harmony in pursuit of shared goals, both globally and at the country level. Discussions are under way in a closed forum of the Gavi Alliance, the Global Fund and the World Bank on a financing platform, which could help. But to be most responsive to country needs and gain the widest international consensus, the process for formulation of a funding platform needs to be open. This is where the UN and the World Health Organization can play a role.

Moving beyond its role as a forum for intergovernmental dialogue and global institutional reform, at the country level the UN's strong presence, legitimacy and institutional neutrality place it well to help individual countries manage the growing flow of external funds for health and especially to help countries coordinate donor-funded programs.

The International Health Partnership, a coalition of international health agencies, governments and donors, may help in this regard, but active, effective leadership is needed. Whether the UN can play this role will be a function of local circumstances, including the skills and drive of UN resident coordinators and the leadership and guidance of the UN System Chief Executives Board, a coordinating committee that is chaired by the UN secretary-general and includes the heads of 28 UN agencies.

National leaders must manage their aid programs in a dedicated and transparent manner. And to work best, national strategies must take into account the views of those providing the money, those distributing the aid and those intended to benefit from it.

In the current international environment, the possibilities for significant health improvements in developing nations have never been greater. But the challenges have also never been greater. ■

Saving Women's Lives in Pregnancy and Childbirth

Adrienne Germain

When I began to work in the field of international sexual and reproductive rights and health 40 years ago, I saw women die from botched abortions and families bury young women who had died in childbirth. I even saw a woman standing by the road whose uterus had fallen out, holding the uterus in her hands. Most, if not all of these losses occurred because local health services lacked the capacity to prevent or treat them. At most, local clinics provided contraceptives, vital but not nearly enough.

Inexcusably, these preventable deaths and misery continue. Every day, nearly 1,000 women die of complications of pregnancy, and every day more than 20,000 suffer lasting disabilities due to preventable causes in pregnancy and childbirth, according to UN estimates. In some countries, maternal deaths and injuries are actually rising. Many of these girls and women give birth and die at home, often alone, in fear and agony. Or, they die in substandard medical facilities, ill-equipped to deal with problems that are routinely managed for women in rich countries or rich women in low-resource countries.

A woman who lives in a country whose health system is weak, such as Cameroon or Pakistan, is many, many times more likely to die of pregnancy-related complications than a woman living in a country with a strong health system. And when a woman dies in childbirth, the infant is far more likely to die because nobody takes care of it.

When confronted with such grave and terrible statistics and images, it is tempting to seek a single culprit. But there is no one culprit. Maternal health is a state of being. It cannot be achieved through a simple technical fix, or health services.

It's Not a Single-Item Agenda

Rather, multiple issues must be tackled: social conditions that prevent women from going to the clinic when they need to; poverty that drives the malnutrition that puts both women and their infants at risk; violence against women by their partners, which makes them afraid to negotiate condom use and which often increases during pregnancy; and failure of governments and donors, as well as the UN system, to prioritize and underwrite the actions needed.

As the leading Egyptian obstetrician and gynecologist Mahmoud Fathalla pointed out decades ago in a now-classic speech on maternal health, women's life journeys are long and hard, too often ending in death as a result of multiple failures on all levels: familial, clinical, social and global.

Although maternal deaths have declined more than 30 percent worldwide since 1990, the Millennium Development Goal to improve maternal health, adopted by world leaders in 2000, is the furthest of the eight goals from being achieved by the 2015 deadline. What are the prospects for substantial progress?

The best news is at the global level. In the last few years, several new global health undertakings have emerged that, in their principles and financing, greatly increase the potential to deliver an integrated package of sexual and reproductive health services that women and girls require for health and to enjoy their human rights fully. The first is the UN Secretary-General's Global Strategy for Women's and Children's Health, which is being supported by public and private donors as well as the governments of 40 countries with high burdens of maternal death.

A second global action, closely (though not deliberately) aligned to the Secretary-General's Global Strategy, is the U.S. administration's Global Health Initiative, which comes with a $63 billion, six-year commitment. This program is meant to strengthen health delivery systems to provide integrated services close to where people live; it is focused on women.

UN Photo/Martine Perret

The UN Population Fund helps Timor-Leste's national hospital make childbirth safer as part of meeting the UN Millennium Development Goals.

A third key is the International Health Partnership, under which countries and their development partners (donors, UN agencies) agree to a single national health policy and budget and coordinate resources to improve efficacy, effectiveness and, possibly, equity in the health sector.

Valuing Women

These sound great, but nothing is ever that easy for women. Generating political will to secure full funding and implementation of these initiatives is a major challenge, which is why the exceptional commitments by the UN secretary-general and the U.S. president offer so much opportunity—opportunity we must maximize while it lasts.

The good news is that saving women's lives in childbirth and supporting their health after birth requires relatively inexpensive and known interventions—not fancy hospitals, new research and technologies or scientific breakthroughs. Many of the services needed do not require medical doctors, but can be delivered by midwives and community health workers.

Rather, we need to concentrate on some basic changes. One imperative is to improve the compensation as well as the working and living conditions of the health workers particularly to address the problems faced by female workers. Another key challenge is figuring out how women can become empowered enough to use health services when they become available.

A key impediment to women using services, to creating political will, and also a major factor in persistently high rates of maternal deaths and injuries, is the low value given to women by societies and even by their families. Gender inequality, feminization of poverty, violence and sexual coercion including in the home, discrimination against women, and myriad other violations of their human rights have all been recognized as contributors to women's ill health and preventable death. These structural factors require investments and action by all segments of society and sustained commitment to long-term social change.

As we work to change these factors we must engage more women in decision-making, in their families and communities as well as the top levels of their governments and the UN. Without women's voices it is nearly impossible to break through the ignorance, stereotypes and prejudice that thwart even the best policy and prevent budget allocations. While not all women will make decisions in support of women, many will. Having more women in power, more girls educated, and more women economically independent has been shown over and over again to make a difference from the home to parliament (witness Rwanda).

My generation has been working for 40 years to put women and girls at the center of health and development policies. Fortunately, a new generation of activists is emerging to take the work of generating political will for the sexual and reproductive health and rights agenda forward. One of the most important investments we can make for women's health and human rights is to support the activism of this new generation and their participation in all levels of decision-making.

Today, we have all the words we need from the highest global leaders, as well as demands from countries. Together we can turn words into a new reality, a just and healthy life for every woman and girl. ■

Talking Points

1. An evolving challenge in global health is epidemics that have no borders and policy responses that must be similarly global in kind. How should the UN, with its global presence and universal membership, position itself in worldwide health campaigns now that aid is increasingly dominated by private philanthropies and nongovernmental organizations?

2. The global allocation of health resources has tightened as many UN member countries attempt to address problems within their own borders, making efficiency more important than ever. Is the best future strategy a narrow but effective "bang-for-your-buck" approach that focuses mainly on the most proven health responses, or should the international community continue its wide-ranging interventions that achieve progress on many fronts but to a lesser degree?

3. So far, progress on the Millennium Development Goal for maternal health has lagged well behind the seven other UN benchmarks. With the 2015 deadline soon approaching and no extension of the Millennium Development Goals in sight, how can efforts to improve maternal health be maintained if not enhanced for some of the world's most vulnerable groups?

4. In the early 2000s, some Muslim leaders in northern Nigeria began warning that the polio vaccine was so unsafe that it could be "un-Islamic," and a few governors suspended vaccination programs, leading to a resurgence of the disease. Should political leaders undermining vital public health initiatives be held accountable by the international community? How could UN-led interfaith dialogue on health issues be used to address concerns of skeptical leaders?

Adam Jones

The skull of a victim from the July 1995 massacre of more than 8,000 Muslims in Srebrenica, Bosnia. Serbian Gen. Ratko Mladic, accused by the International Criminal Tribunal for the former Yugoslavia of ordering the slaughter, evaded arrest until May 2011.

Chasing War Crimes While Changing the Lineup

160 Electing International Criminal Court Judges: Merit Over Politics
Bill Pace and Matthew Heaphy

163 A New Criminal Court Prosecutor
Richard Dicker and Param-Preet Singh

166 70 Years of Evolution in Prosecuting War Crimes
Dan Plesch and Shanti Sattler

171 Talking Points

Electing International Criminal Court Judges: Merit Over Politics

Bill Pace and Matthew Heaphy

Early in the session of the UN General Assembly opening in September, a relatively young international organization will meet at UN Headquarters in New York to elect some of its most important officials and thereby shape its next chapter.

Beginning on Dec. 12, the 116 nations that have ratified the Rome Statute, the governing treaty of the fledgling International Criminal Court, will gather to elect six new judges to replace sitting judges whose nine-year terms expire next March.

The meeting will also select a new prosecutor to replace the outgoing Luis Moreno-Ocampo of Argentina, whose nine-year term ends in June 2012.

In all, the court has 18 judges. Its initial 18, elected in 2003, were assigned by lot to three-, six- or full nine-year terms so that, ensuring a measure of future continuity, only a third of the judges are up for replacement every three years.

Like other elections at the UN, these will be decided largely on the basis of international politics, vote-trading and geographic representation. The candidates, and the question of their qualifications, will have been decided in the nomination period, June 13 to Sept. 2.

International Criminal Court elections, however, were intended to be different, with choices made by merit only.

The world's first permanent international criminal court was established to try individuals for humanity's most heinous deeds—genocide, war crimes and crimes against humanity. From the start, it sought to free itself of the vote-trading of other international elections. At the time the Rome Statute was adopted 13 years ago, participating governments were guided by progressive principles in creating a new framework for the selection of judges.

There was, for example, a major effort to ensure the representation of all major legal systems on the court's bench so that it would not be tilted toward the common law system favored at the UN's ad hoc tribunals, temporary courts that were created to handle particular situations, such as ethnic cleansing in the former Yugoslavia and the genocide in Rwanda.

Gender and Geography Were Goals

The court's creators also insisted on gender and geographic representation, although there were some omissions concerning candidates' legal training and credentials, which probably reflected that international justice itself was very young.

The Rome Statute and later resolutions adopted by the court's governing body set out extensive and detailed provisions on qualifications for candidates.

These require candidates to be nominated to one of two lists, one for those with experience and expertise in criminal law and procedure and the other for those with experience and expertise in international law, designed to ensure diverse legal competence and provide a pool of judges to do pretrial, trial and appeals work. The system also encourages court members to vote for candidates with particular attributes that are underrepresented at the court in the categories of expertise and experience, geographic representation or gender.

For example, men and experts with experience in criminal law will be underrepresented at the time of the 2011 election, thus the rules encourage governments to nominate candidates with these characteristics and require the governments to take these categories into account in the early rounds of voting.

These procedures have helped achieve diversity of experience, expertise, background and gender on the court's bench. They do not, however, guarantee the election of the most highly qualified candidates, nor do they prevent governments from nominating candidates who are not qualified.

So while court members historically have elected a diverse bench, they have not always elected qualified individuals.

As carefully documented by a team of researchers at University College London and Queen Mary, University of London, led by Kate Malleson and Philippe Sands, governments have often decided on which nationality of candidate to vote for even before the nomination period has opened or candidates have been identified. One government may promise in advance to vote for a second government's candidate in exchange for a vote for the first's candidate for the Human Rights Council. It works out well for the vote-trading governments but it does not necessarily bode well for transparency or merit-based nominations and elections.

Water Goes Over the Dam

The problem is that international elections are dominated by a crude political process. Even those governments with the cleanest images have nominated sub-par candidates to senior UN positions. Once the nominations have been made, few elections give weight to candidates' merit or qualifications. This could prove a catastrophe for the International Criminal Court and its supporters.

To succeed, the court must have the most highly qualified judges. To date, its governing body has not evaluated individual candidates, and it has yet to formally establish an advisory committee on nominations, as envisioned by the governing treaty.

It has largely been left to interested outsiders to raise awareness about candidates' qualifications, and, through candidate questionnaires, reports and public meetings, to encourage court members to make evaluations.

There is no panacea for flawed international elections. In fact, outside groups do not agree on how to approach the International Criminal Court elections in general, and specific candidates in particular.

The Coalition for the International Criminal Court, an umbrella organization for 2,500 support groups in 150 countries, established an independent panel on elections, to help encourage governments to nominate the most highly qualified candidates.

Similar to some national bar association procedures, the panel will assess whether each candidate is qualified or not, using the standards set out in the governing treaty. The long-time international jurists Richard Goldstone of South

Africa and Patricia Wald of the United States lead the panel. Other members include the international jurist O-Gon Kwon of South Korea, the former UN Legal Counsel Hans Corell of Sweden and the Chilean jurist and professor Cecilia Medina Quiroga.

The panel expects to issue its first report this autumn.

The establishment of the panel has prompted the court's members to take the first steps to create their own advisory committee, possibly in the coming year, further raising hopes that more attention will be paid to the qualifications of those who, over nine-year terms, will be issuing critical judgments about odious crimes that shock the conscience of humanity. ■

Vincent van Zeijst

The International Criminal Court in The Hague, Netherlands. The court's members will be electing six judges and a prosecutor in December.

A New Criminal Court Prosecutor
Richard Dicker and Param-Preet Singh

In December the nearly 120 nations belonging to the permanent International Criminal Court will make a decision of great impact on future prosecutions for genocide, crimes against humanity and war crimes. When they meet at United Nations headquarters in New York, they will select the next prosecutor to guide the court for a nine-year term.

The court's members have created a search committee that is to use the merit-based criteria in the Rome Statute, which created the court. It is essential that merit prevail over the political and regional factors that all too often prevail in filling senior posts in international organizations. With so many challenges before the growing, but still fragile "system" of international justice, the stakes could hardly be higher.

This selection comes at a critical moment. With its novel mandate and reach, the court met large hurdles at its founding, and difficulties were inevitable for a system designed to adjudicate complex crimes under an innovative international legal regime. Some problems have persisted over its eight years of operation. For example, citing flaws in the prosecution's disclosure of evidence to the accused, the trial judges twice dismissed the case against the court's first defendant. Both times, judges hearing appeals ordered the trial to resume.

To date, all of the court's six cases under investigation are in Africa. As a result, along with the naming of two heads of state and several senior officials as suspects, the court has been criticized, primarily by a handful of North African nations that are not court members, as unfairly targeting Africa.

But Cases Continue to Develop

Nonetheless, it has emerged as the "go to" court to respond to abuses that amount to war crimes, crimes against humanity and/or genocide. The Security Council has referred two situations to the court: Darfur in 2005 and, last February, Libya, upon a unanimous vote. Four African governments have asked the current prosecutor to open investigations into crimes committed on their own territories.

The Office of the Prosecutor is conducting preliminary examinations in eight other countries, but has not yet decided about investigations in Colombia, Afghanistan, Honduras, Guinea, Georgia, Nigeria, Gaza and North Korea. While the prosecutor's office has in recent years increased the public profile of those countries in this phase, there has been limited and uneven follow-up. One lesson is clear: the policies and actions of the prosecutor will be closely scrutinized and subject to criticism, both legitimate and unjustified.

The next prosecutor will face daunting challenges in carrying out the mandate. This mandate is qualitatively different from a national prosecutor's in several ways. The prosecutor must function on a highly politicized, often polarized stage.

The actions of the office are likely to intersect with concurrent military and political initiatives and thus be deemed counterproductive by some diplomats.

The prosecutor must therefore continually root the work in the core principles of criminal justice: impartial application of the law and independence from political influence. These principles are crucial to deflect charges of political motivation while maintaining the legitimacy of the office.

Working in Many Places at Once

Moreover, the court's broad geographic jurisdiction means the prosecutor must pursue work in a number of countries, often simultaneously, and in situations where conditions are insecure, which makes investigations difficult.

Additionally, unlike most national prosecutors, the court has no police force to carry out its orders. This means that the prosecutor must depend on the cooperation of countries, some of which may be complicit in the crimes charged, to apprehend suspects.

Given all these challenges, it is essential that the elements of deal making or regional rotation that are so prevalent in filling senior international positions be curbed. The Rome Statute spells out the criteria: The prosecutor must be a person of "high moral character, be highly competent in and have extensive practical experience in the prosecution or trial of criminal cases."

Some Measuring Sticks to Use

But beyond these broad pronouncements, the statute is silent on what other quality-based characteristics should take priority. We believe a relevant set of practical selection criteria should include the following:
- Demonstrated experience of professional excellence in complex criminal cases.
- The ability to conduct effective and efficient investigations by looking at the totality of the evidence to determine who are the most responsible for the most serious crimes in the court's jurisdiction.
- Demonstrated ability to act with independence and impartiality on a judicial mandate. This includes the ability to ground the work of the prosecutor's office in impartiality and independence from political influence with a long view of success rather than short-term.
- A record of professional excellence in institutional management. Related to this is a commitment and ability to develop a positive work environment for a large staff, based on professional respect and excellence, especially in a multicultural environment. The prosecutor ought to be able to attract and retain the most experienced staff and build not only the office but contribute to strengthening the court overall.
- Demonstrated experience in communicating effectively to varied constituencies. In making justice mean something in the communities most affected by the crimes it tries, the court is at a huge disadvantage because it is situated thousands of miles from where those crimes occurred. The next prosecutor should understand the importance of outreach, and should have a record of conveying complex information in a manageable format.

As political actors, governments do not naturally make this kind of selection on the basis of qualification and principle alone. But here it is an imperative. The nations that created the International Criminal Court to end impunity for the most grievous crimes have a chance to select one of the court's key stewards based on merit. It would be a huge loss if they failed to do this. ■

UN Photo/Ryan Brown

Luis Moreno-Ocampo, the International Criminal Court prosecutor, speaks to reporters after briefing the UN Security Council in December 2010 on the war crimes case against Sudan's president, Omar Hassan al-Bashir, who remains at large and in office.

70 Years of Evolution in Prosecuting War Crimes
Dan Plesch and Shanti Sattler

The year 2011 has seen the war-crimes arrest or conviction of the Nazi John Demjanjujk, the Serbian Gen. Ratko Mladic and the Rwandan Hutu leader Bernard Munyagishari, as well as charges of crimes against humanity brought against members of the Libyan government.

Nevertheless, the optimum means of prosecuting war crimes, genocide and crimes against humanity continues to be controversial. Critics point to the length, cost and remoteness of modern legal processes. They also cite the nearly insurmountable difficulty of prosecuting nationals of major world powers, particularly the five permanent members of the Security Council—Britain, China, France, Russia and the United States.

An assessment of war crimes practice can draw on decades of experience, back to the Nuremberg Trials after World War II. As the 70th anniversary of the establishment of the United Nations War Crimes Commission approaches in 2013, there is an opportunity to reflect on the development of international criminal law. Between the closure of the 17-nation War Crimes Commission in 1948 and the tribunals begun after the end of the cold war, the UN was unable to act and the commission was forgotten.

Structural and procedural changes have unfolded in the nearly 70 years of international efforts to facilitate justice processes. Since 1990 the UN has overseen establishment of ad-hoc international criminal tribunals to consider atrocities committed in the former Yugoslavia, Rwanda, Sierra Leone, Cambodia and Lebanon.

Another Major Shift May Be Ahead

Today it is likely the international community sits on the brink of another significant shift in handling war crimes. The UN is expected to phase out all of its ad-hoc tribunals by 2015, leaving future trials to the International Criminal Court. While that court is legally and functionally independent of the UN, its governing statute gives certain powers to the Security Council and an agreement defines an interdependent relationship between the two.

While each is separate in mandate and scope, the International Criminal Tribunal for the former Yugoslavia, the International Criminal Tribunal for Rwanda, the Special Court for Sierra Leone, the Extraordinary Chambers in the Courts of Cambodia and the Special Tribunal for Lebanon share criticism for limitations. These arise from a collision of the theory of international criminal law with the realities of its application through the UN tribunals. Key problems of the ad hoc tribunals are also apparent in the work of the International Criminal Court.

Long periods of operation, exorbitant costs and general detachment from the populations affected by a conflict are three primary points of controversy.

Exactly how much the international community has spent on international criminal courts since 1993 is remarkable, especially when measured against the relatively low costs of domestic prosecutions. By the time most of the existing tribunals are expected to close by the end of 2015, the international community will have spent nearly $6.3 billion. The tribunal for the former Yugoslavia alone will cost $2.3 billion over its lifetime and the Rwanda tribunal $1.75 billion. The hybrid tribunals for Cambodia, Sierra Leone and Lebanon may come in at lesser, but still significant sums. The cost of the Cambodia court is estimated to total $338 million, the Sierra Leone court upwards of $250 million and the Lebanon tribunal $172.5 million.

Long Proceedings, High Costs

The high costs are directly related to their lengthy operations. The tribunal for the former Yugoslavia is expected to take the longest time and run, through 2014, to 21 years of operation. The Rwanda tribunal is expected to finish in 2012 after 17

Courtesy of Extraordinary Chambers in the Courts of Cambodia

A UN-backed tribunal set up in Cambodia has completed just one trial, convicting Kaing Guek Eav, also known as Duch, for his role in sending 14,000 people to their deaths at the Tuol Sleng prison where he was jailer under Khmer Rouge rule in the 1970s.

Chasing War Crimes While Changing the Lineup **167**

years. The conclusion date for the Sierra Leone court is estimated to be 2012 at the earliest, after more than 10 years. The Cambodia court will likely close in 2015 after nine years and the Lebanon tribunal also in 2015 after six.

The extraordinary time and money these tribunals cost raise questions about the value of justice and what these tribunals accomplish for conflict survivors and the international community. Such questions link to the difficulty of carrying out international standards and practices of justice in the context of primarily civil conflicts in developing countries.

The tribunals for the former Yugoslavia, Rwanda and Lebanon, for example, operate far from the locations of the crimes under investigation and the homes of the victims. Officials cite concerns about safety and political instability in these areas as the reasons for placing courtrooms far away. Programs led by the courts attempt to inform affected populations about their proceedings but meet with varying degrees of success. Additionally, all of the tribunals bring unfamiliar concepts of Western-influenced international justice to countries accustomed to community-level adjudication practices, such as Gacaca in Rwanda and Somroh-somreul in Cambodia.

Looking Back, Planning for the Future

History shows that changes occur in the nature of global conflict, and also in the structure and scope of the UN-promoted international justice initiatives. The UN tribunals have themselves continually evolved.

In the shift now under way, the International Criminal Court, which came into being less than a decade ago, is expected to take on all future trials for extraordinary war crimes, meaning that ad-hoc tribunals will no longer be utilized.

This new shift will do little to address the fundamental questions raised about the special tribunals. The International Criminal Court formalizes concepts of modern international rule of law and global accountability and adds legitimacy to the notion of universal standards of justice. However, the proceedings require a great deal of time and financial support and the delivery of justice ultimately takes place far from the locations of the crimes under investigation.

The UN remains in the early stages of establishing itself as the global facilitator of justice. What exactly the UN ad hoc war crimes tribunals and the International Criminal Court have accomplished is widely debated. With these points in mind, it is critical to acknowledge the challenges as international justice and international criminal law evolve and develop.

A look back 70 years to the operations of the War Crimes Commission reveals stark contrasts. For example, the earlier trials were often conducted close to the crime sites and typically lasted a few days.

In contrast to 21st century practice, during World War II, the then 32 nations of the UN alliance declared in 1943 that accused war criminals would face trials in the countries where the crimes were committed. Subsequently, trials were held by 17 nations supported by the War Crimes Commission in London. The legitimacy and impact of the processes of the 1940s would have been significantly less had the trials all taken place in The Hague, New York or London. Prompt access to justice is an important principle and much might be gained by conducting trials on-site, as was the World War II practice.

Case Files Hidden Away

Sadly, the effective closure to public scrutiny of the tens of thousands of case files and debates on the development of international criminal law, now in the files of the War Crimes Commission at the UN in New York, denies us a potentially valuable resource. To give one illustration, the commission determined that environmental destruction amounted to an international crime. This could serve as a useful precedent in our own time, when such actions are again being debated, but details of the original determination remain inaccessible.

Given the diverse cultures involved today, perhaps more respect in practice needs to be given to local legal custom, especially where it has both broad support and yet appears incompatible with international standards. These standards are set in the foundations laid by the War Crimes Commission and the Nuremberg and Tokyo tribunals, in large part because they proved to provide much more than victor's justice. Twenty-first century prosecutions need to strengthen this key element of legitimacy. The problem remains that the international community appears to prosecute only the vanquished and leaders of weak states out of favor with the West.

The peoples of the nations that have developed international criminal law have much to be proud of in achieving so much in the face of huge obstacles. In improving its effectiveness in the 21st century, there remain important lessons to be learned from the formative years in World War II. ■

APPROXIMATE COST PER INDICTMENT OF EACH TRIBUNAL TO DATE

Former Yugoslavia	$11,800,000
Rwanda	$16,300,000
Sierra Leone	$12,500,000
Cambodia	$28,400,000
Int'l Criminal Court	$35,870,000

Sources:
Ford, Stuart, "How Leadership in International Criminal Law is Shifting from the U.S. to Europe and Asia: An Analysis of Spending on and Contributions to International Criminal Courts" (Sept. 8, 2010). Saint Louis University Law Journal, 2010.

Data on numbers of indictments published by the respective tribunals.

UN Photo/ /Eskinder Debebe

Players from the Single Leg Amputee Sports Club face off in a match in Freetown, Sierra Leone. A UN-backed special court is trying those most responsible for atrocities during the country's 1991-2002 civil war, holding trials in both Sierra Leone and in The Hague.

Talking Points

1. In the coming elections of a new prosecutor and six new judges for the International Criminal Court, the court's member-nations can base their choices either on merit or on the more traditional regional and diplomatic considerations. What personal characteristics should the international community stress in its selections? Should the court consider lifetime appointment of its justices as the ultimate safeguard against outside influence?

2. A major criticism of the UN's international criminal tribunals is that they often operate in locations far from where the crimes occurred. People living where the crimes took place may not be aware of what these courts are doing and how they work, compared to local legal practices. Is it a good idea, then, for future war-crimes trials to be moved to the International Criminal Court in The Hague?

3. The Rome Statute, the International Criminal Court's governing treaty, now requires that judicial candidates be nominated to one of two "experience" lists—criminal law and international law. Given that many acts of genocide, war crimes or crimes against humanity are linked to armed conflict and enemy combatants, should individuals with experience in military law be offered similar official recognition?

4. Prosecution of international criminal law can be limited when it collides with countries' efforts to protect their own interests. How can the International Criminal Court strengthen its gathering of evidence and subpoena mechanisms while also respecting national sovereignty?

UN Environment Program Photo/Peter Prokosch

Polar bears do most of their hunting on sea ice, feeding almost exclusively on the ringed and bearded seals that live beneath the ice. Bears that find themselves trapped on land as the ice shelf retreats can face months of starvation.

Curtailing the Damage to Our Ailing Earth

174 At Climate Talks, Small Steps Add Up to Strides
Karen Freeman

183 Standing Up to a Tide of Garbage
Karen Freeman

185 Talking Points

At Climate Talks, Small Steps Add Up to Strides
Karen Freeman

The earth is getting warmer, and there's no new legally binding deal on carbon emissions on the horizon for this year's major United Nations conference on climate change. The Kyoto Protocol cannot carry the weight of what would be required to keep average temperatures below the level considered dangerous.

The big picture may sound grim, but many of the people at the UN's big annual climate meeting in Cancún, Mexico, late last year must have left with a spring in their step. "Measured against the years of stalemate that preceded it, Cancún was a major step forward," said Elliot Diringer, a vice president at the Pew Center on Global Climate Change, speaking in Mexico in March. "In fact, the Cancún Agreements represent the most tangible progress we've been able to achieve within the UN climate talks in nearly a decade."

Climate change diplomacy is turning a corner. The initial impetus came from the United States, which is pushing for placing some of the obligations of reducing emissions upon some of the biggest developing countries, not just on nations already industrialized. The Kyoto Protocol puts emissions requirements solely on the developed nations who signed up, and that's why the U.S. has never ratified it.

The Cancún Agreements make a nod in the direction of obliging fast-growing developing nations to make commitments to limit their emissions of greenhouse gases. The U.S. makes no secret of its agenda to push for such commitments, and that is expected to provoke heated discussions at this year's UN climate conference, to be held from Nov. 28 to Dec. 9 in Durban, South Africa.

Some Expectations for Durban

Some other things that can be expected at Durban and the preparatory sessions leading up to it include:
- A focus by the U.S. on political agreements, rather than treaties.
- Proposals for the future of the Kyoto Protocol after its first pledge period expires next year. It's already clear that fewer developed nations will be part of the protocol's future.
- Debates over consensus decisions—are they a good idea, and what constitutes a consensus?
- Work on "fast-track" financing and the Green Climate Fund, two big new financing mechanisms to help developing countries combat global warming.

Before, during and after Durban, there will be more maneuvering over the responsibilities of the industrialized countries and of developing countries that are rapidly industrializing. At issue are climate mitigation efforts, which aim to reduce emissions of greenhouse gases, and climate adaptation work, which seeks ways for areas or regions to manage the consequences of climate change.

Todd Stern, the chief U.S. negotiator on climate issues, explained the American position this way after the Cancún conference: "We do not believe in the 'old world' kind of old paradigm, where all obligations go to developed countries and none to even the major developing countries. And it's for a simple reason. I mean 55 percent of global emissions are already coming from the developing world. In the next 20 years, that's going to go up to 65 percent. All the growth in emissions is coming from the developing world."

The U.S. would like to see fast-developing nations agree to a lid on emissions growth as they became wealthier. Countries that are already industrialized would continue to shoulder the burden of cuts in their current levels. When a growing country like China or India "is growing at 6, 8, 10 percent, you can't slam the brakes on completely and say you've got to be making absolute reductions tomorrow," Stern said in Cancún. "It couldn't work."

What is not likely to happen in Durban is a new legally binding agreement. In April, both Stern and Connie Hedegaard, the climate action commissioner for the European Union, predicted this would not occur.

UN Environment Program Photo/Lawrence Hislop

Icebergs near Greenland. Warmer temperatures in the Northern Hemisphere, part of climate change around the globe, are making the ice melt faster, contributing to rising sea levels.

Curtailing the Damage to Our Ailing Earth **175**

A Softer Approach
The UN climate process has been difficult to change because technically it is rooted in legally binding treaties: the UN Framework Convention on Climate Change, a treaty adopted in 1992, and its Kyoto Protocol, dating from 1997. Climate negotiations have had more success recently in the softer legal realm of political agreements, rather than with legally binding deals. That approach has led to such major new initiatives as the Green Climate Fund, a new entity under the UN framework convention that is supposed to mobilize $100 billion a year for climate initiatives by 2020.

From the U.S. point of view, focused political deals are welcome. Even international treaties that are called legally binding can be difficult to enforce—many Kyoto Protocol pledges have not been backed up—so the practical differences between them and political pacts may be few.

But negotiations for a political deal are easier and faster, without ratification requirements for each member nation. It's also harder for a few nations to block a political agreement. So political negotiations are proving a good vehicle for the U.S. to push for what it sees as a more equitable set of commitments obliging the fastest-growing developing countries to shoulder responsibilities.

The recent political deals on climate issues grew out of the Copenhagen Accord, a political agreement that President Obama was able to negotiate at the last minute at the 2009 climate change conference. The elements of that accord were then taken up at the 2010 conference in Cancún, which approved them in the Cancún Agreements. At the Durban conference in December, national delegations will work on how key points will be translated into work on the ground.

One crucial and contentious area will be the Green Climate Fund; another will be the mechanisms for enhanced international monitoring of some climate change actions, including even scrutiny of some developing countries. If the U.S. had been able to get what it wanted enshrined in a legally binding treaty in 2009, it would presumably have done that. But by working through a step-by-step process of successive political agreements, the U.S. is trying to nudge the process in the direction it wants.

A Deal That Broke New Ground
The Cancún Agreements are a good example of a political deal that broke new ground. At Cancún, the governments agreed for the first time to take steps to limit global warming to a maximum rise in average global temperature of 2 degrees Celsius (3.6 degrees Fahrenheit) above preindustrial levels, and they agreed to consider the even more stringent goal of 1.5 degrees C (2.7 degrees F) soon.

Political agreements offer a way around the difficulty of achieving legally binding deals among the adherents (nearly all of them countries) to the UN framework convention. But the UN is not finished with climate treaty questions: the clock is ticking for the Kyoto Protocol.

The pledges made by the Kyoto accord's 193 ratifiers will expire at the end of 2012 and not be replaced unless a new pledge period is ready to go into effect at that time. At a recent session in Bonn preparing for Durban, Christiana Figueres, the UN's climate chief, said she did not think there was enough time for countries to get a legally binding deal to keep Kyoto Protocol mandates in force without interruption because such a pact would have to be adopted and ratified by member nations. "We would assume that there is no time to do that between Durban and the end of 2012," she said. "So countries have realized this—that they actually stand before the potential of a regulatory gap."

The Kyoto accord countries would still have the option of continuing to honor their old pledges or deciding to honor their new ones even before the treaty changes go into effect. Perhaps a political deal may be seen as a stopgap solution, if the current divide between developed and developing nations over the distribution of responsibilities can be crossed.

A big problem for the Kyoto Protocol is that it requires no commitments from the top two emitters of carbon, the U.S. and China. The U.S. never ratified it, and China faces no mandates because of its status as a developing nation. If all current pledges for action were honored, the treaty would still not be able to meet the Cancún Agreements' goal of keeping temperatures to acceptable levels.

UN Environment Program Photo/Lawrence Hislop

The root systems of mangroves help stabilize the coastline in Bali, Indonesia. An archipelago of 17,000 islands, Indonesia is particularly vulnerable to rising sea levels or intense tropical storms linked to global warming.

Backing Away From Commitments

Developing nations enthusiastically support the Kyoto Protocol and want a second round of commitments by industrialized countries after the first expire, but some developed countries, including Japan, Canada and Russia, have already backed away from this. A new round of Kyoto pledges could also lose the support of the European Union, which has been a leader in reducing carbon emissions and in running an emissions trading setup that makes companies pay a price for carbon pollution. The European Union could abandon Kyoto if it does not require more major polluters to take action.

"I can't repeat often enough that it's simply not enough for the EU to simply sign up to a second commitment period," said Jurgen Lefevere, representing the European Commission, at the Bonn meeting on June 17. "We only represent around 11 percent of global emissions. ...We will need a solution for the remaining 89 percent as well."

So what does the European Union want? Lefevere says it seeks "significant progress towards an internationally legally binding agreement that brings the rest of the world's major emitters into a robust regime."

UN Environment Program Photo/Lawrence Hislop

Water sits on the surface of the sea ice near Uummannaq, in northwest Greenland, where the local Inuit population relies heavily on ice coverage for fishing and travel by traditional dog-sled.

But those emitters include countries that are industrializing quickly, such as India, and they look at equity in pollution-reduction requirements and come up with a different answer:

"India, along with other developing countries, has long demanded that all countries should have their atmospheric space allocated based on a per capita endowment," The Times of India contended in a recent article. "They have consistently pointed out that the emissions from the developed world occupy more than their fair share of carbon space in the atmosphere and should be reduced substantially to vacate space for growing economies."

Finding a Fair Yardstick

So are per-capita emissions a fair yardstick? Per-country? Historical emissions? How about carbon dioxide emissions per unit of wealth production? Questions of fairness—to individual countries, to groups of countries and to the planet itself—are fraught and likely to remain so.

Consensus decision-making will also be a sore issue at Durban (such sessions are called a Conference of the Parties to the framework convention) because the Cancún Agreements were adopted despite strong objections from one country, Bolivia, which is not ready to let the matter drop.

"We have had 16 Conferences of the Parties—16," said Pablo Solon, Bolivia's chief climate negotiator, on June 17. "And during those 16 C.O.P.s there were approved 278 decisions. And only one decision ... has been adopted with the objection of a party. During 16 years, only one decision out of those 278."

Mexico and Papua New Guinea are now proposing that some decisions be made by a 75 percent majority vote instead of consensus, but such a change, the UN climate chief, Figueres, pointed out, would have to be an amendment to the framework convention. And that would be "a tall order," she added.

In Search of Financing

A major task for climate negotiators this year will be to put meat on the bones of the Cancún Agreements by figuring out how to set up new financing mechanisms for climate mitigation and adaptation. First, the Cancún pact calls for industrialized countries to make available $30 billion in fast-start financing for the 2010-12 period to help developing nations deal with the effects of climate change and get ready for the projects expected under the more extensive Green Climate Fund.

The deadline for countries to report their fast-start commitments to the UN staff was in May. The World Resources Institute reported on May 20 that 21 developed nations and the European Union had already come close to the goal, committing nearly $28 billion. But some developed countries are already saying many of those resources do not represent new money or new aid programs, and that debate can be expected to continue in Durban.

In February, officials of four developing countries with carbon emissions in the top 20 worldwide—Brazil, South Africa, India and China, called the BASIC group—met in India and criticized the slow release of the fast-start money. The delay is "a betrayal of a grand bargain at Copenhagen," said Jairam Ramesh, India's environment minister. Continued foot-dragging could make the atmosphere at Durban "clouded by doubts and suspicion," he added.

Since it was the BASIC countries that were at the table with President Obama in the negotiations that led to the Copenhagen Agreement, their opinions on the Green Climate Fund are likely to be significant. China's chief climate negotiator, Su Wei, was quoted on Xinhua's English Web site on June 18 as having doubts about another aspect of the fast-start program.

"Some fast-start funds listed by rich countries are not 'new and additional financial aid' as required in Copenhagen, some of which are double-counted," Su said. He also worried that developing nations might be expected to pick up some of the cost of the Green Climate Fund programs. China's priority at Durban, he said, will continue to be a binding treaty to succeed the Kyoto Protocol's first pledge period. That would no doubt keep China from facing any requirements other than voluntary emission restraints.

Management Largely Outside the UN

While the framework convention conference at Cancún voted to set up the Green Climate Fund, its management will be largely independent of the UN. The fund will report to the members of the framework convention but will have an independent board—with half of its members from developing nations and half from developed countries—and an independent support staff. It also will have a trustee, initially the World Bank, to keep an eye on its finances.

"The U.S. is quite keen to have it set up in a professional way," Stern, the chief U.S. negotiator, said at a May 25 hearing before the House Foreign Affairs Subcommittee on Oversight and Investigations, "outside the control of the [framework convention], outside the control of climate negotiators—even though I am one."

The framework convention still has a strong link to the climate fund. The fund is being set up under the Cancún Agreements, a product of a framework convention meeting. A transitional committee appointed by the convention members is working on operating guidelines for the climate fund and is supposed to present them for approval in Durban. Stern estimated that it might take the rest of this year and next to finish setting up the fund and get it working.

Developed countries in the Green Climate Fund are to mobilize $100 billion per year by 2020 to help developing countries. That money can flow through bilateral or multilateral arrangements among nations, and it can come from public or private sources. "Some of that will run through the Green Fund, and some won't," Stern said, adding, "Maybe you would have $10 billion or $20 billion or whatever going through the Green Fund."

Pragmatic Appeal

Much of what Stern had to say at the subcommittee hearing seemed aimed at political considerations and public opinion. The panel is led by Representative Dana Rohrabacher, a California Republican who says global warming is a natural phenomenon and is not caused by human activity.

So Stern made his case for support of U.S. climate policy by appealing to Rohrabacher's pragmatism. "An enormous number of countries are extremely concerned about climate change, see it as a high priority," he said. "If the United States were not engaged—apart from climate change itself, which is in and of itself very important—it would hurt us. It would hurt us diplomatically; it would hurt us in terms of the leverage that we have in the world on a raft of issues. So it matters that we are seen to be engaged and trying to be part of the solution."

Rohrabacher is also concerned that a global climate treaty would decrease the standard of living for millions of people around the world because of the costs of reducing emissions in industry and transportation, and Stern addressed that issue as well. "We do not think that you can approach this problem from the point of view of saying that you're going to clamp down on anybody's standard of living—not a developed country, not a developing country, not the United States, not India," he said. While it will take time, he continued, the only way to solve this problem will be to "break the iron link between the growth of an economy and the growth of emissions."

Many Americans are skeptical about climate change. In a survey taken in May by George Mason University and Yale University, 64 percent said they believed global warming was occurring, compared with 71 percent in November 2008. A little more than half of those surveyed said they were extremely or very sure of their positions—regardless of whether they accepted global warming or not.

Working Against Harder Views

This hardening in American attitudes cannot make it easy for U.S. diplomats working on global warming, and the information reaching the public may contribute to the lack of clarity. For example, one leading climate researcher, Dr. Phil Jones of East Anglia University, said in 2010 that no statistically significant warming had occurred since 1995, only to say this year that warming is now considered significant.

The reason for the different statements, Jones later explained, was that he was asked in 2010 about too short a time span.

"Achieving statistical significance for a trend based on only 15 years is difficult because of the large year-to-year variability in global-mean temperatures," he explained by e-mail. "It is much more climatically reasonable to use longer periods." So the question in 2010 seemed simple, but there wasn't a simple answer.

Solving climate change puzzles is difficult because studying vast areas over long periods of time is inherently difficult. So it is not hard for those who deny global warming to find individual studies that uphold their views. Many are corporate or political figures who may be motivated by economic or political gain. But others are dubious because the data do not always point in the same direction, particularly over short time spans.

For example, when Frank Hill of the U.S. National Solar Observatory and other scientists recently reported that the sun might be going into a relatively quiescent period, many anti-climate change Web sites and blogs interpreted the study as indicating that a little ice age might be approaching.

But Hill disagreed with that interpretation. "It is a huge leap to an abrupt global cooling, since the connections between solar activity and climate are still very poorly understood," he said.

Nonetheless, it is plausible that less solar activity could lead to a temporarily cooler earth. And any cooling could well churn up the global warming debate, complicating the international negotiations.

Feeding Skepticism

Many of those in the skeptic camp seem to distrust the UN as well as the data supporting climate change. That kind of skepticism is fed by such matters as last year's investigation of the Intergovernmental Panel on Climate Change, the UN body that shepherds the writing of scientific reports used by those involved with the issue. The inquiry was prompted by errors in content or procedures of the panel's 2007 assessment report. So the UN asked an organization of scientific academies, the InterAcademy Council, to take a look.

"Those errors did dent the credibility of the process, no question about it," said Harold T. Shapiro, president emeritus and a professor of economics and public affairs at Princeton University, who chaired the committee that reported the InterAcademy Council's findings.

In a speech in Mexico City in March, the Pew Center's Diringer said the UN climate change process may have jumped ahead too quickly at the beginning, without taking the time for the kind of incremental change that he says is a characteristic of many successful multilateral structures. The UN framework convention came in 1992; by 1995, negotiators were looking at legally binding requirements for emissions controls, which were approved when the Kyoto Protocol was adopted in 1997.

"This represented not an evolution, but a radical step-change, moving in one big leap from a largely voluntary framework to a legally binding system of targets and timetables," Diringer said.

Whatever the reasons for Americans' hesitancy on climate initiatives, "without stronger consensus for action at home, the United States cannot commit abroad —and that will take time," Diringer said. "But even apart from the situation in the U.S., the reality is that few if any of the developed countries will take new binding commitments unless China and the other major emerging economies do as well, which they insist they will not. This is the circular conundrum we've been stuck in, literally, for years."

At the end of the recent meeting in Bonn to prepare for Durban, UN climate chief Figueres, looking more tired than she had when the meeting opened, had a straightforward explanation when asked about the slow pace of progress: "If you're in this business, you need to understand that climate is the most important negotiation the world has ever faced. You also need to understand that governments, business and civil society cannot solve climate with one meeting, one agreement." ■

Standing Up to a Tide of Garbage
Karen Freeman

In 1784, a shipwrecked Japanese sailor in the Pacific carved the tale of his disaster into slivers of wood and sealed them into a glass bottle that he cast into the waves. In 1935, the bottle bobbed up near his home village in Japan, its message intact.

Such tales demonstrate that well-sealed buoyant items tossed into the seas can have a long life indeed. But today the vast majority of the trash cast off by societies all over the world, synthetic and buoyant, is both durable and unwelcome when it reaches the oceans. Scientists and environmentalists have gotten the message: it's time to stanch this flood of garbage into the seas and start thinking of ways to clean up what's there.

That was the focus of a conference this spring organized by the United Nations Environment Program and the National Oceanic and Atmospheric Administration, part of the United States Department of Commerce. Representatives from 38 countries attended the gathering, in Honolulu. The UN program and the U.S. agency planned the meeting, the Fifth International Marine Debris Conference, to reach out and build ties among the experts, governments and industries that are involved in the problem.

The conference goal was explained by the UN Environment Program's executive director, Achim Steiner, in a message to delegates: "Marine debris—trash in our oceans—is a symptom of our throw-away society. However, one community or one country acting in isolation will not be the answer. We need to address marine debris collectively across national boundaries and with the private sector."

Working on It at Many Levels

The Honolulu Commitment, which was adopted by the conference, offers a blueprint for such efforts. Through a global network, said Kris McElwee, the Pacific Islands coordinator for the National Oceanic and Atmospheric Administration's Marine Debris Program, "people of all levels, all geographic areas, all capabilities, can do appropriate action and see real outcomes.... People can pick out one string they're going to work on, and then people will report up on a local, regional and global scale."

The Honolulu meeting got substantial cooperation from the private sector, with the American Chemistry Council, PlasticsEurope and Coca-Cola acting as major sponsors.

Plastics are a big part of the problem, but just how big is not known. Oceans cover 70 percent of the earth's surface, and much of that area is unexplored. Plastics slowly break up into tiny pieces in the ocean, and those small pieces are hard to see and study. "One coffee cup lid can make thousands of little pieces," McElwee said. Many pieces can float below the water's surface, and others sink into the water columns or down to the seabed.

So though the term "garbage patch" has been widely publicized, especially to describe debris in the North Pacific, the National Oceanic and Atmospheric Administration says there is no large blanket of seaborne trash visible by satellite or aerial photograph. And while winds and currents can whip together moving spots of surface debris, even experts like McElwee can find visible signs of the pollution elusive.

"The name makes you think you could walk on it, which of course is not true," McElwee said. "I have done one cruise and two overflights and have seen remarkably little debris."

Perhaps an affected area is more a garbage broth or soup than a patch, she suggested; if a ship trawls long enough while taking samples, it will find some pieces of plastic.

To get a clear idea of the scale of the ocean garbage, you can look at the desecrated beaches. Some in Hawaii seem to act as magnets for plastic.

Measuring the Impact Is Tricky

It's hard to gauge the impact of plastics on the animals and plants in the marine environment. A photo of an albatross carcass will reveal small pieces of plastic jammed throughout its digestive system, but that in itself does not prove that the plastic killed the bird. Scientists just don't know how many die prematurely because they ate the pieces of plastic, which look like food.

While it is clear that garbage does not belong in the marine environment, much of the work on the Honolulu Commitment will be done without all the data the experts prefer. Not that people haven't tried to get good data for hundreds of centuries: the ancient Greeks, for example, threw bottles into the sea to learn about currents. Now that modern bottles, like the plastics used for soda, water and shampoo, are washing into the oceans in great numbers, scientists are trying to assess the problem. But the vast reach of the oceans and the unavailability of financing make research progress slow.

One good thing about the problem, McElwee says, is that people and groups around the globe can work on it at a variety of levels, even before research gathers more information. It will take governments, businesses and advocacy groups to tackle the big tasks, like keeping fishing nets and gear from being discarded overboard, and finding new ways to keep plastics and other discards from being washed away in the tide. But individuals can play an important role by keeping the amount of garbage they generate to a minimum, and small groups can clean beaches and encourage others to recycle. There will be plenty of knots to free before the marine debris problem is untangled.

[*A version of this article appeared in The InterDependent, a UNA-USA publication (www.theinterdependent.com), on May 19, 2011*] ■

Talking Points

1. Developed nations are big polluters because their standards of living are largely powered by carbon-based energy; developing nations have significantly increased their emissions as they industrialize, too, arguing that they should be granted the same opportunities for economic growth as the rich countries. How, if at all, should the burden of carbon reduction be divided? Can a successfully binding international carbon reduction treaty, with its potential economic impact, be introduced when developed nations are hurting financially?

2. Fast-start funds—financing mechanisms provided by the developed world to help developing nations deal with the effects of climate change in their country—are currently a sticking point in climate negotiations. Should the developed world have to reduce its emissions and pay for climate remedies in the developing world while emerging economies receive funding without making binding commitments of their own?

3. Another big obstacle to achieving consensus on a new international climate change framework is the hardening attitudes of both doubters and believers in global warming, making domestic support by national governments for "green" initiatives difficult. Can the UN continue to be a major player in garnering public support by advancing the science of climate change, especially given past controversies surrounding the UN Intergovernmental Panel on Climate Change?

4. If major progress on the marine debris problem can be made on the individual, local, state and national levels, is this issue important enough to be taken up by the international community? If so, what role can the UN play in bringing together all parties to reduce pollution of global waters?

UN Photo/Amjad Jamal

Pakistanis affected by widespread flooding get wheat flour and other provisions from the World Food Program in Alipur, Punjab Province, in August 2010.

Appendices

188 Appendix A: Important Dates in United Nations History

192 Appendix B: The UN System

193 Appendix C: Composition of the Secretariat
Compiled by Simon Minching

194 Appendix D: Operations and Budgets
Compiled by Simon Minching

206 Appendix E: Acronyms and Abbreviations

215 Appendix F: Glossary

230 Appendix G: Nobel Prizes

232 Appendix H: Top Contributors of Peacekeeping Funding
Compiled by Simon Minching

233 Appendix I: Top Contributors of Uniformed Personnel
Compiled by Simon Minching

234 Appendix J: Global Summary of the HIV/AIDS Pandemic
Compiled by Simon Minching

236 Appendix K: Millennium Development Goals and Targets

Appendix A: Important Dates in United Nations History

June 12, 1941 Inter-Allied Declaration signed in London, encouraging free people to work together in war and peace.

Jan. 1, 1942 Representatives of 26 Allied nations meet in Washington to sign Declaration of United Nations, in which U.S. President Roosevelt coins the term "United Nations."

Sept. 21-Oct. 7, 1944 U.S., Soviet Union, Britain and China agree on basic blueprint for a world organization at Dumbarton Oaks mansion near Washington.

Feb. 11, 1945 Roosevelt, Churchill and Stalin meet in Ukraine, resolving to establish "a general international organization to maintain peace and security."

June 25, 1945 United Nations Charter unanimously adopted by delegations of 50 nations in San Francisco.

Oct. 24, 1945 The five permanent members of the Security Council and a majority of other signers ratify Charter, creating the UN we know today.

Feb. 1, 1946 Trygve Lie of Norway becomes first secretary-general of United Nations.

Jan. 17, 1946 Security Council, in London, holds first meeting, establishing its procedural rules.

Jan. 24, 1946 General Assembly adopts first resolution, focused on peaceful uses of atomic energy and abolition of weapons of mass destruction.

Dec. 1946 United Nations International Children's Emergency Fund created to provide food, clothing and health care to children suffering famine and disease. Name is later changed to UN Children's Fund but acronym remains Unicef.

Dec. 10, 1948 General Assembly adopts Universal Declaration of Human Rights.

Aug. 21, 1950 Secretariat workers move into offices in the new headquarters complex in New York. Campus eventually comprises Secretariat, General Assembly, Conference Area and Library.

1954 Office of UN High Commissioner for Refugees wins first of two Nobel Peace Prizes, for European work.

Aug. 30, 1955 First United Nations Congress on the Prevention of Crime and the Treatment of Offenders adopts standard minimum rules for treatment of prisoners.

Nov. 7, 1956 General Assembly holds first emergency special session in Suez Canal crisis. Two days before, it established first UN peacekeeping force, called the UN Emergency Force.

Nov. 20, 1959 General Assembly adopts Declaration of the Rights of the Child.

Sept. 1960 Seventeen newly independent states, all but one in Africa, join UN. It marks biggest increase in membership in a single year.

Sept. 18, 1961 Secretary-General Dag Hammarskjöld dies in plane crash on mission to the Congo. U Thant, Burmese diplomat, named to succeed him.

Dec. 21, 1965 General Assembly adopts International Covenant on Social, Economic and Cultural Rights along with counterpart, International Covenant on Civil and Political Rights.

Nov. 22, 1967 After Six-Day War in the Middle East, Security Council adopts Resolution 242, stipulating requirements for end of hostilities.

June 12, 1968 General Assembly approves Treaty on Non-proliferation of Nuclear Weapons.

Jan. 4, 1969 International Convention on the Elimination of All Forms of Racial Discrimination goes into effect.

Oct. 21, 1971 General Assembly admits representative from People's Republic of China, displacing Republic of China on Taiwan.

June 1972 First UN Environment Conference held in Stockholm, bringing establishment of the UN Environment Program.

Nov. 13, 1974 General Assembly recognizes Palestine Liberation Organization as "the sole legitimate representative of the Palestinian people."

Nov. 5-16, 1974 UN conducts conference in Rome on food and agriculture, declaring freedom from hunger as a universal human right.

June-July 1975 UN holds first conference on women, in Mexico City, coinciding with International Women's Year.

May-June 1978 General Assembly holds first special session on disarmament.

May 8, 1980 World Health Organization declares smallpox eliminated.

1981 UN High Commissioner for Refugees receives second Nobel Peace Prize, this for work with Asians.

Nov. 25, 1981 General Assembly adopts Declaration on the Elimination of All Forms of Intolerance and Discrimination Based on Religion or Belief.

Dec. 10, 1982 A hundred and seventeen states and two entities sign UN Convention on the Law of the Sea, largest number of signatures affixed to a treaty in one day.

Dec. 10, 1984 Convention Against Torture and Other Cruel, Inhuman or Degrading Treatment or Punishment adopted by General Assembly.

Sept. 1987 Treaty on Protection of the Ozone Layer, also known as Montreal Protocol, signed.

1988 UN Peacekeeping receives Nobel Peace Prize.

Sept. 2, 1990 Convention on Rights of the Child enters into effect.

April 1991 UN Iraq-Kuwait Observation Mission established to carry out elimination of weapons of mass destruction in Iraq after the Gulf War.

Jan. 31, 1992 Leaders from all 15 members of the Security Council attend first Security Council Summit in New York. The meeting leads to Secretary-General Boutros Boutros-Ghali's report, "An Agenda for Peace."

June 1992 Rio de Janeiro is host to more than 100 countries at the UN Conference on Environment and Development, popularly known as the Earth Summit. Recognition of the importance of sustainable development is major outcome.

Feb. 22, 1993 Security Council establishes first international tribunal to examine human rights violations in the former Yugoslavia.

April 5, 1994 José Ayala-Lasso of Ecuador becomes first UN High Commissioner for Human Rights.

May 6, 1994 Secretary-General Boutros Boutros-Ghali issues Agenda for Development plan to improve human condition.

Nov. 8, 1994 Security Council establishes second international tribunal to investigate Rwandan genocide.

March 1995 World Summit for Social Development held in Copenhagen seeking new commitment to combat poverty, unemployment and social exclusion.

June 1996 Second UN Conference on Human Settlements convenes in Turkey.

Sept. 10, 1996 General Assembly adopts Comprehensive Test-Ban Treaty. It remains to be entered into force.

July 18, 1998 International Criminal Court is established by Rome Statute.

March 1, 1999 Ottawa Convention on antipersonnel mines enters into force.

Sept. 2000 General Assembly adopts Millennium Declaration starting the clock for eight Millennium Development Goals to reduce worldwide poverty by 2015.

Nov. 12, 2001 Security Council adopts Resolution 1377, calling on all nations to intensify their efforts to eliminate "the scourge of international terrorism" in the aftermath of the Sept. 11 terrorist attacks in the U.S.

July 1, 2002 Rome Statue enters into force, and the International Criminal Court begins work.

Aug. 19, 2003 Twenty-two staff members and officials, including Ambassador Sergio Vieira de Mello, killed in a terrorist attack on UN headquarters in Iraq.

Sept. 2005 Secretary-General Kofi Annan presents his report, "In Larger Freedom: Toward Security, Development and Human Rights for All," to a special session of the General Assembly, where member nations discuss significant reform of UN.

Feb. 27, 2006 The 50th session of the Commission on the Status of Women convenes to review the progress and chart new goals.

Jan. 1, 2007 Ban Ki-moon of South Korea succeeds Kofi Annan as the eighth Secretary-General. He is later elected to a second term beginning in 2012.

Sept. 24, 2007 The Future in Our Hands, called to discuss leadership issues relating to climate change, brings together representatives of more than 150 member states.

Jan.1, 2008 UN establishes Joint United Nations/African Union Mission in Darfur to assume peacekeeping responsibility for the war-torn region from the African Union.

May 30, 2008 Convention on Cluster Munitions, first agreement to seek a ban on a particular class of weapons worldwide, is adopted by 107 nations.

Jan. 9, 2011 Southern Sudanese begin voting in an independence referendum held under a 2005 UN-mediated peace deal ending a long civil war. A total of 98.8 percent of voters choose to secede from the north.

March 1, 2011 The General Assembly unanimously suspends Libya's membership in the UN Human Rights Council after forces loyal to Libyan leader Muammar el-Qaddafi launch violent attacks on protesters.

March 17, 2011 The Security Council votes to authorize a no-fly zone over Libya and "all necessary measures" to protect civilians from Libyan government forces, representing a significant affirmation of the Responsibility to Protect doctrine.

March 30, 2011 The Security Council calls on UN forces in Ivory Coast to "use all necessary means" to protect civilians as incumbent leader Laurent Gbagbo resists international demands to cede the presidency following November elections won by challenger Alassane Ouattara. Supported by UN and French peacekeepers, forces loyal to Ouattara seize Gbagbo 12 days later, clearing the way for Ouattara to take office.

June 17, 2011 The UN Human Rights Council adopts a resolution condemning discrimination on the basis of sexual orientation. The nonbinding resolution, approved 23-19, provides a formal process to document human rights abuses against gays and lesbians.

Sources: www.unhchr.ch/chrono.htm
www.un.org/issues/gallery/history/index.html www.un.org/Overview/milesto4.htm
UNA-USA e-news updates www.unausa.org/newsletter

Appendix B: The United Nations System Today

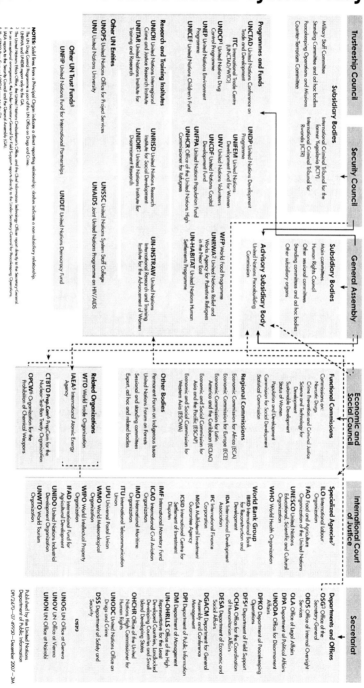

192 A Global Agenda 2011-2012

Appendix C: Composition of the Secretariat
Compiled by Simon Minching

These figures cover the period from July 1, 2009 to June 30, 2010, unless otherwise noted.

The 44,134 worldwide total of staff members in the Secretariat is based as follows:
    15,588 in departments and offices
    2,704 at regional commissions
    23,993 in peacekeeping missions
    1,849 in tribunals

As of June 30, 2010, they held posts at these levels:

Total, under secretaries-general and assistant secretaries-general:	128 (0.3%)
Total, interpreter/reviser/translator category:	754 (1.7%)
Total, field service category:	4,438 (10.1%)
Total, professional category:	10,598 (24.0%)
Total, general service and related category:	27,537 (62.4%)

As of June 30, 2010, the distribution of staff in professional or higher posts:

Post Level	Quantity in Post
Interpreter/Reviser/Translator	754
Professional 1 or 2	1,790
Professional 3	3,833
Professional 4	3,427
Professional 5	1,548
Director 1	510
Director 2	169
Assistant secretary-general	67
Under secretary-general	61

Gender breakdown, professional level and higher:

Post Level	Male Quantity / (%)	Female Quantity / (%)
INT/R/T	347 / 46.0%	407 / 54.0%
P-1/2	828 / 46.4%	962 / 53.7%
P-3	2,231 / 58.2%	1,602 / 41.8%
P-4	2,182 / 63.7%	1,245 / 36.3%
P-5	1,084 / 70.0%	464 / 30.0%
D-1	373 / 73.1%	137 / 26.9%
D-2	129 / 76.3%	40 / 23.7%
ASG	52 / 77.6%	15 / 22.4%
USG	47 / 77.0%	14 / 23.0%

Note: Nationals of 180 countries are represented among the Secretariat staff in posts subject to geographical distribution. There are more than 1,000 nationals in the Secretariat from each of the following countries: Afghanistan, France, Haiti, Kenya, Lebanon, Liberia, Sudan and the United States.

Source: General Assembly document, A/65/360, Sept. 8, 2010.

Appendix D: Operations & Budgets

Compiled by Simon Minching

*United Nations spending is comprised largely of three parts: (1) the regular budget, which is funded through dues paid by UN member nations according to a scale based roughly on the size of their economies; (2) extrabudgetary expenditures, or spending by particular UN agencies (such as the UN Children's Fund Unicef, the World Health Organization and the UN Development Program) financed through additional voluntary contributions by governments, the private sector and individuals; and (3) a separate peacekeeping budget in support of missions of the Department of Peacekeeping Operations, funded via a different scale of member assessments than that of the regular budget. What follows is a brief analysis of each of the three major types of UN spending and their major funding sources.

TABLE 1: REGULAR BUDGET APPROPRIATIONS FOR 2010-2011 biennium, and preliminary estimates for the 2012-2013 biennium (all figures in US$ and rounded to the nearest $100,000; the total does not include extrabudgetary expenditures).

Regular Budget Expenditures:

Part I: Overall Policy Making, Direction and Coordination

    2010-2011 Biennium Appropriation: **$777.6 million**
    2012-2013 Proposal: **$783.2 million (+0.7%)**

Part II: Political Affairs (not including special political missions)

    2010-2011 Biennium Appropriation: **$248.4 million**
    2012-2013 Proposal: **$251.0 million (+1.0%)**

Part III: International Justice and Law

    2010-2011 Biennium Appropriation: **$96.9 million**
    2012-2013 Proposal: **$97.7 million (+1.0%)**

Part IV: International Cooperation for Development

    2010-2011 Biennium Appropriation: **$434.3 million**
    2012-2013 Proposal: **$437.4 million (+0.7%)**

Part V: Regional cooperation for development

    2010-2011 Biennium Appropriation: **$526.5 million**
    2012-2013 Proposal: **$530.0 million (+0.7%)**

Part VI: Human rights and humanitarian affairs

    2010-2011 Biennium Appropriation: **$301.9 million**
    2012-2013 Proposal: **$308.0 million (+2.0%)**

Part VII: Public Information

    2010-2011 Biennium Appropriation: **$186.7 million**
    2012-2013 Proposal: **$186.2 million (-0.3%)**

Part VIII: Common support services

    2010-2011 Biennium Appropriation: **$580.5 million**
    2012-2013 Proposal: **$599.2 million (+3.2%)**

Part IX: Internal oversight

    2010-2011 Biennium Appropriation: **$39.4 million**
    2012-2013 Proposal: **$39.5 million (+0.3%)**

Part X: Jointly financed administrative activities and special expenses

    2010-2011 Biennium Appropriation: **$125.2 million**
    2012-2013 Proposal: **$125.2 million (unchanged)**

Part XI: Capital Expenditures

    2010-2011 Biennium Appropriation: **$61.3 million**
    2012-2013 Proposal: **$67.1 million (+9.5%)**

Part XII: Safety and Security

    2010-2011 Biennium Appropriation: **$239.3 million**
    2012-2013 Proposal: **$241.6 million (+1.0%)**

Part XIII: Development Account

    2010-2011 Biennium Appropriation: **$23.7 million**
    2012-2013 Proposal: **$23.7 million (unchanged)**

Part XIV: Staff Assessment

    2010-2011 Biennium Appropriation: **$517.3 million**
    2012-2013 Proposal: **$526.1 million (+1.7%)**

2010-2011 Regular Budget Appropriation: $4,159,000,000
Preliminary 2012-2013 Budget Projection: $4,215,900,000 (+1.4%)

<u>Provision for Special Political Missions:</u>

    2010-2011 Biennium Appropriation: **$1.0 billion**
    2012-2013 Proposal: **$1,240,200,000 (+24.0%)**

2010-2011 Total Regular Budget Expenditure: $5,159,000,000*
2012-2013 Projected Regular Budget Expenditures: $5,456,100,000* (+5.8%)

*These regular budget figures represent estimates provided by UN documents. Any differences in UN sums from those compiled here are a result of rounding.

Sources:

General Assembly document A/64/6, "Proposed programme budget for the biennium 2010-2011," June 5, 2009.

General Assembly document A/65/560, "Proposed programme budget outline for the biennium 2012-2013," November 5, 2010.

TABLE 2: AGGREGATE UN EXTRABUDGETARY EXPENDITURES FOR 2008-09 & 2010-11 biennium, and the critical UN agencies that receive this funding (all figures in US$).

*Extrabudgetary expenditures are forecasted costs for particular UN agencies and programs not included in the regular budget. They are financed through additional voluntary contributions by governments, the private sector, and individuals. To date, no extrabudgetary expenditure projections for the 2012-2013 biennium have been made, but based on recent history it is safe to assume that there will be an increase— the $9.44 billion extrabudgetary figure in the 2010-2011 biennium was $780 million higher than in the previous two years. The specific agencies mentioned below are typically financed by a combination of assessed and voluntary contributions unless otherwise noted.

Aggregate Extrabudgetary Expenditures:

1) Support Activities

    2008-09 Appropriation: **$831,740,000***
    2010-11 Appropriation: **1,047,590,000*** (**+25.95%**)

2) Substantive Activities

    2008-09 Appropriation: **1,560,210,000***
    2010-11 Appropriation: **1,610,440,000*** (**+3.22%**)

3) Operational Activities

    2008-09 Appropriation: **6,268,540,000***
    2010-11 Appropriation: **6,783,920,000*** (**+8.22%**)

Total 2008-09 Extrabudgetary Appropriation: $8,660,492,300*
Total 2010-11 Extrabudgetary Projection: $9,441,446,200*

Key UN Agencies Receiving Extrabudgetary Funding:

Food and Agriculture Organization

    2010-2011 Total Budget: **$2,200,000,000** (**$1.2 billion** in projected voluntary contributions; **$1 billion** in assessed contributions from member states).

    Expenditures by Focus Area: Food and agricultural outcomes (**$1,562,000,000**); Core functions (**$242,000,000**); Administration (**$132,000,000**); Country office network ($110,000,000); Technical cooperation program (**$110,000,000**); Capital and security expenditures (**$44,000,000**).

Office of the High Commissioner for Human Rights

    2010 Total Budget: **$188,521,800**

    Expenditures by Focus Area: Programs of work and support (**$88,123,300**); Total field presences (**$62,881,200**); Total headquarters- executive management & policymaking (**$23,072,400**); Humanitarian trust funds (**$10,451,200**); Income not allocated (**$3,993,700**).

    2010 Total Voluntary Contributions: **$109,362,504** (**$98.9 million** from member states, **$10.5 million** from international organizations).

UN Children's Fund Unicef

2010 Total Expenditures: **$3,298,000,000**

Expenditures by Focus Area: **$2,943,000,000** in program assistance; **$201 million** in program support; **$154 million**.

2010 Total Voluntary Contributions: **$3,682,000,000** (**$2,083,000,000** from governments, $1,188,000,000 from private sector and NGOs, **$411,000,000** from other sources).

UN Development Program

2010 Total Program Expenditures: **$4,756,524,000**

Expenditures by Focus Area: Poverty reduction and achieving the MDGs (**$1,348,441,000**); Fostering democratic governance (**$1,183,534,000**); Supporting crisis prevention and recovery (**$1,051,996,000**); Other development expenditures (**$664,128,000**); Managing energy and the environment for sustainable development (**$508,425,000**).

2010 Voluntary Contributions: **$970 million** (regular resources- no strings attached); **$4,050,000,000** (earmarked contributions).

UN High Commissioner for Refugees

2010 Total Budget Requirements: **$3,300,000,000**

Expenditures by Focus Area: Refugee programs (**$2,376,000,000**); Internally displaced persons projects (**$726,000,000**); Reintegration projects (**$165,000,000**); Stateless expenditures (**$33,000,000**).

2010 Voluntary Contributions: **$1,863,000,000**

World Food Program

* WFP relies entirely on voluntary contributions to finance its humanitarian and development projects.

2011 Voluntary Contributions (as of June 12, 2011): **$1,624,796,029** (**$1,515,394,179** from governments, **$109,401,850** from the private sector).

2011 Contributions by Focus Area: Protracted relief and recovery (**$724 million**); Emergencies (**$404.8 million**); Other (**$268.3 million**); Development ($120 million); Special operations (**$76.9 million**); Immediate response accounts (**$30.9 million**).

World Health Organization

2010-2011 Total Approved Expenditures: **$4,540,000,00**

Expenditures by Focus Area: **$3,368,000,000** for base programs; **$822 million** for special programs and collaborative arrangements; **$350 million** for outbreak and crisis response.

Voluntary Contributions on Hand (December 31, 2010): **$2,993,000,000**

* These aggregate extrabudgetary figures represent total estimates provided by UN documents. Several key UN agencies receiving these types of funds have not been documented. Any differences in UN sums from those compiled here are a result of rounding.

Sources:
General Assembly document A/64/6, "Proposed programme budget for the biennium 2010-2011," June 5, 2009.

Office of the High Commissioner for Human Rights Report 2010, http://www2.ohchr.org/english/ohchrreport2010/web_version/ohchr_report2010_web/index.html#/management-and-funding

UN Development Program in Action 2010/2011, http://www.beta.undp.org/undp/en/home/librarypage/corporate/undp_in_action_2011.html

UN High Commissioner for Refugees Global Report 2010, http://www.unhcr.org/4dfdbf3915.html

UN Children's Fund Unicef Annual Report 2010, http://www.unicef.org/publications/index_58840.html

World Food Program Annual Report 2010, http://www.wfp.org/content/wfp-annual-report-2010-english

World Health Organization http://www.who.int/about/resources_planning/en/index.html

UN Photo/Albert Gonzalez Farran

A boy gets a haircut in a makeshift barber shop in a camp for internally displaced persons in Cité Soleil, Haiti, in December 2010. A castastrophic earthquake struck Haiti in January 2010, killing more than 200,000 people (including 102 UN personnel) and leaving more than two million homeless, according to the UN Stabilization Mission in Haiti.

TABLE 3: CURRENT PEACEKEEPING OPERATIONS BUDGET AND DATA

*There are currently 14 peacekeeping operations being undertaken by the UN worldwide, and one special political mission directed and supported by the Department of Peacekeeping Operations, the UN Assistance Mission in Afghanistan. All figures provided are based upon the latest available UN data (April 30, 2011); approved budget allocations are for the period July 1, 2010, to June 30, 2011.

Aggregate Data:

> Current peace operations directed and supported by the Department of Peacekeeping Operations: 15
>
> Total number of personnel serving in peace operations: 122,948 (82,278 troops, 15,358 local civilian personnel, 14,669 police, 6136 international civilian personnel, 2,199 military observers and 2308 UNV Volunteers)
>
> Countries contributing uniformed personnel: 115
>
> Approved budget total for the period from July 1, 2010, to June 30, 2011: About $7.83 billion

Operation Specific Data

UN Truce Supervision Organization*
In the Middle East since May 1948

> **Strength:**
>
> Uniformed personnel- Military (149)
>
> Civilian personnel- International Civilians (93); Local Civilians (128)
>
> **Fatalities To-Date:** 50
>
> **2010-2011 Approved Budget:** $60.7 million

UN Military Observer Group in India and Pakistan*
In India and Pakistan since January 1949

> **Strength:**
>
> Uniformed personnel- Military (41)
>
> Civilian personnel- International Civilians (25); Local Civilians (52)
>
> **Fatalities To-Date:** 11
>
> **2010-2011 Approved Budget:** $16.14 million

UN Peacekeeping Force in Cyprus
In Cyprus since March 1964

> **Strength:**
>
> Uniformed personnel- Troops (858); Police (65)
>
> Civilian personnel- International Civilians (38); Local Civilians (110)
>
> **Fatalities To-Date:** 180
>
> **2010-2011 Approved Budget:** $58.16 million, including voluntary contributions of one-third from Cyprus and $6.5 million from Greece

UN Disengagement Observer Force
In Syria since June 1974

Strength:

Uniformed personnel- Troops (1041)

Civilian personnel- International Civilians (41); Local Civilians (104)

Fatalities To-Date: 43

2010-2011 Approved Budget: $47.81 million

UN Interim Force in Lebanon
In Lebanon since March 1978

Strength:

Uniformed personnel- Troops (11,783)

Civilian personnel- International Civilians (341); Local Civilians (653)

Fatalities To-Date: 292

2010-2011 Approved Budget: $518.71 million

UN Mission for the Referendum in Western Sahara
In Western Sahara since April 1991

Strength:

Uniformed personnel- Troops (27); Military (197); Police (4)

Civilian personnel- International Civilians (100); Local Civilians (162); UNV Volunteers (20)

Fatalities To-Date: 15

2010-2011 Approved Budget: $60 million

UN Interim Administration Mission in Kosovo**
In Kosovo since June 1999

Strength:

Uniformed personnel- Military (8); Police (8)

Civilian personnel- International Civilians (147); Local Civilians (236); UNV Volunteers (28)

Fatalities To-Date: 54

2010-2011 Approved Budget: $47.88 million

UN Assistance Mission in Afghanistan****
In Afghanistan since March 2002

Strength:

Uniformed personnel- Military (11); Police (2)

Civilian personnel- International Civilians (402); Local Civilians (1643); UNV Volunteers (60)

2010-2011 Approved Budget: $168 million

UN Mission in Liberia
In Liberia since September 2003

Strength:

Uniformed personnel- Troops (7771); Military (138); Police (1280)

Civilian personnel- International Civilians (460); Local Civilians (980); UN Volunteers (226)

Fatalities: 158

2010-2011 Approved Budget: $524.1 million

UN Operation in Ivory Coast
In Ivory Coast since April 2004

Strength:

Uniformed personnel- Troops (7974); Military (177); Police (1293)

Civilian personnel- International Civilians (402); Local Civilians (741); UN Volunteers (175)

Fatalities: 74

2010-2011 Approved Budget: $485.1 million

UN Stabilization Mission in Haiti
In Haiti since June 2004

Strength:

Uniformed personnel- Troops (8734); Police (3545)

Civilian personnel- International Civilians (531); Local Civilians (1264); UN Volunteers (221)

Fatalities: 164

2010-2011 Approved Budget: $853.8 million

UN Mission in the Sudan
In Sudan since March 2005

Strength:

Uniformed personnel- Troops (9265); Military (488); Police (676)

Civilian personnel- International Civilians (1045); Local Civilians (2790); UN Volunteers (327)

Fatalities: 59

2010-2011 Approved Budget: $1.008 billion

UN Integrated Mission in Timor-Leste
In Timor-Leste since August 2006

Strength:

Uniformed personnel- Military (33); Police (1364)

Civilian personnel- International Civilians (381); Local Civilians (891); UN Volunteers (167)

Fatalities: 10

2010-2011 Approved Budget: $206.31 million

African Union/UN Hybrid Operation in Darfur
In Darfur since July 2007

Strength:

Uniformed personnel- Troops (17,726); Military (226); Police: (5177)

Civilian personnel- International Civilians (1144); Local Civilians (2823); UN Volunteers (468)

Fatalities: 89

2010-2011 Approved Budget: $1.81 billion

UN Organization Stabilization Mission in the Democratic Republic of Congo***
In the Democratic Republic of Congo since June 2010

Strength:

Uniformed personnel- Troops (17,009); Military (731); Police (1255)

Civilian personnel- International Civilians (986); Local Civilians (2781); UNV Volunteers (616)

Fatalities To-Date: 22

2010-2011 Approved Budget: $1.37 billion

---

*Funded from the United Nations regular biennial budget. Costs to the UN for the other operations are financed from separate accounts on the basis of legally binding assessments on all member states. For these missions, budget figures are made on a one-year basis (July 2010 - June 2011).

**Since the deployment of the European Union Rule of Law Mission in December 2008, the Kosovo mission's mandate has been limited to "an increasingly diplomatic and political role targeted on facilitating dialogue and external relations, and fostering minority rights." For more, see: http://www.unmikonline.org/news.htm#1706.

*** In May 2010, Security Council Resolution 1925 announced that the mission in Congo established on Nov. 30, 1999, would be renamed the UN Organization Stabilization Mission in the Democratic Republic of the Congo as of July 2010.

**** The special political mission in Afghanistan is the political mission directed and supported by the Department of Peacekeeping Operations referred to at the top of this table. Figures for total UN personnel deaths to date were not readily available.

Sources:
"UN Peacekeeping Operations Fact Sheet," http://www.un.org/en/peacekeeping/resources/statistics/factsheet.shtm

"UN Political and Peacebuilding Missions Fact Sheet," http://www.un.org/en/peacekeeping/documents/ppbm.pdf

TABLE 4: TOP 10 CONTRIBUTIONS TO THE UN REGULAR BUDGET

Country	Contribution Total	% of Total Regular Budget
US*	$582.68 million	22.000
Japan	$331.86 million	12.530
Germany	$212.36 million	8.018
Britain*	$174.91 million	6.604
France*	$162.17 million	6.123
Italy	$132.40 million	4.999
Canada	$84.94 million	3.207
China*	$84.46 million	3.189
Spain	$84.14 million	3.177
Mexico	$62.40 million	2.356

*Denotes Security Council permanent members. Russia, the fifth permanent member, contributes 1.602 percent of the 2011 UN regular budget, or approximately $42.43 million.

Note: The 2011 UN regular budget is $2,648,538,700. Maximum assessment rate for a member state is 22 percent; the minimum assessment rate is 0.001 percent. All dollar figures are rounded to the nearest $10,000.

Source: UN Secretariat Document, ST/ADM/SER.B/824

UN Photo/Gill Fickling

Villagers in Pessuapa in northeastern Colombia have had to cope with water shortages in recent years due to the effects of climate change in the increasingly arrid territory.

Appendices **203**

TABLE 5: INTERNATIONAL WAR CRIMES TRIBUNALS APPROPRIATIONS Regular Budget

International Criminal Tribunal for Rwanda

Appropriation for 2010-11 biennium: $227.25 million (net)

Appropriation for 2008-09 biennium: $282.6 million (net)

Change: -$55.3 million (-19.59%)

Sources: http://www.un.org/News/Press/docs//2008/ga10804.doc.htm
http://www.unictr.org/AboutICTR/GeneralInformation/tabid/101/Default.aspx

International Tribunal for former Yugoslavia

Appropriation for 2010-11 biennium: $301.9 million (net)

Appropriation for 2008-09 biennium: $342.3 million (net)

Change: -$40.4 million (-11.8%)

Sources: http://www.un.org/News/Press/docs//2008/ga10804.doc.htm
http://www.icty.org/sid/325

The Special Court for Sierra Leone

(Financed by voluntary contributions)

Required 2011 budget: $5.6 million (6 months left to complete court's mission)

Required 2010 budget: $20.5 million

6-month change: -$4.65 million (-45.37%)

Sources: Sixth and Seventh Annual Reports of the President of the Special Court for Sierra Leone (2008-2009 & 2009-2010)

Extraordinary Chambers in the Courts of Cambodia

2011 Total funding requirement: $40.7 million

2011 UN funding estimate: $30.83 million

2011 Cambodian funding estimate: $9.86 million

2010 Final total expenditure: $31.27 million

Change: +$9.43 million (+30.16%)

Source: Extraordinary Chambers in the Courts of Cambodia Revised Budget Requirements- 2010-2011, http://www.eccc.gov.kh/en/reports/eccc-revised-budget-requirements-2010-2011

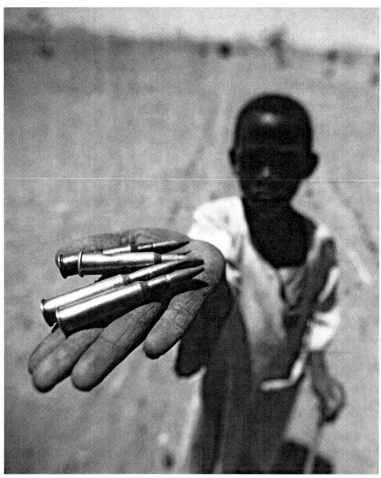

UN Photo/Albert Gonzalez Farran

A child holds up bullets collected from the ground in Rounyn, a village in Sudan's Darfur region, after heavy fighting between government and rebel forces in March 2011. A joint UN-African Union peacekeeping mission has been operating in Darfur since 2007.

Appendix E: Acronyms and Abbreviations

ACABQ Advisory Committee on Administrative and Budgetary Questions

ADB Asian Development Bank

AFDB African Development Bank

AMAP Arctic Monitoring and Assessment Program

AMIS African Union-led Mission in the Sudan

APEC Asia-Pacific Economic Cooperation

APO Asian Productivity Organization

ASEAN Association of South East Asian Nations

AU African Union

BCEAO Central Bank of West African States

BCIE Central American Bank for Economic Integration

BIPM International Bureau of Weights and Measures

BIS Bank for International Settlements

BONUCA UN Peacebuilding Office in the Central African Republic

CAAC Working Group on Children and Armed Conflict

CAPSA Centre for Alleviation of Poverty through Secondary Crops Development in Asia and the Pacific

CARICOM Caribbean Community and Common Market

CAT Committee Against Torture

CBD Convention on Biological Diversity

CBF Committee on Budget and Finance

CBSS Council of the Baltic States

CCE Committee on Central American Economic Cooperation

CCPCJ Commission on Crime Prevention and Criminal Justice

CD Conference on Disarmament

CDB Caribbean Development Bank

CDCC Caribbean Development and Cooperation Committee

CEC Commission for Environmental Cooperation (North America)

CEDAW Convention on the Elimination of All Forms of Discrimination Against Women

CERD Committee on the Elimination of Racial Discrimination

CERN European Organization for Nuclear Research

CESCR Committee on Economic, Social and Cultural Rights

CFA Committee on Food Aid Policies and Programs

CIRDAP Center on Integrated Rural Development for Asia and the Pacific

CIS Commonwealth of Independent States

CMW Committee on the Protection of the Rights of All Migrant Workers and Members of their Families

CND Commission on Narcotic Drugs

COE Council of Europe

COMESA Common Market for Eastern and Southern Africa

COPUOS Committee on the Peaceful Uses of Outer Space

CPA Comprehensive Peace Agreement

CPF Collaborative Partnership on Forests

CRC Committee on the Rights of the Child

CSD Commission on Sustainable Development

CSocD Commission for Social Development

CST Committee on Science and Technology

CSTD Commission on Science and Technology for Development

CSW Commission on the Status of Women

CTBTO Comprehensive Nuclear Test Ban Treaty Organization

CTC Counter-Terrorism Committee

CTED Counter-Terrorism Committee Executive Directorate

CWC Convention on the Prohibition of the Development, Production, Stockpiling and Use of Chemical Weapons

DESA Department of Economic and Social Affairs

DFS Department of Field Support

DM Department of Management

DPA Department of Political Affairs

DPI Department of Public Information

DPKO Department of Peacekeeping Operations
DSS Department of Safety and Security
EBRD European Bank for Reconstruction and Development
ECA Economic Commission for Africa
ECB European Central Bank
ECE Economic Commission for Europe
ECHR European Court of Human Rights
ECLAC Economic Commission for Latin America and the Caribbean
ECOSOC UN Economic and Social Council
ECOWAS Economic Community of West African States
EFTA European Free Trade Association
EPO European Patent Office
EPTA Expanded Program of Technical Assistance (UN)
ESCAP Economic and Social Commission for Asia and the Pacific
ESCWA Economic and Social Commission for Western Asia
EU European Union
EUTELSAT European Telecommunications Satellite Organization
FAO UN Food and Agriculture Organization
GATT General Agreement on Tariffs and Trade
HIPCs Heavily Indebted Poor Countries
HRC Human Rights Council
IADB Inter-American Development Bank
IAEA International Atomic Energy Agency
IBE International Bureau of Education
IBRD International Bank for Reconstruction and Development
ICAO International Civil Aviation Organization
ICES International Council for the Exploration of the Sea
ICC International Criminal Court
ICTR International Criminal Tribunal for Rwanda
ICTY International Criminal Tribunal for the former Yugoslavia
IFAD International Fund for Agricultural Development

IFC International Finance Corporation

IGCP International Geoscience Program

IIC InterAmerican Investment Corporation

ILO International Labor Organization

ILPES Latin American and Caribbean Institute for Economic and Social Planning

IMF International Monetary Fund

IMFC International Monetary and Financial Committee

IMO International Maritime Organization

INCB International Narcotics Control Board

INDES Inter-American Institute for Social Development

INSTRAW International Research and Training Institute for the Advancement of Women

INTAL Institute for the Integration of Latin America and the Caribbean

INTERPOL International Criminal Police Organization

IOM International Organization for Migration

IPCC Intergovernmental Panel on Climate Change

ISA International Seabed Authority

ISDB Islamic Development Bank

ITC International Trade Center

ITU International Telecommunication Union

LDCs Least Developed Countries

MAC Military Armistice Commission

MDGs Millennium Development Goals

MIF Multilateral Investment Fund

MIF Multinational Interim Force (Haiti)

MIGA Multilateral Investment Guarantee Agency

MINURCAT UN Mission in the Central African Republic and Chad

MINURSO UN Mission for the Referendum in Western Sahara

MINUSTAH UN Stabilization Mission in Haiti

MONUC UN Organization Mission in the Democratic Republic of Congo

MONUSCO UN Organization Stabilization Mission in the Democratic Republic of Congo

NAALC Commission for Labor Cooperation (North America)

NEPAD New Partnership for Africa's Development

NPT Nuclear Non-Proliferation Treaty

OAU Organization of African Unity

OCHA Office for the Coordination of Humanitarian Affairs

ODA Office for Disarmament Affairs

OECD Organization for Economic Cooperation and Development

OHCHR Office of the UN High Commissioner for Human Rights

OIOS Office of Internal Oversight Services

OLA Office of Legal Affairs

ONUB UN Operation in Burundi

OPCW Organization for the Prohibition of Chemical Weapons

OPEC Organization of Petroleum Exporting Countries

OSG Office of the Secretary-General

PBC Peacebuilding Commission

UNAIDS Joint UN Program on HIV/AIDS

UNAMI UN Assistance Mission for Iraq

UNAMID UN/African Union Hybrid Operation in Darfur

UNAMIS UN Advance Mission in Sudan

UNAMSIL UN Assistance Mission in Sierra Leone

UNAT UN Administrative Tribunal

UNC UN Command-Korea

UNCDF UN Capital Development Fund

UNCIP UN Commission for India and Pakistan

UNCITRAL UN Commission on International Trade Law

UNCLOS UN Convention on the Law of the Sea

UNCTAD UN Conference on Trade and Development

UNDC UN Disarmament Commission

UNDCP UN International Drug Control Program

UNDEF UN Democracy Fund
UNDG UN Development Group
UNDOF UN Disengagement Observer Force
UNDP UN Development Program
UNECE UN Economic Commission for Europe
UNEP UN Environment Program
UNESCO UN Educational, Scientific and Cultural Organization
UNFCCC UN Framework Convention on Climate Change
UNFICYP UN Peacekeeping Force in Cyprus
UNFIP UN Fund for International Partnerships
UNFPA UN Population Fund
UNGA UN General Assembly
UN-HABITAT UN Human Settlements Program
UNHCR UN High Commissioner for Refugees
UNICEF UN Children's Fund
UNICRI UN Interregional Crime and Justice Research Institute
UNIDIR UN Institute for Disarmament Research
UNIDO UN Industrial Development Organization
UNIFEM UN Development Fund for Women
UNIFIL UN Interim Force in Lebanon
UNIOSIL UN Integrated Office in Sierra Leone
UNIPOM UN India-Pakistan Observation Mission
UNITAR UN Institute for Training and Research
UNMEE UN Mission in Ethiopia and Eritrea
UNMIK UN Interim Administration Mission in Kosovo
UNMIL UN Mission in Liberia
UNMIN UN Mission in Nepal
UNMIS UN Mission in Sudan
UNMIT UN Integrated Mission in Timor-Leste
UNMOGIP UN Military Observer Group in India and Pakistan
UNMOT UN Mission of Observers in Tajikistan

UNMOVIC UN Monitoring, Verification and Inspection Commission

UNOCI UN Operation in Ivory Coast

UNODA UN Office for Disarmament Affairs

UNODC UN Office on Drugs and Crime

UNOG UN Office at Geneva

UNOGBIS UN Peacebuilding Support Office in Guinea-Bissau

UNOHRLLS Office of the High Representative for the Least Developed Countries, Landlocked Developing Countries, and Small Island Developing States

UNOL UN Peacebuilding Support Office in Liberia

UNOMIG UN Observer Mission in Georgia

UNON UN Office at Nairobi

UNOTIL UN Office in Timor-Leste

UNOV UN Office at Vienna

UNPOS UN Political Office for Somalia

UNRISD UN Research Institute for Social Development

UNRWA UN Relief and Works Agency for Palestine Refugees in the Near East

UNSCEAR UN Scientific Committee on the Effects of Atomic Radiation

UNSCO Office of the UN Special Coordinator for the Middle East Peace Process

UNSC UN Security Council

UNSCOM UN Special Commission (Iraq)

UNSDRI UN Social Defense Research Institute

UNSMA UN Special Mission to Afghanistan

UNTOP UN Tajikistan Office of Peacebuilding

UNTSO UN Truce Supervision Organization

UNU UN University

UNWTO World Tourism Organization

WEOG Western European and Others Group

WHO World Health Organization

WFP World Food Program

WIPO World Intellectual Property Organization

WMDs Weapons of Mass Destruction

WMO World Meteorological Organization
WTO World Trade Organization

UN Photo/Ray Witlin

Young girls harvest cotton at an experimental plot in a development project in Nepalgunj, Nepal.

UN Photo/Alexis Duclos

Refugees fleeing violence from an uprising in Libya arrive at the Choucha transit camp in Ras Djir, Tunisia. The camp is run by the UN High Commissioner for Refugees.

Appendix F: Glossary

absolutism A theory of government vesting unrestrained power in a person, a dynasty, a party or an administration.

acclamation An overwhelmingly affirmative vote. If no opposition is indicated, an item of business is declared adopted "by acclamation."

accord A diplomatic agreement that stipulates action on the part of the signers. It does not have the force of a treaty but is often treated similarly (e.g., the Camp David Accords signed by Israel and Egypt in 1978).

act of state The actions of a government for which no individual can be held accountable.

ad hoc For a specific or temporary purpose. An ad hoc committee is not a standing committee.

ad litem A term often used in connection with international courts to describe special judges who participate in only a limited set of cases or over a limited period of time, to supplement the work of the court's regular judges.

aegis Greek for a "shield," thus a power or influence that organizes, protects or shields. Nations join in peacekeeping under the aegis of the UN.

African Development Bank Established in 1964, it provides loans for and invests in its African member states, offers technical assistance for development, promotes investment for development and helps coordinate regional policies and plans. Its members, or shareholders, consist of 53 African countries and 14 non-African countries.

African Union Created in July 2002 to replace the Organization of African Unity. Promotes democracy, human rights and development across the continent and works to increase foreign investment through the New Partnership for Africa's Development.

aggression An act of force; a belligerent action by one state against another.

allegiance Loyalty to a principle, leader or country.

alliance A union of powers or countries created to undertake joint action.

ambassador The highest ranking diplomat who can be sent by one government to another or to an international organization.

amicus or amici curiae In Latin, "friend or friends of the court." Someone who is not party to a legal proceeding. Often identified as "third parties."

amnesty A pardon given by a government to a group or class of people, usually for political reasons.

anarchy Absence of government; a state of lawlessness or political disorder.

annexation An act in which a country proclaims sovereignty over territory beyond its domain. Unlike secession, whereby territory is given or sold by a treaty, annexation is a unilateral act made effective by actual possession and legitimized by general recognition.

appeasement The policy of giving in to the demands of another.

appropriations Funds set aside for a specific use.

Arab League Established on March 22, 1945. Formed to consider cultural cooperation among the Arab states. Its headquarters are in Cairo.

Arab Spring A wave of popular uprisings in the Middle East and North Africa in early 2011.

arbitration A way to settle disputes outside ordinary court procedures by giving an agreed-upon third party authority to make a legally binding decision.

area of operation The portion of an arena of conflict necessary for the conduct of a peacekeeping operation.

area of separation The area between the forces of parties in a conflict where they have agreed not to deploy troops. Sometimes called a demilitarized zone.

aristocracy Government by a small privileged class, usually composed of the hereditary nobility or those conferred status through decree.

arrears The unpaid portion of an assessment for a given financial period.

assessment The amount a member state must pay toward the expenses of the UN in a financial period, as specified in the relevant budget adopted by the General Assembly.

asylum Protection granted by a country to the citizen of another (usually a political refugee).

atrocities Acts of unusual cruelty or brutality, usually inflicted on large groups of defenseless people.

authoritarianism A system of government with a concentration of power in a leader or small elite not constitutionally responsible to the people.

autonomy The right of self-government.

back-channel diplomacy Secret lines of communication, often through an informal intermediary.

barter system The exchange of goods or services without use of money or other medium of exchange, either based on established rates of exchange or bargaining.

BASIC An acronym referring to a grouping of Brazil, South Africa, India and China.

Beijing Declaration An international agreement signed at the Fourth World Conference on Women in Beijing in 1995 affirming the equal rights of men and women and calling upon nations to promote gender equality and the empowerment of women.

bilateral A two-way agreement or exchange.

biological warfare Use of disease-producing agents, like bacteria and viruses, on humans, animals or plants.

bloc An informal grouping of countries.

blockade A maneuver to prevent ships or other carriers from getting goods into a port or region.

Bonn Agreement An agreement on Dec. 5, 2001, creating an interim administration to lead Afghanistan for two years until a representative government could be elected. Elections were held in October 2004.

breach A failure to observe agreed-upon terms; a break or interruption in friendly relations.

Bretton Woods institutions Financial bodies, including the World Bank and International Monetary Fund, which were set up at a meeting of 43 countries in Bretton Woods, N.H., in July 1944 to help rebuild postwar economies and promote economic cooperation.

BRIC An acronym referring to a grouping of Brazil, Russia, India and China.

buffer zone Also known as an area of separation, a neutral space between hostile parties; as a demilitarized zone, an area in which the parties have agreed not to deploy military forces.

bureaucracy An administrative structure usually composed of officials in a hierarchy.

Bush Doctrine Also known as the new National Security Strategy of the U.S., adopted in September 2002, providing for the pre-emptive use of force.

cease-fire An end or pause in hostilities.

censorship The suppression or prohibition of material considered harmful by those in control.

chemical warfare Hostile use of chemical compounds, usually toxic agents.

civil disobedience The refusal to obey the demands or commands of a government or occupying power; violence or active measures of opposition are not used.

civil society The institutions, organizations and behaviors among the government, business world and family. Civil society includes voluntary and nonprofit organizations, philanthropic institutions and social and political movements.

coalition A temporary alliance between two or more political units for the purpose of joint action. In the 2003 Iraq war, the "coalition of the willing" involved primarily the U.S., Britain, Australia and Poland.

Coalition Provisional Authority A temporary administration set up in Iraq by the U.S. and its allies in May 2003 to maintain stability, security and institutional structures until an interim government was established in June 2004.

coercion Forced compliance through fear and intimidation.

cold war The rivalry after World War II between the U.S. and the Soviet Union and their respective allies. More generically, a sustained intensity of economic, political, military and ideological competition between nations, short of direct military confrontation between the concerned parties.

collective security A concept that seeks to ensure peace through enforcement by the community of nations.

commission A body created to perform a function, administrative, legislative or judicial.

Commonwealth of Independent States A union of 12 of the 15 former Soviet republics, created in December 1991 to promote common policies.

communiqué An official document, usually an announcement to the public or press.

Comprehensive Nuclear Test-Ban Treaty Opened for signatures on Sept. 10, 1996, it established a global verification mechanism for nuclear weapons. The treaty says that signers agree not to carry out explosions of nuclear weapons and to prohibit and prevent such explosions anyplace under its jurisdiction or control.

conciliation The process of bringing two sides in a dispute to agree to a compromise.

consolidated appeals process A mechanism used by aid organizations to plan, carry out and monitor their activities; they use this data to produce a humanitarian action plan and appeal and to be presented to the international community yearly.

constituency A body of citizens that elects a representative to a public body.

constitution The fundamental rules and principles under which a state is organized.

constitutionalism The belief that governments will defer to the rules and principles of their constitutions and uphold the rule of law.

convention A practice or custom followed by nations. Some international laws are called conventions, like the Convention on the Rights of the Child.

Convention on the Elimination of All Forms of Discrimination Against Women Adopted by the General Assembly in 1979 as an international bill of rights for women, defining what constitutes discrimination and setting up an agenda for national action to end such differentiation.

Copenhagen Accord A nonbinding agreement on climate change remediation reached in 2009 after participating countries could not agree on a binding treaty.

coup d'état A sudden overthrow of a government.

cross-borrowing Borrowing from one account to meet the needs of another.

Dayton Peace Accords An agreement among Bosnia, Herzegovina, Croatia and the Federal Republic of Yugoslavia in 1995 to respect one another's sovereignty and to settle future disputes peacefully.

delegate A representative.

delegation A group of representatives.

demilitarized zone The area between parties in a conflict where they have agreed not to deploy military forces. It may be placed under control of peacekeepers.

democracy A form of government in which political decisions are made by all citizens. In direct democracy, citizens exercise their control directly through the process of majority rule. In representative democracy, citizens exercise the same right through representatives chosen by election.

Department of Peacekeeping Operations The main UN office dealing with peacekeeping and peace-building.

developed countries Those with more fully industrialized economies, more productive agriculture and a relatively high standard of living. Sometimes referred to as the North.

developing countries Those not fully industrialized, with limited specialization and financial savings. These countries are identified by a population that is outgrowing its resources and who have a low standard of living. Sometimes referred to as the South.

diplomacy The conduct of relations between nations, often through representatives empowered to seek agreements.

diplomatic immunity Special rights for official representatives of foreign governments, including immunity from laws in the country to which they are assigned.

directive A communication in which policy is established or a specific action is ordered concerning conduct or procedure.

disarmament The reduction or removal of armed forces and armaments.

displaced person Someone left homeless as a result of war or disaster. A person fleeing war or disaster who crosses a national border is considered a refugee. People who take flight but never leave their country are considered internally displaced persons.

draft resolution A document prepared for formal debate; it is written in the form of a resolution but has not been adopted.

dumping In relation to trade, the selling of goods in a foreign market below the cost of production, or at lower than they are sold in the home market.

Economic and Social Council A 54-member body elected by the General Assembly to three-year terms. It is responsible for coordinating and overseeing UN economic and social work.

economic growth An increase in a nation's production of goods and services, often measured by gross national product.

embargo A government order prohibiting entry or departure of foreign commercial carriers, especially as a war measure. Also refers to a restriction imposed on commerce by law.

embassy A body of diplomatic representatives, specifically one headed by an ambassador.

eminent domain Also called condemnation or expropriation, this describes the power of government to take private property for public use without the owner's consent.

envoy A diplomatic agent of any rank.

epidemic An infectious disease widespread among the population of a community or region.

ethnic cleansing The expulsion, imprisonment or killing of members of one ethnic group by another seeking ethnic homogeneity.

ethnocentrism Belief in the inherent superiority of one's own cultural or ethnic group.

European Union With its headquarters in Brussels, this organization of 27 countries seeks economic and social progress for a strong European presence in the world and a free and secure citizenship.

exile A prolonged stay away from one's country or community, usually forced. The term can also refer to banishment but is sometimes self-imposed.

extort To get money or other items of value through violence, threats or misuse of authority.

extremist One who supports ideas, doctrines or policies beyond the norm, usually in politics or religion.

facilitator In diplomacy, a neutral person or country bringing warring parties to a meeting with the goal of exchanging views and, possibly, finding preliminary agreement. The facilitator's role is less formal than that of a mediator or a broker in a treaty negotiation.

faction An association of people hoping to influence a government toward actions favorable to their interests; known also as an interest group.

famine An acute general shortage of food.

federalism A system of government in which sovereignty is distributed among a central government and provincial or state governments.

Food and Agriculture Organization Headquartered in Rome, FAO was founded in 1945 with a mandate to raise levels of nutrition and standards of living, to improve agricultural productivity and to better the condition of rural populations.

free trade Trade carried on without governmental regulations, especially international trade conducted without protective tariffs and customs duties.

General Agreement on Tariffs and Trade, or GATT. This 1948 agreement was incorporated into and superseded by the World Trade Organization in January 1995. The 100-plus members of GATT established rules for international trade, with the aim of reducing trade barriers. The World Trade Organization offers a dispute-settlement system to enforce those rules.

General Assembly The central deliberative organ of the UN. Each of the 193 member nations is represented equally and has a vote, and no country has veto power.

genocide Systematic killing to eliminate a whole people or nation.

Global Fund The Global Fund for HIV/AIDS, Tuberculosis and Malaria is a non-UN body initiated by Secretary-General Kofi Annan to raise money to fight deadly diseases in developing nations.

grassroots Originating among ordinary citizens.

gross domestic product An economic measure embracing the total value of all products manufactured and goods provided within a territory (often, per year). Like the gross national product (see below) it is used to assess a nation's economy.

gross national product The value of all goods and services produced by a country's nationals.

Group of Seven (G-7) First made up of the seven most industrialized nations—-Britain, Canada, France, Germany, Italy, Japan and the U.S.—the group now includes Russia and is more often referred to as the Group of Eight (G-8).

Group of Eight (G-8) *See Group of Seven.*

Group of 20 (G-20) A group created in 1999 to promote dialogue and cooperation, particularly on international economic matters, among developed, developing and emerging market nations. It includes 19 countries (Argentina, Australia, Brazil, Canada, China, France, Germany, India, Indonesia, Italy, Japan, Mexico, Russia, Saudi Arabia, South Africa, South Korea, Turkey, Britain and the U.S.) plus the European Union. The International Monetary Fund and the World Bank participate in G-20 meetings as ex officio members. The group is a forum to promote dialogue between developed and developing countries on key economic issues.

Group of 77 (G-77) A group established in 1964 by 77 developing countries that now has 131 members including China. As the largest coalition in the UN, it provides a way for the developing world to promote its collective economic interests and enhance its negotiating strength.

guerrilla A member of an irregular force of soldiers, usually volunteers.

habeas corpus A legal action demanding that a prisoner be brought before the court, to determine whether there are lawful grounds for the prisoner to be detained. The remedy can be sought by the prisoner or by another person on the prisoner's behalf.

The Hague Home to many international courts and tribunals, including the International Criminal Court, the International Court of Justice and the Special Court for Sierra Leone.

head of government The person in effective charge of the executive branch of a government. In a parliamentary system, the prime minister.

head of state The person who represents the state but may not exercise political power. In a parliamentary system, it may be a president or a monarch.

Human Rights Council A 47-nation body established by the UN General Assembly to replace the 53-nation Human Rights Commission, which was abolished in 2006 over what Secretary-General Kofi Annan referred to as its "declining credibility."

human rights law Obligations regulating government behavior toward groups and individuals in political, civil, economic, social and cultural spheres.

ideology A system of beliefs and values.

immunity Exemption from the application of a rule or jurisdiction.

indictment A formal written statement by a court or other authority calling upon a prosecutor to start a trial on specified charges.

indigenous Born, growing or produced naturally in a region or country; native.

inter alia Latin term for "among other things."

interdependence Dependence on each other or one another; mutual dependence.

intergovernmental organization Any body with two or more member states.

internally displaced person *See displaced person.*

interstate Actions between two or more states or countries.

International Atomic Energy Agency Established in 1957, with headquarters in Vienna, this agency serves as the world center for nuclear information and cooperation. It is also the chief inspector of the world's nuclear facilities.

International Court of Justice Also known as the World Court, this is the main judicial organ of the UN for settling disputes between member countries and giving advisory opinions to the UN and its agencies. It does not hear cases brought by or against individual people or private organizations nor does it hear criminal cases.

International Criminal Court A permanent court established in 1998 with jurisdiction over individual people accused of war crimes, crimes against humanity or genocide.

international criminal law This involves violations of international law that point to individual criminal accountability. It provides a legal basis for trying heads of state and the like on charges of genocide, war crimes and crimes against humanity.

International Criminal Police Organization or INTERPOL Established in 1956, it promotes international cooperation among police authorities. INTERPOL has 181 members.

International Criminal Tribunal for the former Yugoslavia Established by the Security Council in 1993, this organization was created to prosecute those responsible for serious violations of international humanitarian law since 1991 in the territory that was formerly Yugoslavia.

International Criminal Tribunal for Rwanda Established by the Security Council in 1994, this organization was created to prosecute those responsible for genocide and other serious violations of international humanitarian law committed in the year 1994 in Rwanda, or by Rwandans in neighbor states.

International Development Association Created in 1960, it provides interest-free loans to the world's poorest countries. It is part of the World Bank group.

International Finance Corporation A member of the World Bank Group, this corporation was founded in 1956. It is currently the largest multilateral source of financing for private-sector projects in the developing world.

international humanitarian law Also called the law of war or armed conflict law, this aims to protect those who are not taking part in hostilities and restricts the methods of fighting between countries or other combatants.

international law Traditionally defined as the agreements and principles governing relations between countries; increasingly it regulates state behavior toward nonstate actors.

International Labor Organization Set up in 1919, it became a specialized agency of the UN in 1946. It seeks to improve working and living conditions by establishing standards that reduce social injustice in areas like employment, pay, health, job safety and freedom of association among workers.

International Law Commission Established in 1947 with a membership of 15 people competent in international law, it encourages progressive development of international law and its codification.

internally displaced person *See displaced person.*

International Monetary Fund Established at the Bretton Woods Conference in 1944, it provides financial advice and financing to countries having trouble with their balance of payments.

Intifada The word has come to symbolize the Palestinian uprising against Israeli occupation.

intrastate Actions within a state or country.

Joint UN Program on HIV/AIDS (Unaids) This body began work in 1995 as the main advocate for global action on HIV/AIDS under the sponsorship of the UN Children's Fund, the UN Development Program, the UN Population Fund, the UN Educational, Scientific and Cultural Organization, the World Health Organization and the World Bank. Today, the UN Office on Drugs and Crime, the International Labor Organization and the World Food Program also sponsor it.

junta A group or council holding governmental power. After a revolution or coup d'état, frequently a group of military officers.

Kyoto Protocol 1997 A treaty resulting from the UN Framework Convention on Climate Change, this agreement outlines goals to limit greenhouse gas emissions and honor commitments made by the signing nations.

League of Arab States *See Arab League.*

League of Nations Organization created after World War I to achieve international peace and security.

least-developed country A country characterized by a low standard of living, limited industrial capacity and long-term barriers to economic growth.

Loya Jirga A Pashtun phrase meaning "grand council." For centuries, leaders in Afghanistan have convened Loya Jirgas to choose new kings, adopt constitutions and decide important political matters. The most recent such process was set in motion by the Bonn Agreement of Dec. 5, 2001.

mandate As it applies to the UN, an authoritative command given by the Security Council or General Assembly to a UN mission or representative.

maquiladora Assembly production of products in Mexico using U.S. resources.

member state One of the 193 countries belonging to the UN.

microcredit The lending of small amounts of money to people unable to provide traditional collateral or security. Microcredit has emerged in places like Bangladesh as a way for people to set up a business and escape poverty.

Millennium Development Goals Eight benchmarks and accompanying targets agreed upon at the Millennium Summit of 2000. It set goals to be reached by 2015 for poverty eradication and developmental progress worldwide.

Millennium Summit Conference A meeting on Sept. 6-8, 2000, at UN headquarters. It gathered 150 heads of state and government to tackle global challenges. The Millennium Declaration outlines the eight Millennium Development Goals.

Montreal Protocol Signed in 1987 and amended in 1990 and 1992, this pact aims to protect the stratospheric ozone layer.

most favored nation The clause in a treaty by which one party or both agree to grant to the other all privileges granted to any third party.

multilateral Involving or participated in by more than two nations or parties.

nation Individuals in a specific geographical area who share a strong historical continuity, common culture and language and are under the rule of one government.

nation-state A sovereign state whose citizens or subjects are relatively homogeneous in factors like language or common descent.

nationalism Loyalty and devotion to a nation, especially a sense of national consciousness exalting one nation above all others and placing primary emphasis on promotion of its culture and interests.

national interest Interests specific to a nation-state, especially including survival and maintenance of power.

nationalize To take over ownership, performed by a national government.

no-fly zone An area over which aircraft are not allowed to fly. Imposing a no-fly zone can involve damaging or destroying aircraft and anti-aircraft installations as well as airports, air bases and their runways.

Nonaligned Countries An alliance of third-world nations seeking to promote the political and economic interests of developing countries. At the UN, this alliance is referred to as the nonaligned movement or nonaligned group.

nongovernmental organization (NGO) A nonprofit organization that contributes to development through cooperative projects, financial and material aid, education and the dispatch of personnel. Some NGOs are accredited by the UN system and can represent their interests before the Economic and Social Council or in other forums.

North Atlantic Treaty Organization or NATO A military alliance formed in 1949 when 12 democratic nations signed the treaty. NATO now has 26 members.

Nuclear Nonproliferation Treaty Taking effect in 1970, this treaty was intended to limit the number of countries with nuclear weapons to five: the U.S., Soviet Union, Britain, France and China. Since then, more than 140 countries have pledged not to acquire nuclear weapons and to accept the safeguards of the International Atomic Energy Agency.

observer mission Unarmed officers sent to observation posts to monitor ceasefires and armistices.

official development assistance Loans, grants, technical assistance and other forms of cooperation extended by governments to developing nations to promote progress.

Organization of American States A regional organization created in 1948 to promote Latin American development. It has 35 members. Cuba was excluded from participation in 1962 but a 2009 resolution opened the door to renewed Cuban participation.

Organization of the Islamic Conference An association of 57 countries and three observer Islamic countries seeking Muslim cohesion in social, economic and political matters.

pandemic An infectious disease affecting a large part of the population in a wide geographical area, often on a global scale.

peace enforcement Also known as third-generation peacekeeping. This does not require consent from the conflicting parties and is undertaken to protect the populace from an aggressor or a civil war.

Peacebuilding Commission An advisory body established in 2006 to support peace efforts in countries emerging from conflict.

peacekeeper A person assigned to help maintain peace where conflict has just ended. Peacekeepers can include civilian staff as well as soldiers, police officers and military advisers.

peacekeeping mission A UN operation, functioning in an impartial and neutral manner, to help maintain or restore international peace and security. After a conflict has ended, peacekeeping can include preventive diplomacy and peacebuilding, based on the consent of the parties involved and relying on a multi-faceted UN role.

peacebuilding mission A project aimed at development and reconstruction in post-conflict regions to ensure that conflicts do not resume.

peacemaking A diplomatic process of brokering an end to conflict, principally through mediation and negotiation. Military activities contributing to peacemaking include military-to-military contacts, security assistance, shows of force and preventive deployments.

permanent five The five permanent members of the UN Security Council, Britain, China, France, Russia and the U.S.

political asylum Protection granted to a person by a foreign government when the applicant demonstrates that he or she would be persecuted or harmed if returned to the country of origin.

political office UN political offices work to support the peace missions through reconciliation and negotiation.

preventive deployment The interposition of a military force to deter violence in a zone of potential conflict.

preventive diplomacy Also known as conflict prevention, this form of diplomacy is geared to prevent disputes from arising.

protectionism The practice of protecting domestic products from foreign competition by placing tariffs and quotas on imports.

protocol A document that records basic agreements reached in negotiations before the formal document is ready for signing.

quorum The number of members of an organization required to be present for conduct of business.

recosting A UN budgetary practice providing for adjustment of foreign exchange rates and inflation assumptions in a budgetary cycle.

referendum The practice of submitting to popular vote a measure proposed by a legislative body or sought by part of the public; a referendum is a direct vote in which an entire electorate is asked to accept or reject a proposal.

refugee *See displaced person.*

regular budget At the UN, includes costs of the Secretariat in New York, the UN offices in Geneva, Vienna and Nairobi, the regional commissions, the International Court of Justice and the Center for Human Rights. More than 70 percent of the UN regular budget is earmarked for staff costs. The scale of assessment (how much each country owes) is based on the principle of capacity to pay.

repatriate To restore or return to the country of origin, allegiance or citizenship.

resolution A document adopted by a committee or body that expresses the opinions and decisions of the UN.

Responsibility to Protect or R2P A doctrine adopted by UN member nations in 2005 holding that the international community was obliged to intercede when a government failed to protect its citizens from genocide, war crimes, ethnic cleansing or crimes against humanity.

rule of law The principle that authority is legitimately exercised only in accordance with written, publicly disclosed laws adopted and enforced in accordance with established procedural steps.

sanction An economic or military measure, usually by several nations in concert, to force a nation violating international law to desist.

Security Council The UN organ responsible for maintaining peace and security. It is composed of five permanent members—Britain, China, France, Russia and the U.S.—and 10 rotating members elected to two-year terms by the General Assembly to represent equitable geographic distribution.

Secretariat The UN organ that runs the daily affairs of the organization. It consists of international civil servants and is led by the secretary-general.

Secretary-General Defined in the UN Charter as the chief administrative officer of the UN and head of the Secretariat. The secretary-general acts as the primary spokesperson and de facto leader of the UN.

self-determination The choice of a people in a given area to select their own political status or independence.

sovereign Supreme power, especially over a body politic; political authority free from external control.

sovereignty Autonomy; the right to control a government, a country, a people or oneself.

stakeholder Someone with an interest in a particular issue or organization.

state-building (nation-building) The concept of rebuilding a post-conflict country, most often so that its sovereignty is recognized by the international community.

state party Countries that are party to—or have joined as a member—a particular group or have signed a particular treaty, protocol or other international document.

sustainable development A term for economic progress that meets the needs of the present without compromising the potential of future generations.

terrorism The systematic use of unpredictable violence against governments or people to attain a political objective.

treaty A formal, binding international agreement. In the U.S., treaties proposed by the executive branch that have been negotiated with a foreign country or international organization must be approved by a two-thirds majority in the Senate and then signed by the president.

tribunal A committee or board appointed to judge a particular matter.

truce A suspension of fighting by agreement.

Trusteeship Council A principal organ of the UN, it was established to help ensure that non-self-governing territories were administered in the best interests of the inhabitants, peace and security. The council suspended operation in 1994 after the independence of Palau, the last remaining UN trust territory.

UN Charter It established the UN and its method of operating and was drawn up and signed by representatives of 50 countries in 1945.

UN Children's Fund or Unicef Founded in 1946 as the UN International Children's Emergency Fund. With headquarters in New York, it is the only UN organization devoted solely to children and their rights.

UN Development Program The main body for UN development work and the largest provider of developmental grant assistance in the UN system.

Universal Declaration of Human Rights A proclamation of the basic rights and freedoms of all people, adopted by the General Assembly on Dec. 10, 1948, and commemorated every year on Human Rights Day.

UN Educational, Scientific and Cultural Organization (UNESCO) A specialized agency working for world peace and security by promoting collaboration in education, science, culture and communication. Based in Paris.

UN Environment Program Headquartered in Nairobi, Kenya, this project provides leadership and encourages partnerships to protect the environment.

UN Framework Convention on Climate Change To counter global warming, this agency seeks to stabilize greenhouse-gas concentrations in the atmosphere and to disseminate technology and information to help developing countries adapt to climate change.

UN High Commissioner for Human Rights A UN office established in 1993 to protect human rights.

UN High Commissioner for Refugees A UN office created by the General Assembly in 1951 to help refugees.

UN Population Fund The largest internationally financed source of population assistance for developing countries. It began its work in 1967.

UN University An international educational institution engaged in scholarly work on pressing global problems. Its two main goals are to strengthen research and educational abilities of institutions in developing countries and make policy-relevant contributions to the UN's work. It was established in 1972 and has its headquarters in Tokyo.

UN Women A new agency, created in July 2010, merging four previous UN programs focused exclusively on women. Full name is the UN Entity for Gender Equality and the Empowerment of Women; it is based in New York.

war crime A crime, like maltreatment of prisoners, in military conflict.

weapons of mass destruction Biological, chemical or nuclear weapons designed to kill large numbers of people at once.

World Bank Established at the Bretton Woods Conference in 1944. As a multilateral lending agency, it seeks to reduce poverty by promoting sustainable growth.

World Food Program The frontline UN organization fighting to eradicate hunger. Its headquarters are in Rome and it began work in 1963.

World Health Organization Founded in 1948 with headquarters in Geneva, this organization promotes technical health cooperation among nations, carries out programs to control and eradicate disease and works to improve the quality of life.

World Trade Organization An international organization meant to liberalize trade. It is a forum for governments to negotiate trade agreements and settle disputes.

Zionism Zionist ideology holds that Jews are a people or nation and should gather in a single homeland. Zionism evolved into an international movement for the establishment of a Jewish community in Palestine and later for the support of modern Israel.

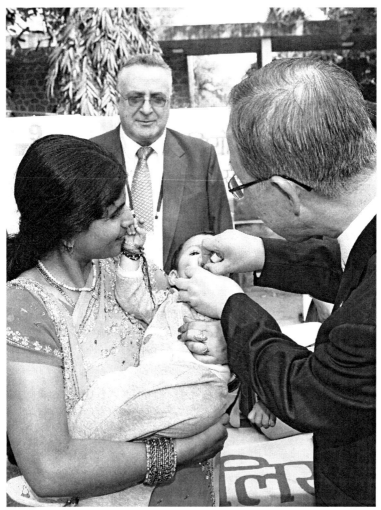

UN Photo/Mark Garten

Secretary-General Ban Ki-moon administers a polio vaccine dose to a child brought by its mother to the UN complex in New Delhi, India.

Appendix G: And the Prize Goes to . . .

Eleven of the ninety-one Nobel Peace Prizes since 1901 have been awarded to people directly related or affiliated with the UN. These extraordinary accomplishments underscore the organization's role as one of the world's foremost peace brokers and a catalyst for socially significant change. Martti Ahtisaari, a former UN under-secretary-general, was the most recent UN-associated Nobel Peace Prize winner, in 2008.

2008: Ahtisaari joined the UN in 1976 in the UN Institute for Namibia, when it was established as the first university in southwest Africa. (It is now called the University of Namibia.) Ahtisaari then rose through the UN ranks, ultimately becoming under-secretary-general for administration and management in 1987 under Secretary-General Javier Pérez de Cuéllar. Ahtisaari won the Peace Prize in recognition of his mediation efforts in Asia, Africa and Europe.

2007: The UN's Intergovernmental Panel on Climate Change and former U.S. Vice President Al Gore were jointly awarded the prize for their work on global warming. The panel was honored for bringing thousands of scientists and officials together to establish certainty on climate change.

2005: The International Atomic Energy Agency and its director general, Mohamed ElBaradei, were honored for their work on nuclear nonproliferation. ElBaradei was a diplomat at Egypt's permanent mission to the UN in New York and worked as senior fellow in charge of the international law program at the UN Institute for Training and Research before heading the IAEA.

2001: The UN and Kofi Annan, the secretary-general at the time, were both awarded the prize "for their work for a better organized and more peaceful world," the Nobel Committee said. Annan was cited for rejuvenating the UN, particularly in working on peace, security and human rights as well as the challenges of HIV/AIDS and terrorism. The committee citation proclaimed that "the only negotiable route to global peace and cooperation goes by way of the United Nations."

1988: UN peacekeeping forces were recipients for operating "under extremely difficult conditions" while contributing to "reducing tensions where an armistice has been negotiated but a peace treaty has yet to be established" and therefore making a decisive effort towards "the initiation of actual peace negotiations."

1981: The Office of the UN High Commissioner for Refugees "carried out work of major importance to assist refugees, despite the many political difficulties with which it has had to contend," namely coping with increasing numbers of refugees flowing from Vietnam and the exodus from Afghanistan and Ethiopia.

1969: On its 50th anniversary, the International Labor Organization, a specialized agency, was honored for succeeding in "translating into action the fundamental moral idea on which it was based"—that is, "if you desire peace, cultivate justice."

1965: Unicef, for acting as a "peace factor of great importance" and for forging a link of solidarity between rich and poor countries and the caring for children.

1961: Dag Hammarskjöld, the second secretary-general of the UN, from 1953 until his death in 1961, was the only person to receive the Nobel Peace Prize posthumously (though he had been nominated before he died). He was instrumental in establishing the first UN peacekeeping force and became deeply involved in the Congo war in the early 1960s and died in a plane crash while on a UN mission in the region.

1954: To the UN High Commissioner for Refugees for its work helping refugees and displaced people in Europe in the aftermath of World War II.

1950: Ralph Bunche, UN mediator in Palestine, received the prize for his mediation of the 1949 armistice between Israel and seven Arab countries. By carrying out these difficult talks, the committee stated, and "by exercising infinite patience," Bunche "finally succeeded in persuading all parties to accept an armistice."

Appendix H: Top 10 Providers of Assessed Financial Contributions to Peacekeeping Operations (2010-2012)

Compiled by Simon Minching

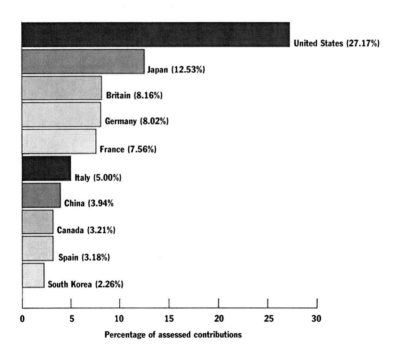

Source: UN Peace Operations, Year in Review, 2010 pg. 83

Appendix I: Top 10 Contributors of Uniformed Personnel to UN Peacekeeping Operations (2010 Averages)

Compiled by Simon Minching

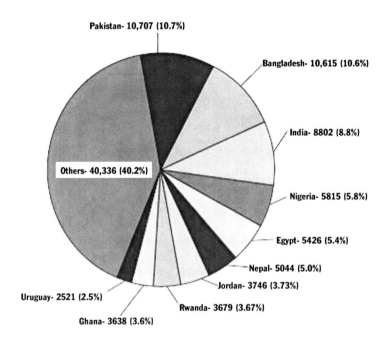

Source: UN Peace Operations, Year in Review, 2010 pg. 83

Appendix J: Global Summary of the AIDS Pandemic
Compiled by Simon Minching

AGGREGATE DATA

People living with HIV/AIDS (2009)	Total	~33.3 million	[31.4-35.3]
	Adults	~30.8 million	[29.2-32.6]
	Women	~15.9 million	[14.8-17.2]
	Under 15	~2.5 million	[2.2-2.7]
People newly infected with HIV/AIDS (2009)	Total	~2.6 million	[2.3-2.8]
	Adults*	~2.1 million	[1.93- 2.29]
	Under 15	~370,000	[230-510,000]
HIV/AIDS deaths (2009)	Total	~1.8 million	[1.6-2.1]
	Adults*	~1.6 million	[1.45-1.74]
	Under 15	~260,000	[150-360,000]

2009 BY REGION

Sub-Saharan Africa	Total	~22.5 million	[20.9-24.2]
	Women	~12.1 million	[11.1-13.2]
	New Cases	~1.8 million	[1.6-2.0]
	Deaths	~1.3 million	[1.1-1.5]
North Africa and Middle East	Total	~460,000	[400-530,000]
	Women	~210,000	[180-240,000]
	New Cases	~75,000	[61-92,000]
	Deaths	~24,000	[20-27,000]
South and Southeast Asia	Total	~4.1 million	[3.7-4.6]
	Women	~1.4 million	[1.4-1.7]
	New Cases	~270,000	[240-320,000]
	Deaths	~260,000	[230-300,000]
East Asia	Total	~770,000	[560k-1 million]
	Women	~220,000	[160-300,000]
	New Cases	~81,000	[47-140,000]
	Deaths	~36,000	[25-50,000]
Oceania	Total	~57,000	[50-64,000]
	Women	~25,000	[22-28,000]
	New Cases	~3700	[2600-5300]
	Deaths	~1400	[1000-1400]

Central & South America	Total	~1.4 million	[1.2-1.6]
	Women	~490,000	[420-590,000]
	New Cases	~92,000	[70-120,000]
	Deaths	~58,000	[43-70,000]
Caribbean	Total	~240,000	[220-270,000]
	Women	~120,000	[100-140,000]
	New Cases	~17,000	[13-21,000]
	Deaths	~12,000	[8500-12,000]
Eastern Europe and Central Asia	Total	~1.4 million	[1.3-1.6]
	Women	~690,000	[600-790,000]
	New Cases	~130,000	[110-160,000]
	Deaths	~76,000	[60-96,000]
North America	Total	~1.5 million	[1.2-2.0]
	Women	~390,000	[310-510,000]
	New Cases	~69,000	[43-120,000]
	Deaths	~26,000	[22-44,000]
Western and Central Europe	Total	~820,000	[720-910,000]
	Women	~240,000	[210-270,000]
	New Cases	~31,000	[23-39,000]
	Deaths	~8500	[6800-19,000]

Source: UNAIDS Report on the Global Aids Epidemic (2010)

Note: The approximation figure immediately following the "~" symbol represents the best estimate of Unaids, with the bracketed figures providing the entire possibility of ranges. For 2009, data were not explicitly broken down into women newly infected with, or dying from, HIV/AIDS. Hence, total regional figures for "New Cases" and "Deaths" are all adults and children, and the data reported for women represent the estimate of those living with HIV/AIDS.

*Because possibility ranges and best estimates for adult figures are not explicitly provided in the report, the derived lower and upper bounds of each possibility range are given by: "Adult+Children Total"- "Under 15 Total"; the best estimate is the midpoint of this range rounded to the nearest tenth.

Appendices

Appendix K: Millennium Development Goals and Targets

GOAL 1: ERADICATE EXTREME HUNGER AND POVERTY

Target 1. By 2015, halve the proportion of people whose income is less than $1 a day.

Target 2. By 2015, halve the proportion of people who suffer from hunger.

GOAL 2: ACHIEVE UNIVERSAL PRIMARY EDUCATION

Target 3. Ensure that by 2015, boys and girls everywhere will be able to complete a full course of primary schooling.

GOAL 3: PROMOTE GENDER EQUALITY AND EMPOWER WOMEN

Target 4. Eliminate gender disparity in primary and secondary education, preferably by 2005, and in all levels of education no later than 2015.

GOAL 4: REDUCE CHILD MORTALITY

Target 5. By 2015, reduce the under-five mortality rate by two-thirds.

GOAL 5: IMPROVE MATERNAL HEALTH

Target 6. By 2015, reduce the maternal mortality ratio by three-quarters.

GOAL 6: COMBAT HIV/AIDS, MALARIA AND OTHER DISEASES

Target 7. By 2015, have stopped and begun to reverse the spread of HIV/AIDS.

Target 8. By 2015, have stopped and begun to reverse the incidence of malaria and other major diseases.

GOAL 7: ENSURE ENVIRONMENTAL SUSTAINABILITY

Target 9. Integrate the principles of sustainable development into country policies and programs and reverse the loss of environmental resources.

Target 10. By 2015, halve the proportion of people without sustainable access to safe drinking water and basic sanitation.

Target 11. By 2020, achieve a major improvement in the lives of at least 100 million slum dwellers.

GOAL 8: DEVELOP A GLOBAL PARTNERSHIP FOR DEVELOPMENT

Target 12. Develop further an open, rule-based, predictable, nondiscriminatory trading and financial system (includes a commitment to good governance, development and poverty reduction, both nationally and internationally).

Target 13. Address the special needs of least-developed countries (includes tariff- and quota-free access for least-developed countries' exports, enhanced program of debt relief for heavily indebted poor countries and cancellation of official bilateral debt and more generous official development assistance for countries committed to poverty reduction).

Target 14. Address the special needs of landlocked developing countries and small island developing states (through the Program of Action for the Sustainable Development of Small Island Developing States and 22nd General Assembly provisions).

Target 15. Deal comprehensively with the debt problems of developing countries through national and international measures to make debt sustainable in the long term.

Target 16. In cooperation with developing countries, develop and carry out strategies for decent and productive work for youth.

Target 17. In cooperation with pharmaceutical companies, provide access to affordable essential drugs in developing countries.

Target 18. In cooperation with the private sector, make available the benefits of new technologies, especially information and communications technology.

Source: UN Millennium Project, 2006

"A Global Agenda" Index

A

Academic Council on the UN System, 117
Afghanistan
  Bonn conference, 50
  civilian casualties, 48
  elections, 48
  female danger ranking, 107
  female UN officers, 85-86
  Internet era, and, 7
  Karzai, Hamid, 46, 48, 50
  Northern Alliance, 46, 50
  Pakistan, and, 46, 50
  Pashtuns, 48
  special rapporteur, 61
  Taliban, and, 46, 48, 50
  UN role, 48-51
  U.S. role, 7, 13, 46-50
Aid & development, 123-141
  2002 Monterrey Conference, 137
  2008 Doha Conference, 127
  aging, 126
  chapter talking points, 141
  donors, 137-141
  economic growth, 125
  environmental challenges, 124-128
  food security, 129-133
  HIV/AIDS, 137, 138, 150-153, 234-235
  Malawi development program, 132-133
  Millennium Development Goals, 134-136, 139
  population growth, xxvi, 124-125, 127
  poverty concentration, 139
  sustainable development, 126-128, 141
  urbanization, 125
  vertical funds, 137-138
Africa
  food security, 129, 132-133
  illicit transactions, 31-34
  international aid, 137
  peacekeeping, 24-25, 80-83
  polio, 144-149, 157
  population, 124-125
  secretary-generals, 103-104
African Union
  Darfur, role in, 191
  electoral assistance, and, 73
  Ivory Coast, role in, 82, 83
  Lord's Resistance Army, and, 25
Ahmadinejad, Mahmoud, 27, 29
Ahtisaari, Martti, 45, 100, 230
Al Qaeda, 46, 50, 87
Al Shabab, 87
Annan, Kofi
  2002 Monterrey Conference, 137
  Global Fund, and, 152
  Nobel Prize, 100, 230
  secretary-general selection, 103-104
  special rapporteurs, and, 59
Arab Spring, 2-17, 29
  democratic reform, and, 3-5
  human rights, and, 6-10
  Human Rights Council, and, 54-55
  Libya, 4, 11-16
  Responsibility to Protect, and, 11-16
  socioeconomic grievances, 2
  Tahrir Square, 1, 3
  UN role, and, 2-5
Assad, Bashar al-, 54

B

Bahrain
  Arab Spring, and, 6, 16
Ban, Ki-Moon
  Bachelet, Michelle, and, 107-108
  Global Fund, and, 152
  Ivory Coast, and, 80-81
  piracy, and, 87
  second term, vii-ix, xxvii, 98, 102, 116, 191
  sexual abuse watchdog, 84
  on UN reform, 99, 115-116
  U.S. relationship, 92, 94-97
Bashir, Omar al-, 77, 165
Bill and Melinda Gates Foundation, 138, 149, 152
Bolton, John, 94, 114
Bosnia
  Responsibility to Protect, and, 11
Bouazizi, Mohamed, 2
Boutros-Ghali, Boutros, 94, 103-104, 190
Brahimi, Lakhdar, 50
Britain
  Libya, and, 15, 95
  Iraq invasion, 13
  nuclear weapons, 35
  veto power, 8, 114
Brookings Institution, 60, 61, 140
Brundtland, Gro, 45, 151
Bunche, Ralph, 100, 112-113, 230
Bush Administration
  AIDS campaign, 95
  Human Rights Council, and, 55, 94
  Iran, and, 27-28
  Taliban, and, 49
  unilateralism, and, 94
Bush, George W. See Bush Administration

C

Carter, Jimmy, 45
Central Africa
  Lord's Resistance Army, and, 20-25
Central African Republic
  Lord's Resistance Army, and, 20, 22-23, 25
  UN mission, 24
China
  carbon emissions, 175, 177, 179
  Iran issue, 95
  nuclear weapons, 35, 39
  sovereignty concerns, and, 13, 57
  veto power, 8, 102, 114
Clapper, James, 26
Clinton, Bill, 94, 151
Clinton, Hillary, 49, 87
Commission on Human Rights, 66
Comprehensive Nuclear Test Ban Treaty, 36
Copenhagen Accord, 176, 179, 180
Congo
  Lord's Resistance Army, and, 20-25, 84
  UN mission, 24
  sexual abuse, 84-86
Condé, Alpha, 72
Conté, Lansana, 72-73
Cuellar, Javier Perez de, 104

D

Darfur. See also Sudan
  civilian attacks, 14, 77, 205
  International Criminal Court, and, 77, 163
  Responsibility to Protect, and, 13, 15
Democratic Republic of Congo
  civilian attacks, 14
  female danger ranking, 107
  Lord's Resistance Army, and, 20-25
  polio outbreak, 149
  sexual abuse, 84
Division for the Advancement of Women, 107

E

Economic Community of West African States, 80-81, 83
Egypt
  Arab Spring, and, 3, 8
  Iran, and, 29
ElBaradei, Mohamed, 100, 230
Entity for Gender Equality and Empowerment of Women
  See UN Women
Environmental challenges, 124-128, 174-185
  Cancún Climate Conference, 138, 174-177, 179-180
  climate change skepticism, 181
  climate talks, 174-182

238 *A Global Agenda 2011-2012*

Copenhagen Climate
  Conference, 138
Durban Climate Conference,
  174-176, 179-180, 182
Green Climate Fund, 174, 176,
  179, 180
marine debris, 183-185
European Union
  climate change policy, 175, 178
  electoral assistance, and, 73
  human rights, and, 58
  Ivory Coast sanctions, 82
Extraordinary Chambers in the
  Courts of Cambodia, 166-167,
  169

F

Figueres, Christiana, 176-177
France
  Ivory Coast, and, 80-82, 95
  Libya, and, 15, 95
  nuclear weapons, 35-36
  veto power, 8, 114

G

Gandhi, Indira, 38
Gavi Alliance, 137, 151-153
Gbagbo, Laurent, 74, 80-83, 191
Gender Equality Architecture
  Reform, 108-109
General Assembly
  Fifth Committee, 115
  First Committee, 36
  Human Rights Council, and,
    54-55, 57-58, 60, 66
  Responsibility to Protect, and,
    11, 13-14
  Second Committee, 112
  secretary-general selection, 102-
    104, 121
  UN Temporary Commission on
    Korea, 41
  UN Women, and, 105-107
Global Polio Eradication Initiative,
  148-149
Goldstone, Richard, 55, 61, 95, 161
Group of 20 (G-20), viii, 120, 130
Group of 77 (G-77), 115-116
Group of Eight (G-8), 30
Guinea
  contested elections, 72-73
  natural resources, 72, 75
  sexual abuse, 84

H

Hammarskjöld, Dag
  death, 189
  generally, 98, 104, 112
  international civil service, 99,
    110-111, 113
  Nobel Peace Prize, 100, 231
  secretary-general reform, 114
Holbrooke, Richard, 97
Human rights, 54-69
  Arab Spring, and, 6-10, 11-17
  developing nations' perspective,
    56-57
  North Korea, and, 44-45
  sexual abuse, 84-86, 91
  special rapporteurs, 59-61,
    66-67
  Western perspective, 56-57
Human Rights Council. *See also*
  Human rights
  Arab Spring, and, 6, 8, 10, 17
  complaints procedure, 66-67
  counterterrorism report, 56
  creation of, 59, 66
  generally, 54-58
  on Israel, 55
  on Ivory Coast, xiv, 55, 81
  on Libya, xiv, 8, 17, 54-55
  on North Korea, 44
  sexual discrimination resolution,
    191
  special rapporteurs, 59-61,
    66-67
  on Syria, 54
  Universal Periodic Review, 59
Human Rights Watch
  Lord's Resistance Army, and,
    20, 23
  "selectivity syndrome," 55
  Sri Lanka, and, 96
Hussein, Saddam, 33, 62-63

I

India
  1971 Indo-Pakistan war, 38
  carbon emissions, 175, 179
  female danger ranking, 107
  nuclear weapons, 35, 37-38
  U.S. nuclear agreement, 35, 39
Intergovernmental Panel on
  Climate Change, 100, 182,
  185, 230
International Atomic Energy Agency
  Iran, and, 27, 30, 39
  Nobel Prize, 230
  North Korea, and, 39, 44
  Syria and, 40
International Commission on
  Intervention and State
  Sovereignty, 11
International Criminal Court
  2008-09 Gaza War, 55
  Coalition for the International
    Criminal Court, 161
  Darfur, and, 77, 163
  indictment cost, 169
  Ivory Coast, and, 83
  judicial elections, 160-162, 171
  Libya, and, 8-9, 14, 54, 163
  Lord's Resistance Army, and,
    23-24
  Moreno-Ocampo, Luis, 160, 165
  North Korea, and, 44
  prosecutor, selection of, 163-
    165, 171
  Rome Statute, 160, 163-164,
    171, 190
  Security Council, and, 9
  war crimes prosecution, 166-169
International Criminal Tribunal
  for Rwanda. *See under* Rwanda
International Criminal Tribunal
  for the former Yugoslavia, 158,
  166-169, 208
International Fund for Agricultural
  Development, 130
International health, 144-157
  as a global concern, 150-153
  global alliances, 151-153
  HIV/AIDS data, 234-235
  International Health
    Partnership, 153, 156
  pandemics, 150-151, 157
  polio, 144-149
  reproductive health, 154-156
International law, 160-171.
  International Criminal Court,
    8-9, 23-24, 54, 83, 160-165, 171
  UN War Crimes Commission,
    166, 168-169
  war crimes tribunals, 166-169,
    `171
International Maritime Bureau, 87
International Monetary Fund
  Bretton Woods institution, 100
  food security, and, 130, 141
  generally, 140
Iran
  2009 election, 28
  centrifuge capability, 27-28
  nuclear issue, 26-30, 39-40
  sanctions, 28-30
  special rapporteur on, 60
  Stuxnet virus, 28, 40
Iraq
  Internet era, and, 7
  Responsibility to Protect, and, 12
  refugees, 62-65
  U.S. invasion, 7, 12-13, 26, 96
Israel
  Human Rights Council, and, 55
  Iran, and, 28
  nuclear weapons, 35-37
  Palestinian conflict, 2, 55, 61,
    95-96
  Vela Incident, 36
Ivory Coast
  disputed election, 70, 74, 80, 95,
    191
  Human Rights Council, and, 55
  Responsibility to Protect, and,
    80, 191
  refugees, 70
  UN intervention in, 80-83, 191

J

Jong-il, Kim, 45

K

Karzai, Hamid. *See under*
  Afghanistan
Khan, A.Q., 35, 39
Kony, Joseph, 21-23
Kuwait
  Human Rights Council, and, 54
Kyoto Protocol
  expiration of, 120, 174

Index **239**

generally, 174, 180
unbinding agreement, 176-177
updated commitments, 177-178

L
Laden, Osama bin, 33, 39, 47
League of Arab States
Libya, and, 15
Libya
Arab Spring, and, xxvi, 4, 6-7, 11-17
Benghazi, takeover of, 15-16
Human Rights Council, and, 8, 17, 54-55
International Criminal Court, 8-9, 14, 163
no-fly zone, and, 14, 54, 95, 191
Responsibility to Protect, and, vi, 11-16
refugees, 12, 52
Security Council, and, 8, 14-17, 54
Lie, Trygve, 103, 188
Lord's Resistance Army, 20-25, 84

M
Middle East
Arab Spring, and, 2-17
nuclear-free zone, 36-37
public support of UN, 5, 17
Millennium Development Goals
2015 deadline, 134-136, 139, 141, 152, 157
creation of, 134, 152, 190
list of, xxvii, 236-237
post-deadline framework, 134-135
President Obama, and, 95
progress, viii, xiii, 134, 139, 157
women's health, 154-155
Mubarak, Hosni, 3
Muntarbhorn, Vitit, 44
Museveni, Yoweri, 21

N
Nehru, Jawaharlal, 37
Nigeria
Ivory Coast conflict, 81
Libya support, 15
polio, 144-149, 157
special rapporteur, 60
North Atlantic Treaty Organization (NATO)
Afghanistan operation, 46, 48
Libya operation, 9, 16, 54
Nuclear Non-Proliferation Treaty, 27, 35, 39, 42, 44, 189
North Korea
Cheonan incident, 42-44
human rights, 44-45
nuclear weapons, 35, 39-40
six-nation Talks, 35, 39, 42
United Nations, and, 41-45
Nuclear Security Summit, ix
Nuclear Suppliers Group, 35, 38
Nuclear Threat Initiative, 36

O
Obama administration
Afghanistan, and, 49-50
conflict minerals initiative, 84
Human Rights Council, 55, 58, 94, 116
UN relationship, 55, 58, 92, 94-97, 116, 121
Obama, Barack. *See also* Obama administration
Afghanistan, 46-47, 49-50
Copenhagen Accord, and, 176, 180
fundraising campaign, 138
Iran, 28
Libya operation, 16
Lord's Resistance Army, and, 25
Millennium Development Goals, and, 95
Responsibility to Protect, and, 96
Odhiambo, Okot, 23
Office of the Special Adviser on Gender Issues and Advancement of Women, 107
Omar, Muhammad, 46
Ongwen, Dominic, 23
Organization for Economic Cooperation and Development, 108, 137
Organization of the Islamic Conference Libya, and, 15
Orr, Robert, 94, 95
Ouattara, Alassane, 80-83, 191

P
Pakistan
1971 Indo-Pakistan war, 38
female danger ranking, 107
Laden, Osama bin, 47
nuclear weapons, 35, 38-39
Taliban, and, 46, 50
women's health, and, 154
Peacekeeping, 71-91
budget and costs, 199-202
Ivory Coast, 80-83
elections, and, 72-75, 91
female peacekeepers, 85-86
personnel figures, 199-202
top funders chart, 232
top personnel contributors chart, 233
Pickering, Thomas R., 50
Pillay, Navanethem, 54, 58

Q
Qaddafi, Muammar el-, 7, 14-16, 54-55, 191

R
Refugee Convention (1951), 63
Responsibility to Protect (R2P)
creation of, 9, 11-12
Darfur, and, 13
Libya, and, vi, 9, 11-16, 191
invasion of Iraq, 12
Ivory Coast, and, 80, 191
Security Council, and, 9, 14
sovereignty issues, 11-12, 17

Rice, Susan, 58, 94, 96-97
Robinson, Mary, 45
Ros-Lehtinen, Ileana, 58, 96-97
Russia
Iran issue, 95
nuclear weapons, 35
sovereignty concerns, and, 13, 57
veto power, 8, 114
Rwanda
International Criminal Tribunal for Rwanda, 90, 166-169, 190, 204, 208
Responsibility to Protect, and, 11

S
Sabin, Albert, 146
Sachs, Jeffrey, 124
Salk, Jonas, 146
Saudi Arabia, 29
Secretary-General. *See also* Ban Ki-Moon
generally, vii, 98-101
Global Strategy for Women's and Children's Health, 155
selection process, vii, 102-104
UN Charter, and, 104, 110, 121
UN System Chief Executive Board, 153
Security Council
Afghanistan, 48-51
Arab Spring, and, 6, 8
Central African peacekeeping, 24-25
Chapter VII, 13, 27
HIV/AIDS, and, 150
International Criminal Court, and, 9
on Iran, 27-28, 51, 95
on Ivory Coast, xiv, 81-83
on Libya, xiv, 8, 14-17, 54
on North Korea, 39, 41-42, 44, 51
nuclear weapons, and, 35, 38
Palestinians, and, 5, 55
piracy, and, 90
Responsibility to Protect, vi, 9, 14
reform, 94-95, 115-116, 120
secretary-general selection, 102-104
on Sri Lanka, 8, 96
on Sudan, 77-78, 165
Sen, Amartya, 100
Somalia
Barre, Siad, 87
female danger ranking, 107
piracy, 87-91
refugees, 18
remittances, 31-34
Transitional Federal Government, 87
South Africa
apartheid, and, 59
South Korea
aid conference, 140
North Korea, and, 41-45
peacekeeping, ix
Security Council, and, ix

South Sudan
  Abyei region, 76
  creation of, 76-79, 191
  new UN mission, 78
Special Court for Sierra Leone
  budget data, 204
  generally, 166, 168, 170
  indictment cost, 169
  total cost, 167
Special Tribunal for Lebanon, 166-168
Sri Lanka
  civilian attacks, 14
  civil war, 8, 57-58, 96
  separatist movement (*see* Tamil Tigers)
Stiglitz, Joseph, 100
Stockholm International Peace Research Institute, 35-36
Sudan. *See also* Darfur
  comprehensive peace agreement, 76
  civil war, 76-78
  debt total, 77
  Lord's Resistance Army, and, 22-23, 25
  National Congress Party, 76, 78
  oil, 77-78
  partition, 76-79, 191
  Responsibility to Protect, and, 13
  sexual abuse, 86
  UN mission, 24, 77-78
Syria
  Arab Spring, and, 6, 16, 54
  Iraqi refugees, 63-65
  nuclear weapons, 39-40

T
Tahrir Square. *See under* Arab Spring
Taliban. *See under* Afghanistan
Tamil Tigers, 8, 96
Trotsky, Leon, 2
Tunisia
  Arab Spring, and, 2-4, 6-7, 15
  Jasmine Revolution, 9
  refugees, 12

U
Uganda
  Lord's Resistance Army, and, 20-22, 25
United Nations (UN)
  aid and development, 123-141
  Arab Spring, and, 2-17
  budget data, 194-204
  "global fault lines," and, 19-51
  important dates, 188-191
  international civil service, 110-113, 121
  international law, 159-171
  management and reform, 93-121
  Nobel Prize winners, 230-231
  oil-for-food scandal, 96, 114
  organizational chart, 192
  top budget contributors, 203

United Nations Association-USA, vi, 50, 104, 120
Universal Declaration of Human Rights, 188
UNAIDS, 150
UN Charter
  adoption of, 188
  Chapter VII, 13, 27
  international civil service, 110
  Israeli occupation, and, 2
  non-intervention, 11
UN Children's Fund Unicef
  aid delivery, 138, 139
  creation of, 188
  extrabudgetary funding, 197
  generally, 150
  Nobel Prize, 230
  Nigeria, and, 144-145, 147-148
UN Conference on Trade and Development, 112, 130
UN Development Fund for Women, 107
UN Development Program
  "Arab Human Development Report," 2
  electoral assistance, 73
  extrabudgetary funding, 197
  piracy courts, and, 90
  remittances, and, 34
UN Economic and Social Council, 140, 152
UN Educational, Scientific and Cultural Organization, 46
UN Environment Program, 112, 183, 189
UN Food and Agriculture Organization extrabudgetary funding, 196
  food security, 124, 127, 130, 132
UN Framework Convention on Climate Change, 176, 179, 180, 182
UN High Commissioner for Human Rights, 54, 58-59, 66
UN High Commissioner for Refugees extrabudgetary funding, 197
  generally, xi, 62, 64,
  Nobel Prizes, 188, 189, 230-231
UN Human Development Index, 72
UN Industrial Development Organization, 112
UN Intellectual History Project, 98
UN International Research and Training Institute for the Advancement of Women, 107
UN Office for Human Rights, 59
UN Office of the High Commissioner for Human Rights, 196
UN Office of the High Commissioner for Refugees, 64
UN Office on Drugs and Crime, 90
UN Population Division, 124
UN Population Fund, 112, 150, 155
UN Secretariat
  Role of Michelle Bachelet, 108

composition of, 193
international civil service, 110, 113
on pandemics, 152
UN System Chief Executives Board, 153
UN University, 117
UN Women, 105-109
  Bachelet, Michelle, 105-109
  creation of, 105, 118, 121
United States
  Central Africa, support for, 22, 25
  climate change policy, 174-177, 180-181
  Global Health Initiative, 155
  India nuclear agreement, 35, 39
  Iran nuclear issue, and, 26-30
  Iraq invasion, 7, 12-13, 26, 96
  Ivory Coast, 95
  Libya, and, 15, 26, 95
  nuclear weapons, 35
  Sept. 11, 2001, attacks, 32, 46
  veto power, 8, 114
Universal Declaration of Human Rights, 10
Universal Periodic Review. *See under* Human Rights Council
U.S. Agency for International Development, 148-149
U.S. Institute of Peace, 30
U.S. State Department Office of Foreign Assets Control, 33
U Thant, 104, 189

W
Waldheim, Kurt, 104
Wallström, Margot, 84-86
World Bank
  Bretton Woods institution, 100
  on food security, 129-130, 132, 141
  generally, 140
  on pandemics, 151
  on remittances, 31
  Stiglitz, Joseph, 100
World Food Program
  extrabudgetary funding, 197
  international food crises, 136, 139
  Malawi, and, 132
  North Korea, and, 45
World Health Organization
  extrabudgetary funding, 197
  HIV/AIDS, 150-151
  partnership building, 153
  polio efforts, 146-147, 149

Y
Yemen
  Arab Spring, and, 4, 6, 16

Z
Zimbabwe
  civilian attacks, 14
Zine, Abidine Ben Ali el-, 9
Zoellick, Robert, 129

Index **241**

Membership Application

Join UNA-USA today and become part of a nationwide movement for a more effective United Nations: The United Nations Association of the United States of America (UNA-USA) is the nation's largest grassroots membership organization and a leading center for dialogue on the UN and global issues. UNA-USA offers Americans the opportunity to connect with issues confronted by the UN and encourages public support for strong US leadership in the UN. UNA-USA is a program of the UN Foundation and is a member of the World Federation of United Nations Associations.

To join online and pay by credit card, go to www.unausa.org/join

To join UNA-USA by mail, please return this form with your check to: BWF/United Nations Association of the USA, PO Box 96397, Washington, D.C. 20090-6397

- ☐ $1,000 Lifetime (one-time dues payment)
- ☐ $500 Patron
- ☐ $100 Sponsor
- ☐ $40 Member
- ☐ $40 Young Professional Member (for members ages 21-40)
- ☐ $25 Introductory (first year only or limited income)
- ☐ $10 Model UN Participant
- ☐ $10 Student

_____
NAME

_____
ADDRESS

_____
CITY, STATE AND ZIP

_____
HOME PHONE / CELLPHONE   BUSINESS PHONE

_____
E-MAIL

Membership in UNA-USA is open to any resident of the US who is committed to the purposes of UNA-USA, a 501(c)3 nonprofit organization.

Read The InterDependent,

the premier online magazine focused on the United Nations, published by UNA-USA.
www.theinterdependent.com